KING OR COVEN

Donald Macpherson
7 Meikle Gardens
Westhill
Aberdeenshire

Aboyne on way back from
Meeting at Cairnshiel
Bridge
4th July 2016
R Lockhead

David Stevenson

KING OR COVENANT?

Voices from Civil War

TUCKWELL PRESS

First published in Great Britain in 1996 by
Tuckwell Press Ltd
The Mill House
Phantassie
East Linton
East Lothian EH40 3DG

ISBN 1 898410 81 X

The Publisher acknowledges subsidy from

THE SCOTTISH ARTS COUNCIL

towards publication of this volume.

British Library Cataloguing-in-publication data
A catalogue record for this book is available from the British Library

Typeset by Hewer Text Composition Services, Edinburgh
Printed by Cromwell Press, Melksham, Wiltshire

For Ian McLeod Stevenson
and
For Neil Alan Stevenson

CONTENTS

ILLUSTRATIONS

INTRODUCTION

This book explores the lives of thirteen individuals who have one thing in common: they lived through 'the troubles', the tumultuous civil wars of mid seventeenth-century Scotland, and had their lives changed by the experience. A few could be claimed to have had a noticeable influence on the course of events, but even they were nonetheless victims of events as well as makers of them, carried along like the rest by the tide and desperately trying to paddle.

Why write about this group of people? Obviously doing so celebrates the individual. These are mainly fairly obscure lives, but there is fascination in them. All too often in history (I plead guilty myself), the individuals are squeezed out. The concern is with high politics and great events, or conglomerates individuals into bald statistics. It is perfectly right that such approaches should have prominence, and immensely rewarding to study history from such perspectives. But we ourselves experience great events as individuals, live our lives as individuals, looking in to our selves, looking out through the defensive ramparts of our eye-sockets at the world. To get the feel of the past as fully as possible therefore, one has to try to look out of the eyes of individuals as well as looking down from great heights of generalisation. Doing this gives fresh perspectives on events, insights into the working of individual minds. Was the battle of Inverlochy a marvellous victory or a terrible defeat? Alasdair MacColla and James Gordon would tell you the one, Robert Baillie and Hope of Craighall the other.

How were the individuals who are singled out in this book chosen? First, by a massive exclusion. I did not want a series of sketches of the great men of the period. It would be silly to deny the central importance in public events of an Argyll, Hamilton or Montrose and the fascination of their careers, but I wanted as far as possible to get below that level, to those experiencing events rather than shaping them. Perhaps I've cheated myself by slipping Johnston of Wariston in, but he is here not so much as a maker and shaker as a man who left a most extraordinary record of his inner life.

So, democratically, exclude the great! But at the other end of society the 'people' are also absent. This is not deliberate. With very rare exceptions, the people are silent. They are not literate, they leave almost no records outside estate papers and court records. I would love to have some of them here, but they are difficult, if not impossible, to access.

Thus this is a book of lives lived in the middle rungs of society, with Craighall and Wariston pushing upwards at the top, Major Weir and John Spalding crouching near the bottom.

Overwhelmingly, the thirteen stars of the book are self-selected. They left memoirs or diaries of some sort concerning their lives or, in a few cases, their lives can be reconstructed from other sources. All were literate, seven at least were university graduates. It is interesting, however, that there is one group in society in which literacy did not inspire memoirs: the nobility. In some cases their lives and personalities could be assembled from other sources, especially their letters. Was writing diaries or accounts of their lives 'not the done thing' in noble circles? Of course, the three very greatest figures, mentioned above (Argyll, Hamilton, Montrose – and one could add Huntly) all had their lives cut short by the headsman's axe or the hangman's noose without time to reflect much on their lives.

Applying crude one-word social / occupational descriptions to the chosen thirteen produces—

  3 gentry
  4 military officers
  2 lawyers
  1 parish minister
  1 Catholic priest
  1 merchant
  1 clerk

Thus, basically, gentlemen and professionals, though they are not to be taken as typical men of their status. Or even as men. The gentry form a particularly untypical group: one publicity-mad bankrupt laird, a lady, and a very retiring minor landlord. The military are no better – two bloody mercenaries, a Gaelic warrior and a junior officer remembered only for sex crimes. Where are the prominent generals, or the large numbers of officers uprooted by war from settled lives?

Not only is the focus by necessity on the middle ranks, but there is unavoidable under-representation of some categories. Only one woman (I hesitate to call women a category) appears, because of women's general social position, and because they were less likely than their menfolk to be confidently literate. Lady Halkett provides splendid compensation, and

Gilbert Blakhal's memoir is as much about three women as about himself. Highlanders too were hard to find, living as they did in a society whose culture, including the recalling of the past, was still largely oral. Alasdair MacColla was not a writing man, but has been dragged into service.

Is this motley crowd worthy of attention, or should it be allowed to wander off into the darkness? Many are 'unimportant', some are distasteful. But to me at least they are vivid, real human beings. They lived. Some things about them I understand and can empathise with, others I can't. I miss them, now that the book is finished.

There are some still who would dismiss such people with a shout of 'off with their heads', denying that they are worthy of remembrance. A pompous reviewer in the *Times* (17 June 1995) recently dictated that to be a 'worthwhile subject for a biography' an individual 'must have done something of importance'. The subject of the biography concerned did not produce lasting art of any kind and she was 'neither a role model nor a history maker and has nothing to teach us'. The writer of the review (also female) perhaps felt a feminist disgust at the biographee concerned for having broken from conventionality only to make a career out of sleeping with (and sometimes marrying) men ranging from an English noble, an Austrian prince, a Bedouin nobleman and the king of Bavaria. Sounds a life more interesting that that of many a 'worthy subject'. To deserve a biography you need to be both Important and Nice. That should kill off the thriving trade in biographies. For a start, step down all the thirteen inadequates in this book.

Obviously, I disagree. I am much in sympathy with a passage from the diary of John Cowper Powys:

> As for me, I tried to do justice to the Death of Christ, but all I could think of was the Death of the two wretched Anonymous Thieves – one on His right and one on His left – who represent the unknown myriads of sufferers who were *not* God in disguise.

Here are thirteen wretched thieves, suffering, but they lived their lives, and I've done what I can to make them live briefly for the reader.

A couple of points relating to conventions adopted. In quotations from sources spelling has been modernised. I have not included footnotes, but as a simpler alternative more suitable to a general work of this nature have provided brief bibliographical notes at the end of each chapter. These are not intended to be comprehensive, but to indicate the main published sources of information regarding the subject of the chapter. In addition, brief lives of all those studied can be found in the *Dictionary of National Biography* (63 vols., London, 1885–1900 and subsequent reprints) – with the exceptions of Thomas Cuningham and Gilbert Blakhal, who failed to make the grade.

SUMMARY OF EVENTS

1560	Reformation. Roman Catholic church overthrown and a Protestant, Calvinist church established in Scotland. In politics, alignment with France is replaced by closer relations with England to protect Protestantism.
Late 1500s	King James VI gradually restores royal power after years of confusion. In religion a split emerges between factions in the new Protestant church. 'Presbyterians' seek a church independent of control by king or bishops. 'Episcopalians' accept king as head of the church, and bishops running it. With the king's support Episcopalian ideas become dominant.
1603	Union of the Crowns: James VI of Scotland inherits the English and Irish thrones as James I. James moves to England.
1618	Five Articles of Perth – a move by James to make changes in worship in the church in Scotland. Widespread unease in Scotland, as the changes are seen as 'English' and 'Popish', imposed by the king through the bishops. Ever since the Reformation Scots Protestants had been obsessed by fear of Catholicism, as the revived Catholic Church of the Counter-Reformation regained much of the territory on the Continent it had formerly lost to Protestantism. With the Articles of Perth, increasing numbers of Scots come to fear that royal control of the church through Episcopalianism is allowing the king to try to push the Scottish church back towards Catholicism.
1618	Thirty Years' War begins in Germany – a confused series of wars involving most European states at one time or another. Though the causes were a mixture of political, religious and social, Scots Protestants tended to see the war simply as a fight for Protestant survival against aggressive Catholicism. Fear and hatred of Catholicism intensifies.
1625	Death of James VI: Charles I inherits his thrones. A well-meaning, earnest man, but too much concerned with principle to be a good politician. Central to his concerns are increasing royal power, and imposing his ideas on the churches of the

three kingdoms. In Scotland unease at his rule is intensified by
the fact that though of Scottish royal blood the new king is
essentially English in attitude, and tends to assume that Scotland
should be anglicised.

1633   Act of Revocation. Vast amounts of land and other property
          formerly belonging to the Catholic church had passed into the
          hands of laymen, especially nobles, both before and after the
          Reformation. The king now takes power to revoke all such
          grants, and thus threatens the property rights of many of the
          greatest men in the country. In reality he has no plans for
          imposing a major upheaval on Scottish society, but political
          incompetence leads to deep fears as to his intentions.

1637   Moves towards further reform of worship in Scotland culminate
          in the imposition of a Prayer Book in Scotland, and again
          political stupidity accompanies an unpopular policy. This proves
          the proverbial last straw. Riots in Edinburgh snowball within
          months into a major rebellion, fuelled by national grievances
          (fear of becoming a province of England), religious fanaticism and
          terror (of Catholicism), and élite alienation (centring on the Act
          of Revocation).

1638   National Covenant sworn as a bond between signatories and
          with God to stand together to force changes in religion on the
          king. Glasgow Assembly of the Kirk: Episcopacy overthrown,
          with royal power over the church abolished, bishops deposed,
          innovations in worship removed. Presbyterian system of church
          government established.

1639   First Bishops' War. Charles I's plans to invade Scotland fail,
          but some fighting between covenanters and royalists in the
          North-East.

1640   Constitutional revolution in Scotland largely destroys royal
          power. Second Bishops' War. Scots invade northern England and
          Charles I, now facing increasing opposition in England, is forced
          to make peace.

1641   Charles I visits Scotland and makes a settlement with the
          covenanters. Scots army withdrawn from England. Irish rebellion
          breaks out: Catholic Irish inspired by the successful rebellion by
          the Scots.

1642   Scots army, to be paid by the English parliament, invades Ulster
          to protect Scottish settlers and Protestantism. Outbreak of the
          English Civil War between Charles I and the English parliament.

1643   The Solemn League and Covenant and a military treaty ally Scots
          and English parliament against Charles I.

1644   Scots army occupies northern England, and with an English parliamentary army defeats the royalists at the Battle of Marston Moor. Rebellion against the covenanters, based in the Highlands and led by Montrose, supported by an Irish Catholic expeditionary force. Successive victories by Montrose undermine the covenanting regime.

1645   Continuing success of Montrose leads to the temporary collapse of covenanting regime, but he is defeated when part of Scots army in England returns. Increasing tension in the alliance between the Scots and the English parliament through the latter's reluctance to establish presbyterianism in England, as promised in return for military assistance.

1646   English Civil War ends in victory for English parliament, but covenanters given little credit for their help. The defeated Charles I seeks to undermine the alliance of the Scots and parliament further by fleeing to join the Scots army in England. But he finds himself held prisoner.

1647   Scots army withdraws from England, leaving Charles I behind as they have found him a dangerous embarrassment. The war in the Highlands against the remnants of Montrose's forces ends. Quarrels with the English parliament (who now hold Charles I prisoner) over a peace settlement grow.

1648   Duke of Hamilton's faction gains power in Scotland and, through an agreement with the king known as the Engagement, leads an army into England to rescue Charles I. The Engagers are defeated by Cromwell's parliamentary army at the battle of Preston. The Engager regime in Scotland collapses and the extremist covenanting 'Kirk Party' seizes power.

1649   English parliament executes Charles I, abolishes monarchy, and establishes the English commonwealth (republic). The Scots refuse to accept their right to do this and proclaim Charles II king of England and Ireland as well as Scotland. Unsuccessful attempt to persuade the exiled king to take the covenants and return to Scotland.

1650   Charles II takes the covenants and comes to Scotland as a puppet king. Cromwell invades Scotland to protect the English commonwealth from the threat posed by Scotland's support for monarchy, and defeats the Scots at the battle of Dunbar. Royalism begins to revive in Scotland, and the Kirk Party's power crumbles as the church splits into minority Remonstrant ('extremist') and majority Resolutioner ('moderate') factions. The latter reluctantly accept that if there is to be any hope of

defeating the English, royalists, Engagers and other 'malignants'
must be allowed into the army, and the king and royalists
allowed real power.

1651   As English military advance continues, Scots launch a despairing
invasion of England, but their army is destroyed by Cromwell at
the battle of Worcester. Charles II flees into exile. The conquest
of all Scotland except for some remote Highland areas is then
completed by the English.

1652   Scotland is incorporated into the commonwealth in a
parliamentary union.

1653   Protectorate established, with Cromwell as Lord Protector of
England, Scotland and Ireland.

1658   Death of Cromwell destroys the fragile republican regime.

1660   The Restoration. After prolonged political confusion monarchy
is restored. Charles II returns, and the parliamentary union of
England and Scotland is abandoned.

1661   Episcopacy restored in Scotland. Large numbers of parish
ministers reluctant to accept this deposed from the ministry in
the years that follow.

1666   Rebellion of religious dissidents in south-west Scotland defeated
at the battle of Rullion Green.

1679   Renewed rebellion by religious dissidents in the south-west
defeated at the battle of Bothwell Bridge.

1685   Death of Charles II; accession of James VII and II, Charles's
younger brother. Fears that Protestantism is in danger grow as
the new king is a Catholic.

1688–9 James dethroned in the 'Glorious' Revolution. William and Mary
(his Protestant son-in-law and daughter) become joint sovereigns.
Attempted rising by 'Jacobites' defeated by 'Williamites' at the
battle of Killiecrankie.

1702   Death of William and accession of Queen Anne.

1707   Union of the parliaments of England and Scotland.

1714   Accession of the Hanoverian King George I secures the Protestant
succession in Britain against the Catholic Stuart claimant.

1715   Jacobite rising defeated.

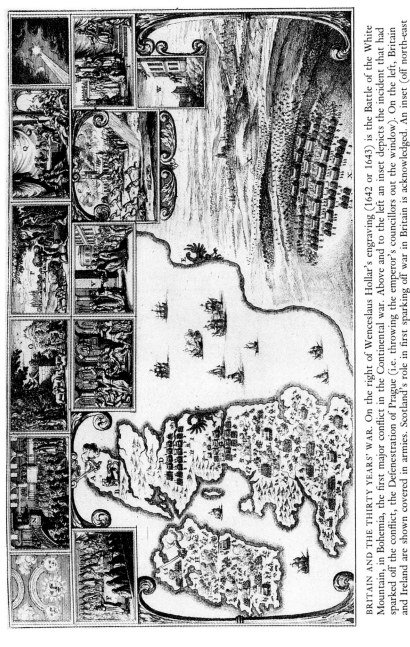

BRITAIN AND THE THIRTY YEARS' WAR. On the right of Wenceslaus Hollar's engraving (1642 or 1643) is the Battle of the White Mountain, in Bohemia, the first major conflict in the Continental war. Above and to the left an inset depicts the incident that had sparked off the conflict, the Defenestration of Prague (i.e. throwing the emperor's councillors out the window). On the left, Britain and Ireland are shown covered in armies. Scotland's role in first sparking off war in Britain is acknowledged. An inset (off north-east Scotland) shows women throwing stools at a bishop when the new prayer book was first used in Edinburgh in 1637. Bohemia and Britain are linked symbolically by a double-headed spread eagle. *By permission of the British Museum, Department of Prints and Drawings.*

ONE

THE SOLDIER OF ILL-FORTUNE:

Sir Andrew Melvill

THE SCOTTISH TROUBLES of the mid-seventeenth century were central to the lives of most of those studied in this book. Sir Andrew Melvill is an exception, but in a sense it is appropriate to start with him, as his career helps set the Scottish, and indeed British, scene in a much wider context. He could be said to be a good European. He moved easily from country to country according to the whims of the job market, returning to his native Scotland for a time only because circumstances seemed to provide opportunities for advancement. But he was not the Eurobusinessman or Eurobureaucrat of his day. We might argue for some similarity with a NATO Eurosoldier, defending good from evil. But he would not have so deceived himself as to pretend to be a peacekeeper. A professional international soldier like Melvill required constant war to make a living. Peace meant redundancy, so he, like thousands of others – many of them Scots – followed Europe's seemingly endless confused wars round the Continent.

Andrew Melvill believed that life had treated him badly, but his reminiscences of his career of hardship and danger indicate that though he certainly suffered many misfortunes, as often as not they were his own fault. Perhaps at heart he recognised this, for his anecdotes of his troubles are not dominated by bitterness. Nor does he dwell on supposed heroic deeds to justify himself. Nonetheless, his memoirs served him well at the end of his active career. They were entertaining enough to catch the attention of his friends and acquaintances. One of these was the Electress Sophia of Hanover, and it was she who sympathetically (or perhaps ironically?) dubbed this battered old mercenary officer a 'soldier of ill-fortune' and showed him favour.

Reading the memoirs leaves the impression that in some respects Melvill was in reality a remarkably lucky man. Death was close on many occasions, and simply having remained alive made him fortunate. Moreover, an initially penniless soldier who not only survived but was able to settle down in old age with a knighthood, a wife and family, the patronage of the electress and other German notables, and the post of major general of the troops of the Duke of Celle, can hardly be judged particularly unfortunate. The great

1

majority of the many thousands of Scots who had enlisted in Continental armies in the period not only experienced hardship and danger like Melvill, but early deaths from wounds, disease or starvation. Given that Melvill was well aware of this, his self-deprecating accounts of his misfortunes surely concealed wonder at the mere fact of survival. Robert Baillie, who will be considered in a later chapter, studied the European wars from afar, at the level of generals and states. Melvill lived many of the wars as one of a host of expendable pawns.

Melvill's part in the Scottish troubles was very limited, incidents in a life packed with a bewildering variety of military experiences as he sold his services around Europe, almost to anyone who offered him pay – though he did draw the line at fighting for Spain. In many ways his varied career typified the life of the mercenary soldier in the Thirty Years' War – except for his survival. Centred in Germany, the Thirty Years' War (1618–48) drew in mercenaries from all over Europe, from Croats, Finns and Cossacks from the east to Scots from the west. Some were motivated in part at least by principle, but lust for adventure and fortune predominated. The Scots won for themselves a special reputation, and a handful rose to high rank and fame. General Sir James Ramsay, for example, became a Protestant hero for his defence of Hanau, of which he was governor. And at one point the siege of the city was relieved by his fellow Scot, Field Marshall Alexander Leslie, of the Swedish army. When Hans von Grimmelshausen produced his great novel of the Thirty Years' War, *Simplicissimus*, Ramsay appears as a character in it, and it is entirely appropriate that the book's scheming soldier hero, alternately victim and oppressor, is in the end revealed to be half Scottish, a nephew of Ramsay.

Andrew Melvill was born in 1624. About his descent, he is at once explicit and guarded:

> I will not say much about the House of Melvill from which I am descended. Suffice it that it has always held a distinguished place among the oldest Houses of Scotland. To this all the histories of the kingdom bear testimony.

In his concern to stress the nobility of his breeding, he glossed over the fact that his father, John Melvill, his grandfather, and his great-grandfather were all parish ministers. This was quite a distinguished little clerical dynasty. Andrew's grandfather James Melvill or Melville was a leading presbyterian activist of his age, author of a famous diary; and James in turn was the nephew of the famous Andrew Melville, the great presbyterian divine. Nonetheless, many would think a parish minister was not quite a gentleman, and at the time when Andrew was writing presbyterianism itself was generally seen as disreputable in aristocratic circles. Therefore he suppressed the clerical element in his family, opting instead for emphasis on more distant but indisputably noble ancestors. However, one characteristic of Melvill was an indirect acknowledgement of his true ancestry: he took pride in the leading role of the Melvilles in pioneering Protestantism in Scotland, and his own Protestant beliefs were one of the few things in his life to which he gave priority – sometimes – over self-seeking and greed.

When he was born, Melvill relates, his father was 'living quietly as a prosperous gentleman in his own home'. No mention of his evidently being the obscure minister of the parish of Newton in Midlothian. But Melvill does admit that his family had declined in status, a fact which he blamed on the leaders of the Melville kin not moving to London with King James VI on the Union of the Crowns in 1603 and thus getting their share of the rich English pickings that then become available to Scots who enjoyed royal favour. Even here he is distorting his family's importance by implying that favour to the greatest of the Melvilles would have affected his father's fortunes, whereas in reality he belonged to a branch of the kin so junior and distant that any fame won by great kinsmen would have benefited him only by a tenuous shadow of reflected glory. Nonetheless, distant kinship and reflections of glory genuinely meant a great deal to Scotsmen, especially perhaps those such as soldiers of fortune seeking to establish themselves abroad as gentlemen and concerned about their social status. Moreover, even where actual kinship could not be proved, Scots assumed that sharing the same surname was evidence of kinship. Whenever Melvill came across another Melville in his career, he could expect a welcome.

To reverse the slide in the family's fortunes, Melvill's father 'had chosen a wife of the House of Kellie'. Her unmarried brother had gone south at the Union of the Crowns and thrived as a courtier, becoming Earl of Kellie, and the Melvills had looked forward to inheriting his fortune at his death. However, when he died in 1639 they found that instead they had inherited only debts. Hard times followed for a family already in financial difficulties. At the age of thirteen Melvill was sent to live with a kinswoman, to relieve his family of the burden of supporting him. Shortly thereafter, she sent him to Königsberg in Prussia to complete his studies and learn languages. What career was envisaged for the young Melvill is unknown, but he may well have been expected to become a merchant, with the benefit of having acquired the languages spoken in the areas Scots traded with in the Baltic.

However, in the age of the Thirty Years' War the temptations of a more active career proved irresistible.

Melvill escaped from his teachers at the age of fourteen and enlisted in a regiment being levied to serve the King of Poland. Life as a soldier offered simultaneously excitement and the hope of riches, of making good through promotion or loot. It was a career especially attractive to youths in Melvill's position, brought up intensely proud of their noble connections by blood, however distant, but through family circumstances forced to earn a living for themselves. Becoming a merchant – or even a parish minister – might have provided a reasonably respectable livelihood, but they were not compatible with noble aspirations. Bearing arms, even if as a paid sword in an unknown cause, even if in the first instance as a common soldier, was honourable. Aristocratic concepts of honour were still largely based on a code of military virtues and abilities. One of the distortions of this code allowed men of many nations with pretensions to gentility but no resources to believe that the very fact of fighting preserved their honour, whatever degradations they might endure, whatever wanton barbarities they might be ordered to commit, however self-seeking their motives.

The youth's – child's, in our terms – military career got off to a slow start. On reaching Poland he found peace had broken out, and he returned to Scotland – perhaps having heard that war between the rebel Scottish covenanters and King Charles I was likely. Arriving in 1639, he found both his parents were dead, their property seized by creditors. His elder brother was serving as a captain in a covenanting regiment, and Melvill was recruited into it and promised promotion – which did not materialise. This was the first of countless times (if Melvill is to be believed) in his career when this was to happen.

He has little to say, unfortunately, about his experiences in the years that immediately followed – evidently because he saw no real action to provide the dramatic incidents that are the backbone of his memoirs. After serving in the Bishops' Wars of 1639–40, he fought in the Scottish army which invaded England in 1644 to aid parliament in the civil war against Charles I. Soon he experienced the privations of a soldier's life. The Scots army in England was badly paid, promotion prospects poor for the many hopefuls who believed that they had a right to it. In 1646 he was cornet of what he described as a company of officers awaiting promotion who, receiving no pay, 'lived upon free quarters wherever our strength happened to prevail': men of honour in their own eyes, but little better than brigands, preying on the peasantry and hanging on the fringes of the army hoping for proper employment. Somewhere in the north of England, local peasants turned on their tormentors and took them prisoner. Typically, what was most galling to Melvill was that he and his colleagues were made to walk on foot while upstart peasants rode their horses and carried their arms, the symbols of their honour.

Handed over to the governor of an unnamed castle, Melvill and his colleagues were held prisoner for two months before being released – and no sooner had they rejoined the Scots army than it withdrew from England (in 1647) and disbanded. Thwarted at home of the chances of glory and honour they craved, Melvill and his elder brother left for the Continent. The latter, on reaching France, set out for Venice, but Melvill stayed and joined the Scots foot guards, which had served the French crown for many generations, 'with the rank of ensign, but with the duties of a sergeant'. Now at last Melvill saw real action, fighting Imperial troops in Flanders and being seriously wounded in the chest at the siege of Lens before moving on to further sieges. 'I could hardly describe our sufferings in this campaign. Hunger and privations were harder to fight than the enemy before us'. A legacy of the campaign was some sort of iron support inserted in his chest after his injury.

Such privations led Melvill to a deed which was to assume great significance in his mind, for he regarded later misfortunes as a just punishment for it. What is really remarkable is the triviality of the deed that haunted him. He stole a taffeta mantle edged with silver lace which was dropped by an officer, and sold it to buy food for himself and a comrade, to 'assuage our gnawing hunger'. Considering the misdeeds with terrible consequences that he later admits to, with only the most cursory indications of remorse, this show of conscience seems out of all proportion. But the petty criminal action offended more against his code of honour as an officer and a gentleman than many bloodier misdeeds. He had stolen from a fellow officer. It was just not the done thing.

Shortly after his 'crime' the punishments for his misdeed began. Straying too far from camp, he and some colleagues were ambushed by a band of marauding Croats in the Imperial service. Finding their prisoners an encumbrance, the Croats resolved to shoot them, after stripping them of their clothes. Here as elsewhere in the memoirs, prisoners were routinely stripped, whether they were to live or die, because clothes were valuable booty. If they were to die, stripping them first avoided disfiguring holes and bloodstains which would reduce the value of the clothing. Melvill, lined up with his colleagues against a wall of a house, was at first resigned to death. But the musket of the Croat assigned to shoot him misfired. Irritated, the Croat hit Melvill with the butt, knocking him down, and then proceeded to reload his gun. The blow shocked the intended victim out of his apathy, and when he saw another prisoner trying to escape Melvill jumped into a moat surrounding the house, forced his way stark naked through a thorn hedge, 'having left part of my skin behind in it', and made good his escape. Eventually he acquired a sack to clothe himself, and fell in with some camp-followers of German troops fighting for Spain and thus allies of the Imperial forces – and of the Croat mercenaries. Melvill managed to pass himself off as a fellow German through his knowledge of the language (it was turning out to be useful to have done some studying in Königsberg after all), and this may well have saved his life.

He was taken to Archduke Leopold's army and treated as a prisoner of war. Straggling behind the army with little attention paid to him, he was mistaken for one of the sick soldiers of the army itself and taken to hospital in Lille. This sounds a stroke of luck, but Melvill describes the hospital as the most horrible and vile place he ever saw, and he was to become well versed in the horrible. But at least he got bread in the hospital, though it needed thorough toasting to kill 'the vermin with which it was covered'. Then he quickly moved on to beg another meal at an Irish convent, before ending up winning the help of a Scottish officer (who, inevitably, knew of his family) serving as lieutenant-colonel of an Irish regiment of the Spanish army. (Any readers who feel they have lost track of who is fighting for whom at this point may be reassured. The whole point of narrating these details of nationalities is to demonstrate the bewildering complexity of the war Melvill was caught up in).

Rather arbitrary prejudice made Melvill reluctant to serve Spain in an Irish regiment. Sometimes in his career he was to serve Catholic masters, but Spain was the arch-Catholic bogeyman in Protestant eyes, and though willing to stretch many a point in his life, Melvill was not willing to serve in Spanish armies. But his luck held. The endless military complexities of the age provided a way out. The Duke of Lorraine, one of the great wheeler-dealer military entrepreneurs of the age, had undertaken to provide forces to serve the Prince of Wales in helping his father, Charles I, who was now a prisoner in England. Melvill obtained a position as an officer in one of the regiments being raised. With great difficulty he rounded up levies and, as ordered, embarked them at Rotterdam to sail to Emden. However, permission to land in Emden was refused, and the levies, convinced (ironically) that they were being hijacked to Spain, mutinied and set sail. Eventually

THE THIRTY YEARS' WAR. The grim reality of military life. A mass execution of soldiers convicted of unauthorised plundering, with other troops paraded to watch. The next victim is being dragged up the ladder, followed by a priest holding out the cross to him. Below, another prisoner kneels to confess his sins. Others, under guard, wait on the left. To the right, a drumhead court martial sits. It looks as though dice are being thrown, and it may be that the arbitrary fall of the dice will decide whether the prisoner will live or die. Print by Jacques Callot.

(after throwing Melvill's servant boy overboard to drown to show that they meant business) the mutineers agreed to submit, provided they were allowed to disembark. But once they had done so the majority, who were Germans, deserted.

With the remnant – a few Scots, Irish and French – Melvill eventually reached Emden, and was sent with them to the island of Borkum for training. However, the execution of Charles I in January 1649 and the establishment of the English commonwealth made it clear that the small forces raised by the Duke of Lorraine were insufficient for any royalist enterprise.

Charles II, as the Prince of Wales had now become, informed Lorraine that his men were no longer needed. Lorraine, seeing Melvill and his men as a bad investment, proceeded to sell them off to Spain, and orders were given for their transportation to San Sebastian. At this point the officers joined the men in mutinying, and the regiment landed in Ostend, and appealed to Lorraine for help. In spite of the fact that he had by now been paid by the Spanish for them, Lorraine received them back again into his own service – and then sold them to Archduke Leopold. Presumably in Lorraine's eyes

Melvill and the others had entered officially into Spanish service. It wasn't his fault they had then deserted, and as deserters from another army he was free to recruit them again into his forces, and then sell them again. Free trade indeed, bringing double profit. It must have been difficult for soldiers in this chaotic war to remember who they were fighting for at any given time.

In the service of his new master the archduke, Melvill was soon involved in the unsuccessful siege of Guise, before moving on to take La Capelle. However, misfortune (or his own folly) still dogged Melvill. Having quarrelled with his colonel and fought a duel with another officer, he was arrested, and missed much of the campaign. He then got permission to go to Breda to join Charles II, who was preparing to leave for Scotland to assert his claim to the English throne with Scots help. Having agreed to travel to Scotland to fight for Charles, Melvill returned to Flanders to free himself from his obligations to Lorraine and the archduke. Perhaps the former had not sold him to the latter, but just rented him out. Anyway, honour required that Melvill get proper clearance from superiors before leaving the Flanders war. He then set out to make his way to his native land.

In a countryside overrun with soldiers and robbers the journey from Ypres to Bruges was hazardous, the danger of being robbed of his modest possessions great. He therefore sold everything he owned except a scruffy old coat, and sewed all his money into a belt which he then sewed round his arm. This he covered with horribly blood-stained bandages and splints. However, he overdid the disguise of a penniless wounded soldier, tying the bandage so tightly that his arm swelled up and caused him real agony.

Perhaps this added to the plausibility of his performance, for the disguise served its purpose. By the time he reached Bruges, Melvill had been repeatedly searched by bands of thieves, but all he lost was his hat and shoes. His old coat must have been in a revolting state, for no one thought it worth stealing. From Bruges he walked to Rotterdam, and there joined up with a German captain of horse, also travelling to Scotland to take advantage of the career opportunities offered by a new war. However, fear of English naval patrols prevented them finding a passage. They therefore bought a boat and found a shipwrecked Scots pilot willing to guide them to Scotland. Though the English fleet was sighted, they reached Montrose safely after a twelve-day voyage – though shortly thereafter the boat (and the capital it represented) was wrecked, their baggage and servants lost.

Hastening to Perth, Melvill was graciously received by Charles II, who promised him a place in the army he was about to lead into England. Sent to the north with the Duke of Hamilton to raise levies, Melvill was returning to court when the second incident in his life occurred which was to haunt him, and which he was to blame for later misfortune. At a river crossing he was unable to attract the attention of a ferryman on the opposite bank until he fired a shot from his pistol. Carrying unexpectedly far, the ball hit and fatally wounded a child on the far bank. This was a misdeed much more serious than the stealing of a cloak, and if the emphasis Melvill gives to his remorse seems strange in a memoir so full of the horrors of warfare, the explanation probably lies in the fact that though the child's death was accidental he accepted his responsibility, and the child was not the casualty of military action. Elsewhere in the memoirs he has much to reveal that is not to his credit, but he was usually justified in his own mind by the fact that he was acting a legitimate role of man of arms in time of war.

Shortly after this incident Melvill marched into England with the Scots army, and shared in its massive defeat by Oliver Cromwell at the battle of Worcester in September 1651. Again, it is hard to know whether Melvill is to be condoled with for his sufferings, or congratulated for his remarkable escapes. Knocked from his horse and captured during fighting in the town streets, he was about to be stripped of his clothes when a passing officer ordered his captors to desist, claiming the captive for himself. As they quarrelled over their prize, one of his original captors, furious at the prospect of being deprived of his rightful booty, shot Melvill in the stomach. Thus Melvill did not even have the consolation of being wounded in the heat of battle, or even as a hated or feared enemy. He was shot simply to ruin his clothes, which were regarded as more valuable than his life.

Gravely wounded, Melvill met with alternate compassion and callous brutality from enemy soldiers and officers who encountered him. After he had lain all night on a gun-carriage, an English officer, seeing there were still signs of life, had him taken to a poor woman's house to be looked after. But then the house was pillaged by English soldiers who stole everything, including the bed he was lying on. Dragged from the house, he was flung in a ditch, pinned down under a corpse thrown in after him. The poor woman and her daughters rescued him, however, and bedded him down on some straw. At his request they sent to 'General' Douglas, 'a near kinsman of mine on my mother's side and my very good friend'. In fact there does not seem to have been any Douglas of that rank in the Scots army, so it seems that, typically, Melvill has inflated the rank of his relative. Douglas, who had lost an eye in the battle and been taken prisoner, sent his surgeon to tend Melvill.

In the months ahead Melvill gradually recovered, cared for by the women who had taken him in, even though they had to go begging to support him. His brother, he heard, was among the Scots prisoners transported to serve as labour in the plantations of the West Indies. It is unlikely that he ever returned. Melvill himself was in danger of capture when a Cromwellian soldier burst into the house and identified him as a Scots royalist. But the old boys' network of the mercenary trade saved him. The English soldier had served in Holland, greeted Melvill as a comrade in arms, and revealed that he himself was at heart a royalist!

After three months Melvill was well enough to leave Worcester, and set out to walk to London – in the rather elaborate disguise of a German tailor suffering from dysentery. Thus he again took advantage of the knowledge of languages gained in his years on the Continent, rather than speak English in an accent which would identify him as a Scots fugitive. And again he reaped the advantage of looking so revolting even by the appalling standards of these wars that no one investigated him too closely.

Reaching London, he lodged for a time in what was evidently a brothel (he is a bit coy about this) and he met up with a fellow Scot on the run, passing as a Dutch sailor – and, almost inevitably, he found a Melville kinsman to help him. The latter fitted him up with a new disguise as a Dutch merchant and lent him money to buy a passage to the Continent. The two would-be Dutchmen escaped successfully to Rotterdam, though a third Scots escapee foolish enough to 'speak Scottish' to soldiers when embarking was captured.

This ended Melvill's involvement in Scotland's wars. But his complex and undistinguished military career in the years ahead saw him involved in innumerable further adventures and escapades. Participation in the French civil wars known as the Fronde brought him imprisonment in Paris, an attempt by Jesuits to force his conversion to Catholicism as the price of freedom, and a spell as a bodyguard to the Cardinal de Retz. Service in a Scots unit in French pay commanded by the exiled Duke of York (later James VII and II) followed, but ended ignominiously when Melvill irresponsibly left his troops in search of a supposed cache of food, eager as he admits 'for my share of the booty'. His men were attacked and defeated in his absence, and he himself was captured by Croats in the Spanish service. Mistakenly identified as a deserter, he was in danger of execution. Glorious death (in his opinion) he had often faced in the past, but execution as a deserter was the most ignominious fate he could imagine. He was also getting pretty fed up with Croats constantly popping up and trying to kill him.

THE KING OF FRANCE'S SCOTS GUARDS at the Coronation of Louis XIII. The figures in the foreground can be recognised as members of the elite Scots Guards by the crowned 'L' on their uniforms. Andrew Melvill commanded a personal Scots Guard formed to protect Cardinal de Retz, and later served with the Scots Men at Arms, a much older formation. But he never made it to the king's own guards. W. F. Leith, *Scots Men at Arms and Guards in France* (2 vols., 1909), i, 144. *By Courtesy of the Trustees of the National Library of Scotland.*

At the last minute his true identity was established, and before long he was back with the French. In 1655 he left that service and made his way (losing all his baggage *en route*) to Amsterdam. Moving on to Königsberg, he joined the levies of the Elector of Brandenburg as part of a force which aided Charles X of Sweden in an invasion of Poland in 1656. Again Melvill's obsession with loot added incident to his life. Out with a small force on a fruitless sweep in search of pillage in a countryside already ravaged by Cossacks, he captured two Jews and threatened them with death unless they could reveal where some booty could be found. After one was shot (accidentally, Melvill assures us), the other promised to guide him to a treasure, a sack of money hidden in a marsh. But when recovered, the sack proved only to contain copper coin – better than nothing, but not the riches hoped for. However, the incident intensified Melvill's lust for loot, and belief that Jews could lead him to it.

Shortly afterwards he was in charge of the garrison of a small town when a Jew promised to lead him to another treasure. Led by the 'cursed desire I had to become rich', Melvill placed himself in great danger by setting out to find it. He achieved nothing, and in his absence the town he was supposed to be defending was pillaged and burnt by Cossack raiders. They herded great numbers of Jews into the synagogue and burnt them. 'I will not attempt to express my chagrin' at 'my evil destiny', lamented Melvill. Seldom is reaction so unequal to the event. The long list of employers who failed to promote the soldier of ill-fortune had a point. He was irresponsible to the point of being ridiculous, totally unreliable.

Melvill's self-defined misfortunes continued. He could not even revenge himself on the Cossacks, for they were working in alliance with Charles X. He captured a party of aristocratic ladies, but a senior officer claimed them, thus thwarting Melvill's drooling hopes of a rich ransom. Soon Brandenburg withdrew from the alliance with the Swedes, and Melvill was among the forces returned to Prussia. By 1658 he was in Swedish service, raising troops in Germany in support of Charles X's invasion of Denmark. The death of the Swedish king in 1660 led to Melvill's regiment being disbanded, and excited by news of the restoration of Charles II in Britain, he hastened to London in search of reward for his services in the Worcester campaign. But all he got was a gracious reception, and a promise that his services would not be forgotten. This hardly being enough to live on, Melvill sadly returned to Germany, where there were always wars to join. This time he joined forces raised by the Elector of Cologne to fight under the emperor against the Turks in Hungary. Predictably, by his own account he

met with misunderstandings and failures to acknowledge his just deserts —
but also with good luck which ensured his survival at one point. In an
incident in the 1664 campaign he found his helmet uncomfortable and gave
it to a servant to wear. The force of 500 men he was commanding was
then overwhelmed by Janissaries — who proceeded to behead his servant,
assuming from his special helmet that he was the commanding officer.
Melvill did not try to explain the error, but hid before making his way
back to his army.

Melvill was now forty, with the end of his campaigning days in sight.
But at last, through his endeavours against the Turks, he began to receive
some recognition. It is interesting, in judging his memoirs as a source, that
the only part of his Turkish campaign that he mentions is the helmet
incident. Entertaining self-deprecation takes precedence over what must
have been distinguished service. Otherwise, when he was passing through
Vienna after the 1664 campaign, the emperor would hardly have sent him
a gold chain and medal. In Cologne the elector went one better, sending
his portrait mounted in diamonds on a gold chain.

Soon thereafter, in 1665, Melvill entered the service of George William,
Duke of Hanover, who soon became Duke of Celle on the death of his elder
brother. Melvill became commandant of Celle, charged with guarding the
town. At last he had a settled, permanent position: not a very exalted
one, and he had not the riches he had lusted after. But it was a lot better
than continuing to wander around in search of employment. However, his
campaigning was not yet over. In 1666 he was with troops from Celle and
other German states which relieved Bremen from siege by the Swedes —
though he was not allowed to go with a force dispatched to help the
Venetians against the Turks in Crete. Melvill still had hopes that he might
end his days back in Britain, for in 1667 he visited London. He found
Charles II kind as ever: but he declared that he was unable to reward
everyone who had fought for him in the past. Sourly Melvill observed
that many of the most prominent men at court were former enemies of
Charles, and that 'the good Prince gave no thought to anything but to his
mistresses'.

Back in Celle, Melvill was involved in some campaigning in the petty
quarrels of local princes, then in 1673, after the French had invaded the
Netherlands, he was with German forces sent to Alsace in alliance with
the Dutch. In this campaign in 1675 Melvill fought in his last battle. He
was on the winning side, but when the French overran the position he was
holding, he not only received eighteen wounds but was trampled into the

ground by the advancing French soldiers. Yet the following year he was
sufficiently recovered to campaign against the Swedes (allies of France)
– and receive further slights and disappointments. 'I realised that I was
already well on in years, covered with wounds, and yet without substantial
material advancement, and without the prospect of obtaining such'. But in
1678 the wars ended, and Melvill was rewarded by the office of high bailiff
of the county of Gishorn, and the rank of brigadier.

'Since then, nothing of importance has happened in my life' as Celle was
at peace – though he was advanced to the rank of major-general. When
he finished writing his memoirs is unknown, but at that time he recorded
himself as happy in the midst of his family, and even happier that God had
granted him time to meditate upon Him and His mercies. Perhaps there is
some recognition here that his long career as a soldier needed extensive
piety to balance moral accounts.

Yet, as his memoirs show, he was not ashamed of his life – a few isolated
incidents apart. He had led the honourable life of a soldier, and ended up
with a position suited to his much-vaunted noble birth. His anecdotes of
his life seem to have given him the reputation of something of a character
– though how far he can be believed in detail is dubious. He may not have
striven for an image of heroism and achievement, but he certainly made
himself colourful. He intrigued the Electress Sophia, sister-in-law of the
Duke of Celle, whose attention was drawn to him when a marriage was
proposed between him and a lady in her household. Sophia described him
in 1667 as

> a Scotsman called Melville; soldier of *ill*-fortune I call him, for a cannon-shot
> has carried away part of his chest, which is only supported by an iron
> contrivance. With all his valour he has won no greater prize than his
> present charge.

The wedding duly took place, Sophia remarking bitchily that the lady
'seems to prefer half a man to no man at all'. Clearly he was a notably
battered figure even before the occasion in 1675 when he received eighteen
wounds (by his own account – sixteen according to Sophia), eight of them
on the head. She was amazed by his fast recovery.

> I verily believe that the Scots are descended not from Adam but from the
> serpent. One cuts them into sixteen pieces like Melvill and they all join
> together again

– though he was evidently left with a permanently maimed hand.

The high bailiff of Gishorn lived on in comfortable obscurity until 1706. In 1680 he ensured that the noble status of his children would be recognised by obtaining (like other Scots exiles) evidence of his noble descent from Scotland — far from accurate, but impressive enough for the purpose. It was not his nobility, however, or his military achievements that preserved his memory, but his memoirs, published in French in Amsterdam in 1704 at the wish of the Electress Sophia. The opening words of the memoirs perhaps reflect Melvill's realisation that his career was not altogether creditable: 'It is the most difficult task imaginable to speak of oneself in such a manner as to please every one'. But it is his frankness about his failings which gives his autobiography credibility — though some allowance should be made for his selling himself as an engaging rascal. His lack of detail about his involvement in Scotland's wars is infuriating, but he presumably felt that they would not be of much interest to his European readers.

Nonetheless, his narrative is of interest for the way in which it presents Scotland's troubles not just in the well-known context of Britain's civil wars, but in a much wider perspective of endlessly fluctuating alliances and wars on a European scale. To a career mercenary like Melvill, war was everyday work, whether in Hungary or in Scotland. The general impression to emerge from his memoirs is a horrifying one. Not war as an occasional trauma, but permanent war, war as a way of life, war sickening in its casual barbarity. As Melvill crisscrossed central Europe, his anecdotes and tales give us snapshots of devastated countrysides, marauding troops of every variety having in common only the fact that they are brutally parasitical on the civilian population. Civilians are mentioned only when they are having food, lodging and money extorted from them, or — on a few occasions — when giving succour to Melvill when his fortunes are at their lowest.

As to the man himself — unscrupulous, prepared for atrocity as a matter of course — perhaps all one can say in his defence is that he was no worse than many, many thousands of others of his age, who would have supported his values and acted like him. It is a disquieting thought.

His career was composed mainly of defeats, but he came out of it reasonably well — in material terms — in the end. The story may have seemed to him a miracle of survival. But it might well be concluded that it was a miracle that contributed nothing worth having to human experience — except that it allowed him to detail the horrors of the period and his part in them. If his account of his career seems a confused chaos of wars, that is what it was, meaningless except in its demonstration of how often Scottish pride in the heroism and achievements of its mercenary soldiers abroad is misplaced.

FURTHER READING

Memoires de Monsieur le Chevalier de Melvill, Géneral Major de Troupes de S. A. S. Monseigneur le Duc de Cell, & Grand Baillif du Comté de Gishorn (Amsterdam, 1704).

An English translation of the memoirs by Torick Ameer-Ali was published as *Memoirs of Sir Andrew Melvill* (London and New York, 1918).

TWO

MERE HASTY BABBLEMENTS?

Mr Robert Baillie

ANDREW MELVILL SETS Scotland's wars in a context of endless swirling Europe-wide bloodshed. Robert Baillie followed the continental wars of the 1630s from a distance, but not merely as a casual observer. He was involved in that he knew that their outcome could threaten his religion, and that reactions to foreign war could cause instability in Britain. War can be infectious. When domestic war did indeed arrive, his focus naturally changed. Battles in central Europe took second place to battles at home. Moreover, he quickly came to be not just a commentator, but a significant player in Britain's complex dance.

Baillie became widely known – as the author of many publications on the bitter controversies of the age, and as a scholar outstanding for depth of learning, this being reflected, it was said, in his knowledge of thirteen languages. (Even Urquhart of Cromarty, seldom admitting being second to anyone, only claimed twelve.) Some of his work lay outside the study, for not only did he play the role of parish minister and become well known in church assemblies, but he became an ecclesiastical diplomat negotiating with the English in the obsessive but futile attempt to persuade them that – to put it cynically but not altogether unfairly – God was a Scotsman.

Having taken part in dead controversies in past ages would hardly have been enough to preserve Baillie's name in later times much beyond an obscure footnote or two. But, in a sense, Baillie lives. The books he published, on which he no doubt thought any fame would rest, lie unread, and he is remembered instead (occasionally, at least) because of an informal, unacademic work that he would probably have been horrified to see published at all. What posterity has valued highly has been his *Letters and Journals*, especially his many letters, frequently hasty, often very long, addressed to his cousin William Spang, Scots minister at Veere, the Scots staple port in the Netherlands. Often the letters turned into journals, with Baillie hastily noting down each day the most important developments in public affairs – especially of course those in which he was involved himself.

Thus in later generations Baillie's *Letters* became recognised as sources

AN
HISTORICALL
VINDICATION
OF THE
Government of the Church of Scotland,

From the manifold bafe calumnies which the moft
Malignant of the Prelats did invent of old, and now lately
have been publifhed with great induftry in two
Pamphlets at LONDON.

The one intituled *Iſſachars burden, &c.* written and
publifhed at Oxford by *John Maxwell,* a *Scottiſh* Prelate,
Excommunicate by the Church of *Scotland,* and declared an
unpardonable Incendiary by the Parliaments
of both KINGDOMS.

The other falſly intituled A Declaration made by King *James*
in *Scotland,* concerning Church-government and Presby-
teries; but indeed written by *Patrick Adamſon,* pretended
Archbiſhop of St. *Andrews,* contrary to his own conſci-
ence, as hinſelfe on his Death-bed did confeſſe
and fubfcribe before many Witneſſes
in a Write hereunto annexed.

By ROBERT BAYLIE Miniſter at *Glaſgow.*

Publifhed according to Order.

London, Printed for *Samuel Gellibrand* at the Brafen-
Serpent in *Pauls*-Churchyard, 1646.

TITLE PAGE OF ROBERT BAILLIE'S *An Historical Vindication of the Government of the Church of Scotland* (London, 1646). Here Baillie in his role as a leading presbyterian propagandist refutes publications by two Scottish episcopalians, as part of the campaign to persuade the English to establish presbyterianism. *By Courtesy of the Trustees of the National Library of Scotland.*

indispensable to historians. But not all judgements on them were entirely favourable. The great nineteenth-century historian Thomas Carlyle denounced them in typically extreme terms: 'As to composition, nothing can be worse written than these Letters are, mere hasty babblements, like what the extempore speech of the man would be'. And having decided the word 'babblement' was appropriate, Carlyle used it repeatedly. One of the ironies of history dictates that while few can now endure the endless extravagant rhetorical gestures of Carlyle's style, the informality of Baillie seems much more accessible. And Carlyle does acknowledge some virtue in Baillie on this point, by accepting that the very simplicity of the *Letters*, the fact that they often seem closer to everyday speech than polished prose, gives them an attractiveness, a feeling of immediacy, lacking in other sources. The composition is indeed often chaotic, as Baillie switches – or rather wanders – from narrative of national events to details of his own doings; from family anecdotes and news of friends to theological controversy. If only he had had a word processor . . . And yet, a sterilised, rewritten, rearranged Robert Baillie would lose most of his distinctiveness and charm.

The letters began as part of an exchange with William Spang before the troubles began. Baillie was keenly interested in European affairs. He wanted to follow the progress of Europe's multifarious wars, to hear about the fortunes of Protestantism and its Catholic enemies. He wanted to know what the latest books being published on theology and religious controversy were. By Baillie's account, it was remarkably difficult to get such news of Continental affairs in Scotland, and many academic books could not even be bought in London. So, Spang (whose letters unfortunately don't survive) provided him with the foreign news he thirsted for, and in return, he sent Spang information about what was going on in Scotland. At first at least Baillie got the best of the bargain. He was living in the country, and must have found Scots news hard to obtain – and anyway there was not much exciting going on in Scotland.

Baillie was born in Glasgow in 1602. Though his mother was the daughter of the town clerk and his father a merchant burgess, the indications are that the family was not a particularly prosperous one. Mother was a widow who had remarried, and father seems to have been a pretty obscure figure in the town. Baillie must have done well at the grammar school, for he moved on in 1617 to the university. Having received his AM (as the MA was then called) in 1620, he would have liked to do what his richer contemporaries were doing: travel on the Continent. But he hadn't the money, and settled for touring in Scotland instead, visiting relatives (which kept the cost down) in Edinburgh and a number of other major towns. He then returned to Glasgow to study divinity, having decided to become a parish minister. On completing his studies, however, he first became a regent (teacher) at Glasgow University, which was a common move for a would-be minister awaiting a suitable parish. Not only did being a university teacher provide a living, it gave an opportunity to make a name for yourself, to attract favourable attention and patronage from those who had parishes to offer.

This happened in Baillie's case. The Earl of Eglinton, father of one of his students, presented him to the parish of Kilwinning in Ayrshire in 1631. He settled in quickly, and vigorously opposed a suggestion that he be moved to an Edinburgh parish. Whatever the prestige of the capital, he modestly felt himself best suited to a country parish:

> It has pleased God so to join my heart to my people, and theirs' to me, ever since my entry among them, that to speak of a departure it were to break not my heart alone, but [those] of many hundreds that are glued to mine.

There were, however, other reasons than the personal. Baillie, like Eglinton and his parishioners, was presbyterian in his inclinations, and in Glasgow had been taught by a number of men who (like himself) were to be among the most eminent covenanting divines opposing royal religious policies. His attitude to changes being made in worship and theology by Charles I was that he could not in conscience adopt some of them himself, but equally he felt at this time that he could not publicly denounce them or take part in resistance to them. Such defiance of the king, the supreme magistrate, could not be justified.

In Edinburgh as capital of Scotland pressure to conform, to set an example to the rest of the country, was strongest. Baillie would have been under pressure to practise many 'English Ceremonies', and to denounce, for example, those who refused to kneel at communion. His freedom to preach against 'Arminianism and Papistry' would have been lost. He was prepared to compromise, even to practise kneeling at communion, the most controversial of recent 'innovations' in worship, but he wanted to retain as much freedom and flexibility as possible. In the obscurity of Kilwinning he had this, as well as the love of his parishioners. He also gained a wife there: Lilias Fleming, whom he married in 1632.

Robert Baillie began copying the letters he wrote to Spang – or some of them – into a letter book in about 1636. The first few pages are missing, and the earliest surviving letters date from 1637 – just the right moment for the historian of the troubles. Perhaps he already suspected that great events were at hand in Scotland, and wanted his own record of them.

The babblements – or those which survive – begin, and in January the first line of the first letter reveals Baillie's anxiety about the new prayer book. Orders for using it in worship had been issued, and like hundreds of others Baillie wanted to see a copy. All were suspicious, because the new book had not been printed yet, so they feared there was a plot to get ministers to promise to use a form of service they had not been allowed to see. This piece of official bungling was to prove characteristic of the regime in the controversies that followed. The prayer book might well be an 'apple of contention' which would banish peace from the church for ever, Baillie predicted. Not for ever perhaps, but certainly he was right for the rest of his life and beyond; and the contention was to be far more bitter than he could ever have imagined. But, as over the proposed move to Edinburgh, Baillie showed himself straddling to some degree the divide between presbyterian and episcopalian – in a way which was probably very common but was written out of history by contemporary propaganda and sectarian historians. Baillie was deeply disturbed by the new form of worship in the church. Nonetheless, he accepted the king's authority – though he thought the church was increasingly corrupt:

> Bishops I love; but pride, greed, luxury, oppression, immersion in secular affairs, was the bane of the Romish Prelates, and cannot have long good success in the Reformed.

Thus by inclination Baillie was a respecter of authority, but the interactions of events and his conscience in the years that followed forced him into defiance. Just after the tumultuous reception of the prayer book in Edinburgh in mid-1637 the Archbishop of Glasgow asked Baillie to preach at the synod of Glasgow in favour of the book and its predecessor, the book of canons. Presumably the assumption was that Baillie was respected by men in both the emerging camps – and that he was a man who did what he was told. On this occasion he didn't. He had not studied the books in enough detail to preach on them, he replied. This sounds like prevarication, but he continued boldly: from what he had seen of the books, he was not satisfied. Moreover, most ministers and other people he had come across expressed 'great displeasure' at the books. So wrote the archbishop's 'very loving Friend, and obedient Servant'. The refusal to preach turned out to be wise. The minister who preached in his place earned the dislike of all in the synod – and was thoroughly beaten up in the streets of Glasgow afterwards by a mob of piously infuriated women.

Soon Baillie was active in the local organisation of a national campaign of supplications against the prayer book. But he had deep fears about where the cause he was now involved in might lead. Having described to Spang the increasing defiance centred in Edinburgh, he brooded:

> What shall be the event, God knows: there was [was there?] in our Land ever such an appearance of a stir; the whole people thinks Popery at the doors; the scandalous pamphlets which come daily new from England, add oil to this flame; no man may speak anything in public for the King's part, except he would have himself marked for a sacrifice to be killed one day. I think our people to be possessed with a bloody devil, far above anything that ever I could have imagined.

Earlier he had feared the disaster of the church splitting in two. Already by October 1637 he thought 'bloody civil war' more likely. To punish the nation's sins, God was going to 'give us over unto madness'. Indeed in spite of involvement in the resistance movement, Baillie feared for his own safety because he was a 'moderate'. He might have been loved in the past 'yet, I think I may be killed, and my house burnt upon my head' because he refused to go along with extremists.

Such dangers did not prevent him continuing to stand up for his own beliefs. When the National Covenant was drafted in February he indicated that he could not accept it if it committed supporters to abolishing bishops, or if it provided for the possibility of using force defensively to resist the king. Instead of being rewarded with assassination, Baillie found that changes were made to the text to pacify him. By this time he was becoming a respected and very active figure among the leading ministers of the resistance movement. To lose his support would be an embarrassment. More generally there was anxiety that the new covenant should act as an impressive public show of unity, and its authors were ready to make concessions in detail to ensure it did not instead prove a cause of division.

The National Covenant appealed – ostensibly – to the past, to legality, to true Protestantism, and against popery, against illegalities, against attempts to undermine godly religion. It earnestly stressed loyalty to the crown, but in reality was a declaration of defiance, indeed of rebellion. Baillie continued full of worries about the future 'Our main fear [is] to have our religion lost, our throats cutted, our poor country made an English province'. Unless God intervened 'I take the religion, liberty, and peace of our land, houghed [hamstrung] and clean overthrown for our days'. Nobody could accuse him of optimism. Nor, indeed, of irrational faith that the cause would triumph through its righteousness or divine support.

Triumph it did, however. The king's attempt at crushing the covenanters in 1638 proved such a masterpiece of incompetence that it collapsed without a war being fought. The covenanters proceeded to a general assembly to reform the Scottish church. Baillie, typically, had worries. In particular, an assembly could not be held legally without the king's permission. However, royal consent was eventually obtained, Baillie's tender conscience satisfied.

In the midst of dramatic public events he records very little of his family life. But one vivid cameo is inserted at random, with no logic except his concern for his family:

> My second boy, Harry, a most pretty child, of two years old, about eleven hours, following his mother to the brewhouse, is unattentively near the caldron full of seething wort.

The child took hold of the cauldron, which tipped over. Most of the contents missed him but 'some of the scalding wort gushed out upon the babe'. He could have been 'burnt to death', but the scalding was limited to the back of his head, his neck and one hip, and his face was 'safe'.

> My heart had been overmastered with grief, if so unworthily my pretty child had either been deformed or killed ... there is grief in the want [lack] of children, and as much in having of them.

A commonplace sentiment: how many parents have echoed it down the centuries?

Within a few weeks Baillie was back on the national stage, as a member of the 1638 general assembly. His recognition of the importance of the Glasgow Assembly was indicated by the great length of the 'story' of it that he compiled for Spang. Here Baillie's prose is more formal and ordered. But still the personal comments and stray minor anecdotes find their way in. His account of the assembly is perhaps the most important of the surviving unofficial historical sources for it. Yet the asides are often as valuable as the main narrative. They set the mood, bring events alive.

The king's commissioner, the Marquis of Hamilton, tended to be late in arriving in the morning. The reason? As the king's personal representative, he was under orders to behave like the king. This meant he had to eat a 'magnificent and very sumptuous' royal breakfast every day, and this took time. It was hard for members to get to their seats, often causing long delays, because so many folk crowded into the cathedral, making a great din and clamour. Was this a vice common to all nations, or attributable to peculiarly Scottish rudeness? Or was it just the zeal stirred up by the covenanting cause? More orderly behaviour in religious buildings could be learnt from the pope, Turks, or pagans, he added (certainly a thought he would not have wanted to be published). Such gems catch the reader's attention, stimulating the mind's eye.

Such trivia apart, Baillie had one issue on his mind above all others. Was the National Covenant compatible with episcopacy? To satisfy moderates like Baillie himself, the covenant had only said the existing bishops should be punished for their sins, but not that their office would be abolished. But most covenanters assumed that abolition was implicit. Baillie had spent 'many a sorrowful day' considering the issue. In the assembly he declared for one of his customary compromises. Bishops should be removed from the church. But episcopacy should not be ruled to be unlawful. It could be lawful in other Protestant churches for episcopacy to continue. Baillie had similar quibbles when it came to the abolition of changes in worship made by the 1618 Five Articles of Perth. But of course these were not mere quibbles to him – nor to his opponents. They were points of principle, and after the assembly he wrote to several of the covenanters' leaders explaining his reservations in detail and asserting that they should not be grounds for persecution. But though he was infuriating his fellow covenanters on some points, Baillie changed his mind on one central issue in a way satisfying to them. Further study led him to the conclusion that, after all, armed resistance to the king could be justified. Decision on the matter was urgent for him, for after the Glasgow Assembly abolished bishops there was no doubt that there would be war – and indeed it was known that the king was preparing to invade.

Again, in this First Bishops' War of 1639, the king was humiliated, Spang duly being provided with an account of how royalists in Scotland had been crushed and the king had failed to invade when he realised how strong the covenanters' forces on the border were – forces which included Robert Baillie as chaplain of the Earl of Eglinton's regiment. He had a pretty aggressive concept of the role of a military chaplain. He supplied half a dozen 'good fellows' with muskets and pikes, his boy (servant) with a sword – and himself with a pair of pistols and a sword. But these, he hastened to add, were for protection against robbers. His official tasks were only to pray and

GLASGOW CATHEDRAL, scene of the General Assembly of 1638 which defied the king, overthrowing episcopacy and setting up a presbyterian church. Robert Baillie supported this revolution, though with some lingering anxieties and doubts. Detail from a late seventeenth-century print by John Slezer, from his *Theatrum Scotiae*.

preach. The work that made his time as a chaplain invaluable to posterity, however, was his unrivalled description of the Scots army's camp, of its officers and soldiers, their behaviour and morale. Voluntary psalm singing, praying, Bible reading. But unfortunately also some swearing, cursing and brawling.

Once back in Kilwinning, Baillie was soon threatened with another upheaval, in the form of a move to transfer him to the ministry in Glasgow. He continued, however, to lack ambition for a pulpit in a major burgh, and again he managed to hang on to his rural parish. Thus when the Second Bishops' War came in 1640 Baillie found himself playing the role of chaplain in the same regiment as the previous year. Before he set out for the army on the eastern borders he embarked on a new strand of activity. He produced, anonymously, his first publication, *Laudensium Autokatakrisis. The Canterburian's Self-Conviction*. William Laud, Archbishop of Canterbury, was loathed and feared by the covenanters as one of those mainly responsibly for the religious policies in Scotland which had caused the troubles. The book was devoted to the destruction of his supposedly 'popish' beliefs and those of his supporters, and to arguing that such ideas were as dangerous in England as Scotland. England should not, therefore, be making war on Scotland, but acting with her against the common enemy.

The book was written at the suggestion of Archibald Johnston of Wariston, one of the most extreme and inflexible of the covenanter leaders, and he revised the text before publication. It is hard to know how to interpret this. Why did he ask Baillie to produce this propaganda work? He might have been expected to be one of those most ready to denounce the troublesome minister who had made a nuisance of himself at the Glasgow Assembly. Certainly the incident shows again that Baillie was regarded as a particularly learned country minister. Or was there some thought of diverting Baillie from making trouble on controversial issues by employing his talents on a task on which he could be trusted?

In 1639 the covenanters had waited in vain for the king to invade. In 1640 they decided to take the initiative and force a decision. On 20 August the army crossed the River Tweed without opposition. Baillie describes how the troops of cavalry stood in the river to break the force of the current, while the infantry regiments waded across downstream – including their colonels, who dismounted to set an example for their men. There had been competition among the commanders for the honour of leading the invasion, so lots had been drawn. The winner was the Earl of Montrose, 'to whom I think it was very welcome'. This was perhaps a rather ironical comment on Montrose's passion for glory. But there is also, in a longer perspective, irony that chance dictated that the leader of an invasion directed against King Charles was, within a few years, to become a royalist general.

Within days there was a more eventful river crossing. The army forced the passage of the Tyne in the face of an English army, which fled. Newcastle surrendered, but Baillie admitted that the Scots didn't know what to do next. They were so short of supplies that many were deserting, yet they didn't want to take food from the English. If local Englishmen began to rise against them as looters, and forces from the rest of England began to concentrate against them, the outlook would be grim. Part of the trouble was that the covenanters had genuinely expected active support in England. They had generously invaded England to free the English from 'popery' and other such horrors. When the Scots came, the happy English would surely help them:

> If the English will now be beasts, and dastardly cowards, they must lie without any man's pity under their slavish servitude for ever.

However, the situation soon stabilised, as the king despaired of military success and agreed to open negotiations.

Baillie returned to Kilwinning, but hardly had time to settle back into the routine of parish minister when he was summoned again to England. He was to return to the Scottish headquarters at Newcastle, and bring with him a number of copies of his *Canterburian*, and all the sources and papers which had been used in writing the book. No explanation was given, but later his role was defined as trying to convince English Laudians of their errors. A more specific task was probably already in mind for him, however. The Scots were determined to bring about the downfall of Archbishop Laud, working in conjunction with his many English puritan enemies. Not only was he evil and ungodly, but the covenanters could never feel their revolution was safe while he influenced the king. Scots commissioners were to go to London to negotiate peace – involving parliament as well as the king – and Baillie was to join the delegation as one of the leading anti-Laud experts.

Baillie's journey first to Newcastle, then London, inspired his first surviving letters to his wife, Lilias. 'I know thou does now long to hear from me,' he starts one letter with confidence. Whether she liked the contents is impossible to know: brief, though heartfelt, references to her and their children, something on his own activities, a lot of miscellaneous public news. And what did she make of the short note announcing 'It is laid upon me to give his little Grace [Laud] the last stroke, to make, as we hope, his funeral'? The stroke was to be the Scots-led prosecution of Laud as 'the prime incendiary', the person primarily responsible for the troubles. This gloating anticipation of helping bring about someone's execution is unexpected, given what Baillie has revealed about himself up to this point. It may be that the 'funeral' was meant metaphorically, as a reference merely to Laud's downfall. But by this time calls for Laud's death were being made, and given the virulence of Baillie's loathing for him and fear of the danger to true religion that he represented, hope for his execution is quite possible.

Laud was not to die on the scaffold for some years, but compensation was offered by the trial of the Earl of Strafford, lord lieutenant of Ireland and regarded as second only to Laud as an 'incendiary', a lighter of the fire of the troubles. Baillie attended the trial, writing a detailed description of it, with his usual informal asides and comments. When at one point the accused broke down during a speech, weeping when mentioning his first wife, Baillie recorded that explanations offered ranged from the charitable through the cynical to the libellous. Genuine grief? A rhetorical device to win sympathy? A delaying tactic as he had forgotten part of his speech? Or guilt because he had hit her and killed her when she found 'one of his whore's letters'? Strafford was duly convicted and executed. Baillie mentions neither, though in advance he had predicted hopefully 'when we get his head, then all things will run smooth'. Whatever he had meant about Laud's fate, bloodlust is certainly present now.

Most of his months in London were, however, spent in argument and writing against Laud and similarly inclined divines. Among the results of this were several treatises which were published after he returned to Scotland, in addition to new editions of his *Canterburian*. In England as well as Scotland, it was books that made his name. Baillie at last set off for home in June 1641. Travelling up the east coast by sea, he resolved never to do so again after experiencing stranding on a sandbank, a storm, a leaking ship, and narrowly avoiding being wrecked on rocks. But as usual God did his stuff, 'blessed be his name'. Baillie was not home long before he was off to the general assembly in St Andrews, and then (judging by some of the detail he gives) to attending some of the Scottish parliament's meeting in Edinburgh).

1642 brought further, more permanent, upheaval. He accepted an invitation to return to his old university of Glasgow, as joint professor of divinity with an old friend, David Dickson. The reasons for his agreement to leave Kilwinning at last were mixed. Perhaps the events of the past few years had developed his taste for writing and teaching, and made him wish to be rather closer to the centres of events than in a rural parish. And had he indeed shown arrogance, going against God's will by refusing so many offers of moves in the past? By this time all three of Scotland's other universities had approached him to accept chairs. A more practical reason for change was that the Earl of Eglinton had failed to pay most of his stipend for a number of years, and, when asked, refused to pay up. Maybe this was one result of Baillie's occasional troublesome doubts and qualifications on controversial issues, or maybe the earl was in genuine financial difficulties, having put his money where his conscience was in supporting the covenanting armies. Certainly on a few occasions Baillie's outspoken preaching – especially on drunkenness – had caused offence.

Whatever his motives, Baillie thus decided to accept what was, given the pressures on him, virtually inevitable. The move to Glasgow was complicated by family sickness and sadness. His wife was poorly for a year, and often 'near death'. His youngest daughter, 'a very pretty child', was 'removed' by death. On reaching Glasgow, his wife and sons were 'very sick of a fever'. Was God showing His disapproval of him settling in Glasgow, Baillie mused. This is one of many examples in the *Letters* of the almost universal habit of individuals reading divine messages to them in the fates of others. Logic surely suggested that this indicated that these 'others' were less important to God than the recipients of the messages. The 'others' could be disposed of to instruct or to warn those lucky enough to receive divine help in this way – though unfortunately these messages were often bewilderingly hard to interpret. How could Baillie really believe that his baby girl was dead as part of advice from on high on his career development? As will be seen later, Johnston of Wariston was at one time scared stiff that God would make him ill to teach his wife a lesson.

Baillie was soon busy with more orthodox teaching schedules, modestly declaring himself 'a mere novice' but clearly proud of how much he was getting done. But there were plenty of distractions: church assemblies of various sorts to attend and keep him busy as a leading member; dangerous political squabblings in Scotland to analyse. As he had always done, he kept an eye on Europe's wars. Now there was civil war in England to watch as well, and the Irish civil war in which a Scots army was involved.

Soon Baillie was himself caught up again in public affairs, though at first largely as an observer in the making of the Solemn League and Covenant, whereby the Scots allied themselves with the English parliament in return, among other concessions, for the English agreeing to introduce presbyterianism in England and Ireland. In the general assembly of 1643 'it was received with the greatest applause that I ever saw anything, with so hearty affections, expressed in the tears of pity and joy by very many grave, wise, and old men'. Tears, it was to be proved in the long term, were appropriate, but not tears of joy.

Scots Commissioners were to be sent to London to negotiate with an assembly – the Westminster Assembly as it was to become known – about religious uniformity between the nations. Baillie was chosen to be one of them. Predictably he objected. Apart from anything else, he would not (as things were planned) have time to go home and sort out his affairs; and his wife was pregnant and likely to die of grief if he went south in such dangerous times. Eventually he wangled his way out, and set off for Glasgow 'with joy for my liberation unexpected'. He rejoiced too soon. Before the end of 1643 he was summoned to join the other church commissioners in London, and this time he agreed to go. He was not to see his family again, except for one short visit, for three years.

The reason for the length of his stay in England was primarily that many of the English members of the assembly were deeply opposed to the presbyterianism promised as the price of military help from the Scots. Their endless delaying tactics combined, as Baillie saw it, with an English national characteristic. They talked too much, both in parliament and assembly, and would never get to the point. 'The unhappy, and unamenable prolixity of this people, in all their affairs, . . . is like to undo them'. 'We are vexed and overwearied with their ways. God help them'. Still, progress was made, and at the beginning of 1645 Baillie was summoned to the general assembly in Edinburgh to report on this. He then returned to Glasgow and his family. But his hopes of staying there were short-lived, for he was promptly ordered back to London. His problem was that he was so highly respected that his presence at the Westminster Assembly was regarded as vital.

Getting there took longer than anticipated. His ship (he had after all ventured to travel by sea again) was blown by storms to Holland. This was a crisis which turned out to have a bonus attached so far as Baillie was concerned. He had never been abroad before, and a taste of Calvinist Holland was welcome. He visited William Spang; he went to Rotterdam; he frequented bookshops, buying works he could not get in Britain. Indeed he was strongly tempted to linger indefinitely, and needed some persuading to return to London and duty. But in rather late and abbreviated form he had had the Continental excursion he had longed for in adolescence.

Meanwhile, whether the work of the assembly would have any point to it depended on the outcome of the English civil war. After many fears and setbacks, Baillie had been able to rejoice at the joint Scots and English victory over the royalists in July 1644 at Marston Moor. But soon he had news of a new war to weave into his narrative, and one that did not go well: the landing of an Irish force in the Highlands under Alasdair MacColla, and command of it being taken by the Earl of Montrose. How were the victories of these royalists, enemies of God, to be interpreted? Baillie was conventional. God was letting the godly covenanters be defeated because they were not sufficiently godly. As this was because God himself had failed to humble and soften the hearts of the people, it seemed a bit hard to terrify them into 'real reformation' by the horror of mass bloodshed, but His ways were not to be questioned.

Later Baillie changed his interpretation. God had resolved to humble the Scots for their excessive pride at military success in England, deliberately choosing to have them not only repeatedly defeated, but defeated dishonourably. Not only was the royalist force much smaller than its covenanting antagonists, it was made up of savages, barbarians – 'naked Scots Irishes'. But eventually even Baillie, the minister with, as it were, a professional training in finding glib interpretations of the Lord's frequently puzzling actions, admitted that he was 'amazed' at God allowing these 'barbarous men' a fifth victory in battle. Moreover, He had sent a major epidemic of bubonic plague to sweep southern Scotland. Still, Baillie hung on to his faith with determination. There must be 'love at the bottom of all this bitterness'. It was 'one of the deeps of divine wisdom, which we will adore'. That was what Baillie wrote in a letter probably intended for widespread circulation in Glasgow. In the privacy of writing to Spang he was more explicit. Not only was he amazed, he could not understand God's treatment of Scotland. Certainly for Him to humble the land for its sins was explicable. But why had He gone so far beyond what anyone had expected – and, implicitly, beyond what Baillie thought justified?

In October came good news at last: the defeat of Montrose at Philiphaugh and the dispersal of his army, a 'great mercy' from the Lord, though Baillie's reaction was restrained. At the time it was far from clear how decisive the victory had been. No one could have predicted that Montrose would never again raise a credible army.

At last, at the start of 1647, Baillie was allowed to return north, leaving a permanent memorial of his exile in London in the form of a number of published treatises on controversial issues. But though he was soon in Scotland, home was impossible to reach. Plague had reached Glasgow, and all who could had fled from the burgh. By chance or design, Baillie ended up back in Kilwinning, which was one of the places at which the refugee university was holding classes – and it may well have been where his family had fled to. But plague quickly spread through the countryside, and Baillie took his family to Edinburgh (now plague-free) for safety. Soon new dangers joined the 'pestilence'. Relations with the English parliament deteriorated rapidly, and the unity of the covenanters collapsed as many allied with royalists in the Engagement, planning to rescue King Charles from imprisonment in England. Most of the ministers of the church opposed the Engagers, so church-state conflict emerged. As the Engagers took over

government and successfully raised an army, Baillie found another cause
for amazement:

> Our State has now found, which scarcely could have been believed, that,
> contrary to the utmost endeavours of the Church, and all their friends,
> they can raise and maintain an army, and do what they will at home
> and abroad.

Baillie believed in separation of church and state, thus that the church should
not interfere in civil matters. Nonetheless in a sense he clearly thought that
the church should be supreme, for it was the conscience of the state, and the
state should listen to it. Naively he had taken it for granted that in case of
dispute, state would defer to church. How could he be so ill-informed on
the realities of power? Given his fascination with the politics of Britain and
Europe, it is hard to understand except in terms of faith. A faith strong
enough to see bubonic plague as a gift from God was strong enough to
think mere politicians could be swept aside by God's church.

However, if the Engagers were distressingly unimpressed by ecclesiastical
arguments, they were most certainly influenced by worldly, military force.
Their bungled invasion of England in 1648 led to their total destruction
by Oliver Cromwell at the battle of Preston. Deprived of its army, the
Engager regime in Scotland collapsed, and the 'Kirk Party' regime, in
sympathy with the church, took power in Scotland. But new disaster
soon followed. The English executed Charles I. The Scots immediately
proclaimed his son Charles II, thus making a new conflict between the
countries almost inevitable – and sending Baillie on his travels again, as
one of the church's delegates sent to the exiled new king at The Hague
to negotiate terms on which he would be allowed to return to Scotland.

Baillie was deeply impressed by the new teenage monarch – the fact that
Charles had already begun his long and distinguished career in fornication
(and indeed had an illegitimate son) was carefully concealed from the pious
Scots. Even so, the mission was a failure. Charles would not make all the
concessions demanded by church and state, no agreement was reached, and
the commissioners sailed home disappointed.

In spite of all his service, Baillie soon found himself in trouble, if
not danger. The Kirk Party faction now in power in the church was
determined on the severe punishment of Engagers, especially ministers.
Men were deposed from their ministries not only for positive support for
the Engagement, but for failing to have been active enough in opposing it.
Baillie thought this far too harsh, and said so. In the 1649 general assembly he

made his opinion clear in a number of cases, refusing to vote for depositions. He stood up bravely for John Strang, the principal of Glasgow University, accused of heretical tendencies by the zealous purgers now in power. By all this Baillie earned distrust – and mutterings about his own 'malignancy'. Such was the prevailing climate of bitterness that the man who on several occasions in the recent past had had to take evasive action to avoid being elected moderator of general assemblies, now found himself in danger of prosecution for lack of commitment to the cause.

Aware of the danger he might be in, Baillie's reaction seems to have been to retire to Glasgow and get on with his job as professor of divinity, avoiding involvement in controversy. For ten months there are no entries in his letter book. Did Baillie stop writing, or stop keeping copies, for fear of incriminating himself? The first letter he recorded after the gap was one addressed to Baillie himself, and recommended what he was probably doing anyway: 'Get you to your book and your work, and meddle not', wrote Robert Blair, another prominent minister, for by acting as he had in the 1649 assembly he would defile his conscience and destroy his name, 'which already suffers not a little'.

The kirk soon had too many other crises on its hands to agonise over whether Baillie might be tinged with malignancy. Charles II returned to Scotland in 1650 as a covenanted king, but this provoked an English invasion. Shattering defeat at the battle of Dunbar followed, and in a note on one of his sermons Baillie recorded 'sad weeping' both alone in his room and with his family. The kirk began to tear itself apart on an issue of principle arising from the disaster. Should only the godly be allowed to fight the English, or, since that policy had contributed to defeat at Dunbar, should royalists and Engagers be recruited, provided that such malignants repented their pasts? The Remonstrants, a substantial minority concentrated in the west, argued for an exclusive, purged, army, and went so far as to raise their own army. In the synod of Glasgow Baillie was hesitant about expressing his own view. He expected the pressure would be to vote against admitting Engagers to the army, but he was opposed to this. Yet 'I loved not to appear in contradiction to some violent men' – the fanatical Remonstrant leaders. After much prayer, however, he was 'brought to a necessity of contradicting'. His protest was to be a passive one. He decided to be absent from the debate – but then decided, 'not daring to take that course', to attend. Absence might lead to his being denounced. Then, when the crucial debate came, Baillie was delayed by other business, and when he reached the synod the crucial debate had just

ended. He did not have to deliver his opinions after all. Divine providence
had helped him out.

Presumably it was also divine providence which soon brought Oliver
Cromwell to Glasgow. Baillie fled to the offshore island of Cumbrae, hitching
a lift with Lady Montgomery – but left his family and goods behind, such
was his confidence in the likely good behaviour of the English army. As
Baillie realised, Cromwell's journey west was more a propaganda mission
than a military one, as he tried to win support from the Remonstrants.
Cromwell not having success with this policy, shortly afterwards another
English force was sent west and routed the godly Remonstrants' army of
the Western Association. Baillie was in Perth at the time, so again escaped
the English occupation of Glasgow.

However, Baillie soon had to get used to English rule. A nine-month
gap (one short letter apart) in his recorded letters in 1651–2 covers the
culminating defeat of the Scots and their king at the battle of Worcester,
the English conquest of virtually all the rest of Scotland, the setting up
of a provisional government, and moves towards a political union (on
English terms) of England and Scotland. Baillie was staunchly against the
'tender' – the English offer of parliamentary union. But in the years ahead
he was to be mainly involved in another union: the attempt to re-unite the
church by an agreement between the extremist Remonstrants and the more
moderate party, the Resolutioners. The latter began to depose ministers in
the opposing faction from office. In response the Remonstrants 'protested'
that the 1651 general assembly was illegal, and held their own assembly.
The climax of humiliation came in 1653 when each party sought to hold its
assembly at the same time in Edinburgh, and both were impartially dispersed
by hated 'sectarian' English puritan soldiers. Is it chance that there are so
very few letters to William Spang preserved from 1649 to 1652? Or had
Baillie no wish to record the years of disaster and shame, of conquest and
schism in the church? The further gap, from 1652 to 1654, probably has a
different explanation: Scotland's English rulers and the Dutch were at war,
interrupting the posts.

In the confused situation in Scotland, Baillie managed to be in both
a majority and a minority position simultaneously. At the national level
his stance as a Resolutioner meant he was a supporter of the majority.
But Glasgow and the west were the strongholds of the Protesters or
Remonstrants. In local courts he could find himself in a minority. And
English intervention could complicate matters further. It imposed on
Glasgow University as principal a man who was not only a Protester,

but a minister deposed from the ministry by his opponents. For himself, Baillie expected that his turn for deposition, as professor of divinity, had come. To the stress of this fear was added in 1653 the sadness of the death of his wife, Lilias – which does not even get a mention in his surviving letters, a culminating demonstration that his letters had ignored his family for years, concentrating instead on public affairs.

In 1654, however, a family snapshot appears – because Baillie wanted to enlist Spang's help with a family problem. Seventeen-year old Henry (Harry), his second son, was a student at Glasgow University and doing well. One of the best scholars in his class, hard-working, well-liked, virtuous: in all, very well qualified to become a parish minister. Baillie was very keen for him to do this, and the boy had assumed that that was where his future lay. Now the boy, perhaps demoralised by the bitter feuding in the church, had told his father that he had decided that he really wanted to be a merchant. Baillie's reaction is revealing. Henry should finish his current year at university. If by then he had not changed his mind, Baillie would help him become a merchant. What the university had to offer as training was irrelevant to a merchant, so he asked William Spang if his son could stay with him in Holland, and there learn French and Dutch, learn to keep accounts, and be given some practice in trading, under supervision. Baillie was not the sort of father who believed that he would lose face, even honour, if his son failed to obey orders over a career. The boy's own choice of a career was respectable enough, and better a contented merchant than an unhappy, probably incompetent, minister.

However, the result of Henry's Dutch venture must have been just what Baillie had hoped. Having gained some insight into the life of a merchant, Henry decided after all that the career of a parish minister was preferable. Soon he was back in Glasgow, 'as diligent a student as ever, without any inclination to merchandise'. Henry was back on course for the ministry. His elder brother was ahead of him, intended for the same destination. But 'My sweet boy Rab' was to die in 1658 without achieving a parish. Before he died, he confided to his father that he had had for many years an assurance of salvation. One of the signs of this was that 'in the world he never had pleasure', though the Scriptures had often been his delight. This was clearly a comfort to Baillie. Lack of pleasure was an encouraging sign, indicating the presence of divine grace.

Much space in Baillie's letters in the 1650s is taken up with the minutiae of in-fighting by church factions in Scotland, though interspersed now and again with sketches of the state of Scotland under English rule: the

country quiet with garrisons occupying it; widespread poverty; collapse
of trade; threats posed by English religious policies. Cromwell's death in
1658 brought a mixed reaction. It was welcome in many ways, but 'We
were feared for trouble after his death'. Luckily 'all is settled in peace'.
Little did he know: there were indeed troubles in the following months.
But after a period of political confusion, an outcome emerged far better
than Baillie could have hoped for: Charles II was restored to his thrones,
English conquest of Scotland was cancelled.

What was to happen about religion and the covenants? Developments in
England filled Baillie with foreboding. Before it became clear what settlement
would be made in Scotland, Baillie had a personal problem to settle, however.
The principalship of Glasgow University was, it was indicated, Baillie's, if
he wanted it. He dithered. 'Age and weakness' suggested refusal. In his
eyes there had been no legitimate principal since Dr Strang had been forced
into resignation in 1650. Since Strang's death in 1654, Baillie believed, the
principalship had been 'no less than my due and just deserving'. Indeed,
almost his hereditary right, as he had married as his second wife Strang's
daughter Helen.

Now that the Remonstrant upstart who had been intruded into the
principalship had himself been deposed, what was Baillie to do? The job
might be his due, but he was 'far averse from changes and advancement'.
He was loath to leave his chair of divinity – which was consistent with
his reluctance to leave Kilwinning long before. But principal he became –
probably not all that reluctantly in reality – when he heard it was the king's
will. Baillie's promotion, implicitly accepting the new regime's religious
policies, was a propaganda triumph for it. A former leading covenanter
spokesman and propagandist had endorsed it. But it was not a happy
endorsement. Writing of the covenants and of the persecution of ministers
more extreme than himself, Baillie displayed a sadness – sometimes only
implicit as he carefully narrates events without comment.

Soon he had a much greater sadness to lament. Before the end of 1661
episcopacy was restored in Scotland – or rather, assumed to exist. Baillie
was grief-stricken. But he was evidently ready to continue to serve in a
prominent position in what was now an episcopalian church, under the
authority of an archbishop. He was aging, in poor health and demoralised.
His last letter (May 1662) was, appropriately, to Spang. He managed to fit
in discussion of the material for a gown sent from Holland for his wife – even
that had turned out to be the wrong size. Generally the tone was gloomy. He
had been ill for six weeks, his doctor diagnosing scurvy. 'It were a favour to

me to be gone'. Scotland had suffered so much for Charles II, at Dunbar and Worcester and elsewhere, but in spite of this presbyterianism was being destroyed. Bishops were back. The new Archbishop of Glasgow had visited the university, and Baillie had told him of his opposition to 'his way' and refused to use his 'styles' (formal modes of address) – though typically, he had apologised for this. As to persecution of ministers, 'It's the matter of my daily grief, and I think it has brought all my bodily trouble on me, and I fear it shall do me more harm'.

> My hearty service to your dear kind wife, and all your sweet children. I rest, after the old fashion, your cousin to serve you. R. Baillie.

So he signed off to Spang, to his role as a historian, and, in the event, to his life. He died in August, and those who have been reading the *Letters* are likely to feel that they have lost a friend.

Robert Baillie had begun his career as a minister who believed in bishops and their authority, who had some doubts about innovations in worship and yet practised at least some of them. He could best be described as an episcopalian, but a conservative one with no zeal for change in the church. Politically he believed that nothing could justify disobedience to the king. In 1637–9 he moved on to becoming an enthusiastic presbyterian, willing to take part in the deposition of bishops on charges ranging from the significant to what now seem the silly – like curling on frozen lochs on the Sabbath. And he was soon to justify war against his king. He remained not just a loyal but a leading presbyterian for twenty years, a great denouncer of bishops. But when episcopacy returned in 1661 he was ready to live with it in the church – though making clear his disapproval.

What is to be made of this career as it swerves about? An obvious conclusion would be that this was a man who was always with the winners, whose flexible conscience conveniently allied with the majority. There is an element of truth in this. But there are factors in mitigation. It is a type of career pattern common to a great many parish ministers (and university staff) in these decades of high emotion, great fears, and disastrous consequences of making the wrong decisions. Deposition from the ministry in most cases meant total ruin, loss of home and income, reducing minister and family to poverty. It meant ostracisation, sometimes exile. If some deposed bishops, who might have hoped for support from the king, had almost starved after 1638, what might an ordinary minister expect? Practical arguments could be powerful influences on principles. And there were of course genuine principles. Baillie and others could argue with justice that the 'episcopal' church they had been loyal to up to the 1630s was not the same as the 'popish'-inclined church of the book of canons, prayer book and suchlike horrors.

Baillie personally could also point out that at critical turning points he had argued and questioned, often courting unpopularity by doing so. He had needed to be genuinely convinced. There is a paradox here. He was a worrier. He was often fearful. He refers on a number of occasions to his tendency to silence, to keep quiet on risky issues. Yet on a number of occasions he spoke out when others didn't dare. Perhaps it was the very fact that he recognised his own tendency to timidity that made him force himself to speak out.

Only one description of Baillie survives – and it seems designed to confuse rather than inform: 'The little monk of Kilwinning'. Just that. Enigmatic, inspired by the fact that there had once been an abbey at Kilwinning. It suggests a retiring, bookish man. Personal information in the *Letters* is infuriatingly sparse. But their tone and other information provides a picture of a man happy before the troubles with doing the pastoral work of a rural parish, liking his parishioners, earning and valuing their respect. He also enjoyed his academic work as a professor of divinity and the chances for research and publication it gave him. But the troubles meant that all too often he was called away from Kilwinning and Glasgow. He proved effective as a propagandist, as a preacher, in verbal debate, in pamphleteering, but while some of the time at least he relished being involved in great events, the impression frequently given is that he longed to be back in his study, or with his family. At times, in his official capacities, he could be harsh, in controversy bitter. However, given the age and its depths of sectarian hatred, it would be unrealistic to expect otherwise. And certainly Baillie was less of a hater than most. The general impression is of moderation. He didn't revel in controversy, but was usually saddened by it, even when himself taking part. Often – though by no means always – he had some human sympathy for defeated enemies.

Had Robert Baillie chosen a motto for himself, he would no doubt have gone for something pious. But perhaps the most suitable would have been 'All I want is a quiet life'. He didn't get it. He would have had a better chance of one if he had kept his head down. But occasionally he had felt obliged to pop his head over the parapet and say 'Hey, I'm not happy about this'. So he got noticed, his ability recognised, and was dragged, nervous but flattered, into public life. His lasting reputation, however, has come not from public involvement but from his private 'babblements'. The ways of his Lord were indeed mysterious.

FURTHER READING

R. Baillie, *The Letters and Journals of Robert Baillie*, ed. D. Laing (Bannatyne Club, 1841–2. An earlier edition had been published in Edinburgh in 1775).

T. Carlyle, 'Baillie the Covenanter', *Critical and Miscellaneous Essays* (5 vols., London, 1899), iv, 226–60. The essay was first published in the *London and Westminster Review*, no.72 (1842).

F.N. McCoy, *Robert Baillie and the Second Scots Reformation* (Berkeley, 1974).

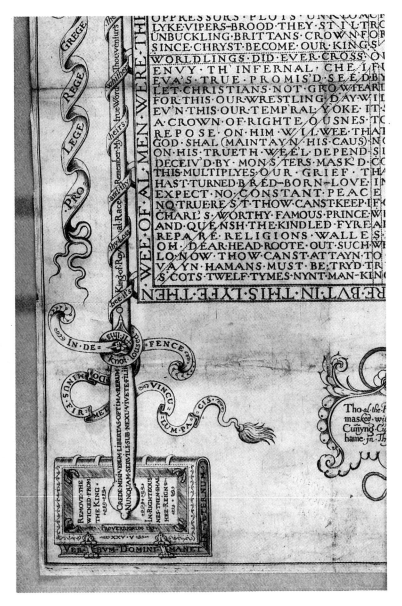

SIR THOMAS CUNINGHAM'S THRISSELS BANNER. On the left the sword of
authority rests on the Bible representing God's will underlying lawful authority.
On the sword's tip stands the national emblem, the thistle. Five rings form the
links between the sword and the banner. They stand for nobility, gentry, burgh
ministers and commons, all faithful covenanters working to hold together the
king's authority (sword) and the true church (the banner itself). But, Cuningham
explains, if the bonds linking king and church break, the five rings will remain
attached to the banner. The Scots will thus be loyal to church rather than king
if forced to choose between them. *By Courtesy of the Trustees of the National Library
of Scotland.*

THREE

THE BEARER OF THE THRISSELS BANNER:

Sir Thomas Cuningham

THOMAS CUNINGHAM FOUND career opportunities in the civil wars not as a soldier, but as a supplier of arms to the covenanters. Yet there is little doubt that conviction was at least as important as profit in determining his actions, and the strength of his commitment to Scotland's cause was demonstrated by his strange and elaborate contribution to covenanting propaganda, the Thrissels (Thistles) Banner.

When the civil wars began Cuningham was in an ideal position to help the Scottish rebels. His father had settled in Veere, the staple port through which all Scottish trade with the Netherlands was supposed to pass. There was a long-established Scottish community in the town, and Thomas's father and namesake had become one of the Scottish factors who, as deputies to the conservator, supervised the trading links between Scots and Dutch merchants. Though strictly speaking forbidden to trade in his own right, the elder Thomas did so, and died a prosperous man in 1623. His family life was complicated: he 'appears to have had five wives and an enormous number of children'. The younger Thomas had already become a factor by 1621, and married a Dutch girl four years later. But 1625 was an unhappy year for him in two other respects. He and six other Scots factors were forced to confess to a variety of misdoings, including buying up foodstuffs in times of shortage and re-selling them at higher prices to Scots merchants. And in the same year Sir Patrick Drummond was appointed conservator, a royal appointment which was unpopular with the Scottish royal burghs and with the Scots community in Veere itself.

The squabbles between conservator and factors took on a political dimension after the troubles began in 1637. Drummond remained loyal to the king who had appointed him, while Cuningham and other Scots factors came out in support of the covenant. Drummond raged impotently as they organised the sending of arms to Scotland, and at the way in which Scots merchant ships continued to reach Veere in spite of the king's attempts to impose a naval blockade on rebellious Scotland. Not only that, but before sailing from Scotland shipowners and merchants were compelled by the covenanters to undertake to return to their war-torn country with cargoes

41

of munitions. Eventually, in 1640, the Scots in effect deposed Drummond and replaced him by Cuningham, though cautiously they merely stated that he was appointed to carry out all the duties of conservator. They might be in rebellion against the king, but nonetheless they avoided challenging outright the king's prerogative right to appoint conservators.

It is at this point that Cuningham began his own narrative of events, his *Perfect Accompt, Memorial, or Quotidian Record of the most Considerable, Material and Remarkable Passages, Specially Respecting and Relative to the Public Commissions and Employments laid Upon Me . . .* This is less than half the full rambling title of his manuscript memoir, *Observantly Collected by Me.* The work opens with an 'Introduction, or the Moving Cause and Manner of my First Appearing upon the Public Theatre'. Scotland had for long time 'groaned under prelatical hierarchy'. The 'insatiable pride' of the bishops had produced a division between king and people, and horrified the reformed churches of Europe. In these circumstances

> how was it possible for any true patriot and orthodox Christian to play the neuter and live at rest abroad, while his dear country and nation was so pitifully shaken at home?

Religion and justice, the pillars of government, were undermined. A major theme of Cuningham's work, it becomes clear, is justification, both of himself and of the cause of the covenants:

> I clearly discerned a misinformed and highly offended Prince on the one hand; on the other hand his loyal oppressed and humbly supplicating subjects, and between both a faction of arrogant incendiaries crying 'no Bishop, no King'.

This was the standard covenanting interpretation of the situation: they were loyal subjects, but were making a stand against 'incendiaries' who had misinformed the king and were leading him astray. Every subject had a duty to oppose magistrates or sovereigns who acted contrary to the laws of God and nature in ways destructive to themselves and the commonwealth.

Cuningham's personal response was, as he pompously describes it, to utter 'a shrill-sounding voice as a warning shout or stentorian exclamation in an unpractised style of poesy, under the title of the Thrissels-Banner'.

The thistle banner of 1640 was an extraordinary design in the form of a flag. The flagpole from which it flew was a sword, its hilt resting on the Bible, a thistle balanced on its point: religion and nation were the causes the covenanters had drawn the sword to defend. Usually the symbol of Scottish nationhood was the lion, but the lion was specifically the symbol of the crown, and that was obviously inappropriate when the self-proclaimed patriots were opposing the king. Therefore the thistle took over, backed by the St Andrew's cross, to indicate national unity.

The flag itself was entirely covered with a closely written inscription, with the crosses of St Andrew and St George superimposed, signifying the Union of the Crowns. Another inscription ran round the border of the flag, and further inscriptions were to be found by reading along the lines of the two crosses. Bible, sword and just about everything else in the design were littered with pithy texts supporting the covenanting cause.

The text on the flag itself, reading downward the first letter of each line of the inscription, produces the cheerfully subversive doggerel:

Woe to them that control us
We'll fear God, then Carolus [Charles].

The diagonals of the St Andrew's cross on the flag read (rather incoherently):

When only Thrissels King our faithful steward born St Andrews cross enjoyed, we joyed by truth's plantation.

Reading the lines of the St George's cross added:

But since the doubled cross of Britain's chief was worn, Worldlings did ever cross our peace and Reformation.

All had been well for religion in Scotland until the Union of the Crowns not only deprived Scotland of the presence of her king, but had led to him falling under evil religious influences – though this message is rather garbled by the demands of the acrostic containing it.

The main inscription on the flag contained a rather more extended analysis of the situation in Scotland brought about by Satan seeking 'to re-establish his decayed whorish throne of spiritual adultery', and an account of the reactions of the Scots, the 'faithful Thrisselists'.

The symbolism of the banner was so elaborate that Cuningham supplied a printed 'Explication' elucidating it. The banner itself was engraved on copper and 200 copies were then printed on white satin, 1800 on paper. These he had distributed in Scotland and 'everywhere abroad'. Though the satin copies may have been meant for public display there is no indication that they were ever used as flags. As a design for a flag the banner was absurd, far too cluttered and detailed to be comprehensible. Rather it was a symbolic banner of defiance.

The Thrissels Banner was a notable tribute to the sincerity of Thomas Cuningham in his support for the cause of the covenant, but in practical terms his value to the covenanters rested on his work as an arms supplier. This is the main theme of the factual parts of his journal. It opens with a transcript of the letter he received from the covenanters' ruling committee, the committee of estates, in 1640 congratulating him on the Thrissels Banner, and proceeding to detail the events surrounding the deposition of Drummond as conservator and the appointment of Cuningham himself to replace him as conservator – an economy with the truth, as he had been appointed to carry out the conservator's functions, but not to the office itself.

The journal then moves on to detailing Cuningham's services to the cause, listing the munitions he and two Scots partners had supplied. He evidently had not provided arms for the army raised by the covenanters in 1639, but his contribution in 1640 was massive. The list was headed by a fully armed frigate, and included twelve 'great brazen cannon' and over 15,000 muskets.

The Bishops' Wars were soon over, but in 1642 a new opportunity to serve both the cause and profit himself arose. Cuningham got the contract to provide all the arms for the Scottish army being sent to Ireland. Eight ships brought 10,000 swords and sword-belts, 6,000 muskets and bandoliers, and 4,000 pikes to Scotland. Moreover, he invested as an 'adventurer' in the Irish wars, equipping two frigates and sending a shipload of corn to help the English parliament in its war with the Irish Catholic rebels, payment being promised in land to be confiscated from the rebels. But by this time civil war had broken out in England, and he agreed to one of the frigates being diverted to securing the Isle of Wight for parliament.

By 1644 the involvement of a new Scots army in the English war as an ally of the English parliament led to further demands on Cuningham, and he persuaded two Dutch merchants, Adrian and Cornelius Lampsins, to put up the money to send further massive arms shipments to Scotland and Newcastle (which was garrisoned by the Scots army): 10,000 muskets and bandoliers, 12,000 swords and sword-belts, 500 pistols and holsters, and large quantities of gunpowder and match. By now Cuningham was not only conservator but 'ordinary agent' in the Netherlands – Scotland's diplomatic representative – struggling to gain official recognition from the Prince of Orange and the states general, a task complicated by his battle to obtain recognition as conservator as well.

EDINBURGH in the mid-seventeenth century. In this view of the capital from the south the castle stands high on the left, and the city and then the Canongate trickle down the ridge to Holyrood Palace at the right.

However, he still found time to involve himself in new ventures on his own account. Early in 1645 he agreed to hire to Scotland three ships (carrying 32, 14 and 10 cannon respectively) and 200 men to protect Scotland's merchant shipping. But the committee of estates decided it could not undertake any new expense, the country being

> in a very lamentable extremity under a doubled affliction of God's destroying angel devouring as fast in the South as the bloody sword in the hand of Montrose made havoc in the North.

Not only was the covenanters' regime threatened by the military triumphs of Montrose in the north, but the Lowlands were being ravaged by bubonic plague. And there was worse to come. In August Montrose's culminating victory at Kilsyth led to the temporary collapse of the covenanting regime, some refugees who ended up in Veere giving Cuningham first-hand accounts of the situation in Scotland. Within days, however, the equally astonishing news of Montrose's defeat at Philiphaugh arrived, a 'signal overthrow of that Arch-destroyer of his own country and nation'. The news continued to be good: royalists in the north driven back into obscure corners; the

royal cause collapsing in England; the king fleeing to join the Scots army at
Newark. As negotiations for a settlement proceeded, Cuningham anxiously
reminded those involved that he was still owed £10,000 Scots, plus interest,
for arms supplied in 1640–1, as well as his pension as Scots agent and
money due to repay the Lampsins the capital they had advanced in 1644.
The English parliament had undertaken to pay this last debt, but growing
tension between parliament and the Scots, and the withdrawal of the Scots
army from England, defeated Cuningham's hopes of being able to secure
payment. In Scotland an army still had to be maintained to pursue the
remnants of the royalists in the north, and the regime was in no position
to pay its debts. The committee of estates was ready to accept that
Cuningham was owed huge sums, but payment was a different matter.
Worse followed. In 1648 the Engagers, an alliance of moderate covenanters
and royalists, won control of the regime, and asked Cuningham to supply
arms for the army with which they intended to rescue the king from the
English parliament. Cuningham refused to oblige. The Engagement was
destructive to the 'joint Parliamentary interest of both nations', which
was 'the sole inducing motive to my bypast undertakings'. He came back
to Scotland to try to obtain payment of the debts due to him, but once
he had refused to supply new arms he had no hope of generosity from the
enraged Engagers. All he got was the sympathy of 'honest patriots'.

The report of the destruction of the Engagers' army in England was
greeted with joy by Cuningham: Scotland had passed back into the control
of 'approved peers and patriots'. But such comment on events was by
now being buried in Cuningham's journal by a blow-by-blow account
of endless attempts to get payment for the arms supplied in the early
1640s. In 1649, by Cuningham's estimate, the Lampsins were still owed
over £16,000 sterling.

1650 brought some diversion from his own financial concerns, when a
delegation from Scotland arrived at Breda to negotiate for the return of
the young Charles II to Scotland. But Cuningham found that not all the
duties expected of him were congenial. The commissioners were desperately
short of cash, and demanded that he get the Scots factors at Veere to make
them a loan. This was not willingly given, but eventually 'promises and
threats' by the commissioners extorted 50,000 guilders (£5,000 sterling).
However, on this occasion Cuningham got some reward for his services:
Charles, having reached an agreement with the Scots delegation, summoned
him to his presence, recognised him as conservator and Scots agent, and
knighted him. Cash in hand might have been more welcome. As the sword

of knighthood touched his shoulder, did Cuningham recall the sword of his Thrissels Banner, the sword of the Bible and the thistle? Perhaps it was partly consciousness of his new status that led him at first to ignore requests to help ship the king's horses to Scotland, deeming it 'unsuitable' work. Typically, once he did get involved in the matter he soon uncovered the fact that those undertaking to take the horses had inflated their charges far beyond what was justified.

If Cuningham's hopes of getting payment of moneys due to him were roused by having the support of the king as well as the Scots parliament, they were soon dashed, as the invasion of England led by Charles II ended in the disaster of Worcester, and the armies of Oliver Cromwell conquered Scotland. As if that was not enough, Scotland was then absorbed into the new British commonwealth, which soon found itself at war with the Dutch. Peace was restored in 1654, and Cuningham continued his obsessive calculations in papers explaining what was due to him and the Lampsins. At this point the journal ends abruptly:

> I closed this Memorial at Campvere, being ready to depart thence . . .
> to take passage for London. The Lord protect and direct me, and grant
> his blessing upon my honest intentions and endeavours, so as I may with
> comfort return to my family, amen.

Needless to say, his mission in London was to try to get the new British parliament to accept responsibility for the remainder of the cost of supplying arms in 1644. His stay in London lasted several years, partly because of his 'inability' and 'infirmities', and there were complaints that he was neglecting his duties as conservator. Then with the Restoration of monarchy in 1660 came dismissal from the post of conservator. Sir Patrick Drummond was restored, and the Scots in Veere were so anxious to win the favour of the new regime that he was installed as an elder of the Scots church in Veere and titled conservator even before he had been commissioned by the king. Cuningham fell on hard times. In 1662 he was still hopefully petitioning the crown for £800 sterling due to him, and was reported to 'suffer much from want of the money and from disease'. But when he died, in 1669 or 1670, he was still an elder in the Scots church in Veere. Thus in spite of the bitterness of past conflicts he was not entirely ostracised after the restoration of monarchy and episcopacy in Scotland; and on the other hand he was prepared, though no doubt with sadness, to serve in a church in which the dreaded hierarchy of bishops had been restored. The hardship he suffered, moreover, appears to have been exaggerated, no doubt to support his claims for money. His family continued to thrive, both before and after his death. His eldest son, the third Thomas, worked as a factor in Veere, while his second son, Arnold, was elected to the town council in 1663 – and ten years later became burgomaster. In 1668 he was still trying to obtain payment for money advanced by his father in 1651 for transporting the king's horses.

Cuningham's journal is at once aggravating and invaluable. The outbursts of covenanting zeal in 1640 provide a most revealing account of the depth of his convictions, of why he felt he had to support the covenanters, of how he squared this with declarations of loyalty to the king by asserting that the latter was being misled. The narrative then becomes overwhelmingly concerned with his endeavours to secure his position as conservator and agent, and of his attempts to obtain payment for services rendered. Much of this, a detailed narrative supported by endless transcripts of letters and other documents, makes tedious reading. The merchant rather than the man dominates. Only occasionally does he comment on the conflicts that tore Scotland apart, and his position in the spectrum of covenanting beliefs can be charted by the fact that in 1648 he sided with the zealots of the Kirk Party in opposition to the Engagement. But in 1651 he supported the settlement with Charles II, rather than join the small extremist minority of Remonstrants who virtually disowned the king. The wider value of his work lies in the details of how Scots armies – in Scotland, England and Ireland – were supplied with arms in 1640–44. Scotland could supply the men for the wars of the three kingdoms, but needed to look overseas to arm them. Cuningham describes not only the numbers of weapons, the weights of ammunition, but how they were transported to Scotland, and the financial deals and bills of credit used to pay for them. Sober businessman, perhaps at heart Dutch as much as Scots, he combined financial expertise and religious conviction in writings which provide a unique insight into the mechanics of war which underlay Scotland's great military efforts in these years.

FURTHER READING

T. Cuningham, *The Journal of Thomas Cuningham of Campvere, 1640–1654, with his Thrissels-Banner and Explication thereof*, ed. E.J. Courthope (Scottish History Society, 1928).

FOUR

A PRIEST AND HIS LADIES:

Gilbert Blakhal

GILBERT BLAKHAL WROTE to protest against the way he had been treated by three women he had served as chaplain, and to counter malicious rumours about his conduct. He had served them faithfully, going far beyond his duty and putting himself in great danger. Yet two of them repudiated him in fury. The third didn't positively reject him – but caused him problems by dying inconveniently. Blakhal was not convinced about virtue being its own reward. He felt he deserved more.

A Breiffe Narration of the Services done to Three Noble Ladyes presents his case. This does not sound hopeful. Works devoted to expressions of grievances are seldom rewarding. But Blakhal does not whine – much. He is robust, aggressive, indignant in his writing – as he tended to be in life. Moreover, he cannot resist embellishing his tale with lively anecdotes about his adventures. He had his grievances, but revels in recalling his life.

Without grievances, Blakhal would not have written, and readers would have been deprived of a window into a hidden corner of Scotland in troubled times, into a world of priests and the remnants of a Catholic nobility secretly trying to preserve their faith.

Nothing is known of Blakhal's birth or death. Apart from one or two obscure references, he exists only in the period in which he recorded his services to his three ladies. That he bore an unusual name is some help in tracing his origins, for the Blakhals were concentrated in Aberdeenshire and he mentions having two Blakhal cousins in the area. Certainly his religion was consistent with an origin in the North East, for though it contained only a scattering of Catholics in the early seventeenth century, compared to the rest of Lowland Scotland it was a concentration.

Before he embarked on a career as a priest, Blakhal served as a soldier – for a considerable period, judging by skills he acquired. Indeed it is likely that he was an officer. However, a dramatic career change was signalled when he entered the Scottish College in Rome in 1626 to study for the priesthood. Four years of theology later he was ordained. Of the handful of students at the college some chose to enter the Jesuit order, but Blakhal decided to remain a secular priest. The choice was one of some significance,

THE GORDONS AND CATHOLICISM. The 1st Marquis of Huntly erected these
panels over the entrance of his newly-built castle of Strathbogie (now Huntly) in
1602, asserting his status as the greatest noble of the north of Scotland. His own
coat of arms is surmounted by that of the king and queen, indicating that he
holds his lands from the crown, whose authority he represents. Above the royal
coat came religious symbolism, boldly proclaiming the Catholicism of the Gordons
two generations after Protestant Reformation had triumphed in Scotland. It was
under the ultimate protection of the House of Huntly that priests like Gilbert
Blakhal operated in the area. But under the covenanters that protection collapsed.
The 2nd Marquis of Gordon, as Patrick Gordon laments, was unable to protect
his heritage. His enemies captured the castle, and hacked the 'idolatrous' Catholic
imagery off the panels. *Courtesy of Historic Scotland.*

for the Catholic mission in Scotland was bitterly split between the Jesuits and seculars. There were only a tiny number of priests struggling to survive in a hostile sea of Calvinism, yet they wasted a good deal of energy in factional squabbling and trying to undermine each other's work.

Blakhal, however, settled first not in Scotland but in Paris, as confessor to a Scot, Lady Isabelle Hay. This was the first of his three noble ladies. It is hard to know whether Blakhal in his relations with her was unlucky (as he presents himself) or rash. Almost immediately he took up his post he became involved in a furious dispute – though not primarily with Lady Isabelle. Her father, the Earl of Erroll, had sent her to France when she was in her early twenties. It may have been hoped that a suitable marriage into a noble Catholic family could be arranged, for she was equipped with a birth brieve (such as Andrew Melvill was to obtain later) so she could produce evidence of her illustrious noble ancestry. In France she was entrusted to the care of a Mr James Forbes, a cousin of Blakhal. It was presumably Forbes who had got Blakhal his job, and he soon regretted it.

Forbes planned to advance himself by marrying the aristocratic girl in his charge, and set out to woo her. She became embarrassed by the frequency with which he visited her, seeing it as threatening to her reputation. She asked Blakhal to 'admonish' him, which he did 'very mildly'. From what the priest reveals about his personality elsewhere, it seems mildness was not something he was skilled at, and evidently mildness was not perceived by Mr Forbes. He reacted furiously, and a violent argument almost led to a fight.

Doubtless there were faults on both sides. Forbes's subsequent rages and coarse abuse concerning his charge indicate his character. He would not let her have any more money until, he raged, she knelt and kissed 'his bare breech'. Blakhal's lack of tact in telling Lady Isabelle full detail made matters worse. His letter to her about the affair reduced her to tears: she would never have believed that Blakhal could be so bitter, she said – his priority, it seems, had been complaining that he had been badly treated, rather than considering her feelings. He confessed shamefacedly that the letter had been 'very satiric' – and he was supposed to be on her side.

He also zealously related to her the crude things Forbes had been saying. When Forbes came to see her, she denounced him, saying (not unreasonably) that she would not 'kiss his stinking breech'. Failing to persuade her that he had not said such things, Forbes gave up: 'all is lost, women can never forgive'.

One crisis was followed quickly by another for Blakhal. Lady Isabelle's brother (now the Earl of Erroll on their father's death) wrote telling her that he would not be sending her any more money from Scotland. He had decided that she should have two choices as to her future: join a religious institution, or return to Scotland for a marriage he had arranged. Lady Isabelle's inclination was towards a religious life – especially as the husband on offer in Scotland was a Protestant – and she had already moved temporarily into a nunnery. Blakhal set out to find a suitably aristocratic institution for her to settle in. This involved travelling to Brussels in the Spanish Netherlands and tackling the Spanish viceroy, the Infanta Isabella Clara Eugenia. What he hoped for was a place for Lady Isabelle in an order of canonesses where the women lived a religious life together according to set rules – but didn't take vows committing themselves for life as nuns did.

Boldness and a glib tongue got Blakhal an audience – and the offer of a place, when there was next a vacancy, with the canonesses of what was regarded as an élite order in their house at Mons. On a visit to inspect it, Blakhal was treated to an unorthodox but clearly much appreciated fashion show. One of the canonesses – 'one very beautiful lady' – modelled the various habits and vestments they wore at different times. No doubt a noble lady considering joining a religious order needed to take into account what the clothes were like.

Returning to France, Blakhal brought Lady Isabelle to Brussels to meet the Infanta, who proved gracious and friendly. Blakhal was deeply impressed by the Infanta, awarding her what was no doubt his ultimate accolade: in some respects she was better than a man. With her patronage Lady Isabelle's future seemed secure. Joy gave way to despair, when the Infanta died suddenly. But Blakhal with his usual persistence was soon bustling round the court trying to discover whether her favour to Lady Isabelle was still valid.

It was. In the few days of fever before her death not only had the Infanta found time to confirm Lady Isabelle's right to a place at Mons and the revenues that went with it, but had gifted her a pension until a vacancy became available. Now that she was settled, Blakhal decided to return to Paris – a journey enlivened by one of several encounters on his travels with 'cavaliers'. These were soldiers, either unpaid and making a living as best they could, or waiting for a campaign – and therefore paid employment – to begin. They regarded themselves as men of honour – but in reduced circumstances (like Lady Isabelle!). They were acting only through necessity, they explained earnestly, and indignantly rejected the suggestion that they were robbers. But, in effect, they were highwaymen. Blakhal – by his own account – behaved with calm bravery, cheekily negotiating to hand over a nominal sum to satisfy the cavaliers – whose willingness to accept such a deal does something to support their claims not to be mere thieves. Not for the last time, his military past proved useful in giving Blakhal confidence in dealing with such situations.

Something worse than an encounter with cavaliers soon followed for Blakhal. He wrote an account in a letter of what had happened in Brussels. This news was passed on to Lady Isabelle's family in Scotland. It won him their gratitude (previously they had tended to believe various lying stories about him). But it roused Lady Isabelle to fury. Before she herself had had time to tell her family what had happened, this pushy priest had presumptuously rushed in with his account – presumably hoping to gain favour. She never wrote to him, or referred to him, again. So from the first of his noble ladies he received no 'reward and thanks' for his services.

Blakhal stayed three more years in France, and his decision to leave in 1636 was evidently the result of receiving a legacy from an employer. He could afford to travel and support himself while seeking new employment. Proceeding by way of London, he set off for 'home', as Scotland still was to him. 'We were merry, and made a good voyage' on horseback through England. Here as elsewhere Blakhal indicates that he was not averse to a few – or more than a few – drinks. Spending some time in an English Catholic household, Blakhal immediately found himself involved in the Jesuits-versus-seculars feud, as the former sought to discredit him. Finally, in August 1637, he reached Scotland.

He could hardly have chosen a worse time to arrive. It was only ten days since the Edinburgh riots against the king's religious policies, branded as 'popish', had begun the troubles, though the collapse into war was not yet predictable. Intense anti-Catholic panic was spreading fast. No wonder Blakhal hastened north to Aberdeenshire, where he might expect some support. Not, however, from the Jesuits, though there was one useful exception. He obtained from the superior of the Jesuits permission to minister in six scattered gentry houses. This was better than nothing, but hardly satisfactory. He spent only one night a month at each house. The rest of the time he – plus horse and servant – lodged in taverns at his own expense.

The obvious thing might seem to be to approach the Hays of Erroll, but Blakhal was very conscious that Lady Isabelle had accused him of trying to curry favour with them, and did not want to seem to give credibility to the charge. Even when one of her elder sisters wrote asking him to come and see her, he refused. This seems unnecessarily churlish, especially as the lady concerned was Sophia, Lady Aboyne, her deceased husband (Lord Aboyne) having been a younger son of the Marquis of Huntly, the greatest Catholic in Scotland. Eventually Blakhal was persuaded to meet her. He evidently expected reproaches, but instead was received graciously and thanked for his services to her sister. One of the qualities in others that Blakhal most appreciated was their being 'thankful', ready to acknowledge services done for them. Lady Aboyne, he quickly concluded, had this virtue in large measure – 'the gratitude of her noble heart, wherein she exceeded all women, as I do believe'.

Searches for a permanent base proved difficult, though he stayed several times with Lady Aboyne. One offer of employment was rejected because the lady concerned was suspected of involvement in the burning of the Tower of Frendraught, a notorious atrocity (or possibly accident) in which Lady Aboyne's husband had died. It was another aspect of the Huntly connection that lost him another job. The dowager Lady Huntly intervened to prevent her daughter, the Countess of Moray, taking Blakhal on – evidently because he was not a Jesuit. But the problem was not just the Jesuit one. Most priests in the area seem to have been hostile to Blakhal, and to have persuaded most Catholic landlords to refuse him access to their houses. Insecurity was often the issue, as priests feared a newcomer might win patronage or employment from their own employers, at their expense.

However, in the end this hostility worked to Blakhal's advantage. Lady Aboyne's resident priest, already discontent, was infuriated at her favour to him, and walked out. Blakhal got his job – the best possible, in his opinion, because of her character and generosity. When he ate in his chamber (where a priest lived concealed for much of his clandestine existence) he got at every meal four dishes of meat, wine and ale. And his own servant went to the kitchen to choose his food for him. In other Catholic houses the priest was merely sent up a trencher of food chosen by others. Food, like drink, was important to Father Blakhal, not least because it indicated the status he was being accorded.

Moreover, Lady Aboyne soon agreed that he should come out of the closet. He 'could not endure' being virtually a prisoner much of the time in his chamber – and therefore an object of intense curiosity whenever he was glimpsed. First he asked if he could dine with the servants; the countess replied that he could dine with her and her daughter. The servants gradually got used to seeing a priest around in public. He then began to show himself

EDINBURGH CASTLE, engraved from a drawing by James Gordon, minister of Rothiemay, 1640s. The name 'Arx Pvellarvm' translates as 'Castle of the Virgins', a reference to the legend that the castle had never been 'taken'. However, deflowerment came at the end of 1650, when the castle surrendered to Oliver Cromwell. One indignant Scot exclaimed, 'It was alwayes before called the Maiden Castle, but henceforth call it the Prostitut Whore' (J. Fraser, *Chronicles of the Frasers* (Scottish History Society, 1905), 372).

outside Aboyne Castle. Soon, he boasted, there was no man better known in the parish, 'nor better loved by the best sort', even by Protestants (except for one gentlewoman, whose ambition was to wash her hands in his blood). So much for the effectiveness of the covenanters' campaign against Catholics. And so much for the modesty of this priest. In reality, the political situation may have helped him. Most of the local Protestants would have been episcopalians and royalists, themselves feeling under threat by this time (late 1638) from the covenanters – and less likely than usual to see a few Catholics as a danger.

Blakhal's services to Lady Aboyne spread far beyond religion. She referred to him as her priest, her chamberlain, and the captain of her castle, and he detailed his services under these headings.

As priest he said mass for her very nearly every day. He preached to her, and Catholics among her household, neighbours and tenants, on Sundays and holy days. Periodically he went on trips to Aberdeen, then up to Huntly, zigzaging between a small group of Catholic houses on the way, before returning to Aboyne. Thus priests employed in the household of noble protectors helped preserve the faith of a wider Catholic community. But in 1642 came an unwelcome extension of Blakhal's religious duties. Lady Aboyne fell ill. He sustained her through a long sickness, and his last duty was to supervise a clandestine burial according to Catholic ceremonies. Again, from his second lady, he received no reward. This time, it seems it was Blakhal's own fault: he had refused her offer of a legacy, to avoid charges of using his position for profit. Pride made him a hard man to please. No reward was insulting; offered reward was potentially damaging to his reputation. In this case an additional consideration may have been that he knew that Lady Aboyne had very little to give anyone.

Blakhal seems to have stumbled into acting as chamberlain, supervising Lady Aboyne's revenues by accident, on realising that she had problems. Her finances were in a mess, not least through cheating by trusted servants, and, it seems, a generosity on her part which amounted to fecklessness. The task of restoring order proved hopeless, because she failed to back him up. Crooks remained in her employment because she was too soft-hearted to dismiss them – especially if they could claim some sentimental ties to her family. She let tenants pay their rents a year or more in arrears. 'My lady deserved, in some manner, to be deceived' because of her folly, and relatives showed no interest in her plight and didn't attempt to help her.

Nor had she thought to make provision for defence of her castle in increasingly threatening times. When Blakhal settled there in 1638, weapons available consisted of a pair of pistols, owned by a man who had never fired them, and swords owned by servants. As Blakhal remarked, swords were not much use in defending houses from attack. Soon under his supervision there were twenty-four firearms in the house – including 'a very wide carbine' which was loaded with nine or ten pistol balls. This weapon he carried himself on his journeys through the country. The church militant. There had been hopes of benefiting from shiploads of weapons sent to Aberdeen by the king to arm his supporters, but bungling meant that most ended up in 'rebel' – covenanter – hands. When Lady Aboyne sent to her brother-in-law, the Marquis of Huntly, for some of the remaining arms he scornfully replied that 'ladies were not ordained for fighting' and supplied none. Ironically, in the years ahead Huntly was to prove himself a military incompetent of a high order.

There is further irony in that the most threatening force the castle needed to be defended against consisted of some of Huntly's own men, a band of about forty Highlanders from Badenoch who appeared at the castle gate demanding lodging and money. Under Blakhal's supervision a show of strength led them to back down and accept food sent out to them as all they would get. Shortly afterwards another Highland band of Huntly's vassals appeared, Camerons from Lochaber, 'a wild kind of people'. When denied access, they began to loot houses in the area. But a well-planned little expedition led by Blakhal surprised them and forced their surrender. These episodes give a strong impression of the degree of the priest's military experience – and it is at this point that he makes his only specific reference to his former career. He told the leader of the Cameron gang, 'Know that I was a soldier before you could wipe your own nose'.

Next, in this local anarchy that the feuding of covenanter and royalist had brought to the north, a party of Stewarts, Highlanders from Atholl, turned up demanding money. But they proved a fairly peaceable lot, and settled for some food and a night's lodging with tenants on the estate.

As priest, chamberlain and captain, Blakhal was (by his own account) invaluable to Lady Aboyne, suffering as she did the twin disadvantages of being a widow, and of being a personality incapable of running her household and estate. One of the reasons for the repeated incursions of the not-so-gallant Highlanders was that they calculated that a house run by a woman would be easy prey – and they may also have heard that she was a particularly easy touch. She became fond of Blakhal as well as grateful to him, and his consciousness of this was to get him into trouble. Years later, he said (or so it was reported) that she had loved him better than any man living. No romantic connotations were intended, but his account of his services to her was an extended attempt to show that he merited her love. This was necessary because Lady Aboyne's daughter, Henrietta, was furious at the rumour of a jumped-up priest, a nobody, claiming the love of a noble lady.

This was the more unfortunate as Henrietta Gordon was the third of Blakhal's noble ladies. As with the first of them, her aunt Lady Isabelle Hay, hard and devoted work by him on her behalf culminated in his losing her favour through some slight, real or imaginary. As she was dying, Lady Aboyne had been fearful for the future of her only child. Already fatherless, once she lost her mother as well Henrietta (who was aged about fifteen in 1642) would probably be put in the household of 'some heretic to pervert her'. The dying woman begged Blakhal not to abandon Henrietta 'and save her soul, if you can'. Blakhal decided that the only thing to do was to get the girl to safety in a Catholic country. Her grandmother, the dowager Lady Huntly, had settled in France to avoid the troubles in Scotland, so Blakhal resolved to go there to seek her assistance. But, knowing her character, he was not too hopeful; so he planned that if that failed, he would try to get help from Anne of Austria, the Queen of France. One thing he never lacked was confidence.

Nor did he lack a sense of honour, based on his concept of himself as a gentleman. As he was making preparations to leave for France this nearly got him into more trouble. Going into an inn, he was horrified to find it packed with drunken covenanter soldiers. But honour would not permit him to withdraw. Further, instead of keeping the low profile which would have been wise for a priest in disguise, he got drunk and ended up having a furious quarrel with the captain of the soldiers, who had asked him who he was in a manner Blakhal thought not suitable for addressing a gentleman. The squabble could have ended fatally, but eventually a drunken reconciliation took place.

Danger was not yet over, however, for the covenanters' intelligence seemed unusually good in reporting his movements, even though he managed to remain one step ahead of them. Sneaking on board a ship at Aberdeen bound for Veere got him out of Scotland – but of course into Protestant Holland. There he hitched a lift on a Dutch warship (which sounds folly) and finally reached France.

Having taken a post in a household in Normandy to support himself, Blakhal began his campaign to provide for Henrietta Gordon. Approaches to Lady Huntly proved fruitless. Blakhal spoke pretty plainly about her meanness towards her granddaughter. As it turned out it didn't matter: she died within a week, so any promises she had made would have been fruitless – 'but meritorious unto her own soul', added the priest. Pious or malicious?

Next stop, the Queen of France. Friends laughed at the absurdity of the idea that she would not only support a poor and obscure Scots noblewoman, but pay to bring her to France. But Blakhal was single-minded. He had promised Lady Aboyne to do all he could to save her daughter for Catholicism, and would persevere whatever the odds. Soon he was at court at St Germain, and though he knew no one there he quickly wheedled his way into the queen's presence with his tale of woe. Henrietta was not only descended from the Marquis of Huntly but from the Earls of Erroll, constables of Scotland, a leading noble family renowned for its valour for nine hundred years. Her father had died a Catholic martyr in the Tower of Frendraught, praying as the flames consumed him – and indeed converting one of the lairds trapped with him to the true faith. (How this was known, since all in the tower were killed, Blakhal does not reveal.) Lady Aboyne, Blakhal told the queen, had lived on in a widowhood of melancholy piety, until her death had left her poor daughter, Henrietta, at the mercy of her heretic relatives.

As with the Infanta, Blakhal's convincing tongue prevailed against all the odds. The queen agreed to support Henrietta at court until some position was available whereby she could support herself. And because the priest was worried that his travelling to France with a young girl would cause scandal, he got a letter from the King of France to Henrietta urging her to make the journey. Writing direct to her and not to her tutor (guardian), the Marquis of Huntly, was intended to protect the latter, for it was illegal to be involved in taking Catholic youths to Catholic countries for their upbringing. Blakhal, with his usual thoroughness, also got a back-up letter from the queen on some pretext. The real reason, which he could not admit to, was that Louis XIII was unwell, and the priest feared his death would invalidate his letter.

Blakhal now set off for Scotland to collect his charge. In France the trouble was again highwaymen, but with four pistols, a broad-barrelled 'musketon' loaded with nine pistol balls, and a sword, he managed to deter several gangs from attack. In England the trouble would be the 'combustion' – the civil war. He decided that it would make sense to travel by sea direct to Scotland. But the first four ships bound for Scotland to call at Dieppe he avoided, because there were passengers on them who knew him and would compromise the secrecy of his mission. At last, after eight weeks, he sailed. He didn't quite avoid England, in the event. A great storm would have wrecked the ship if it hadn't been driven to safety at Holy Island – where he found the locals praying fervently for ships in distress in storms, their prayers urging God that the ships might be wrecked and their cargoes washed ashore.

Opting for land travel, Blakhal rode the few miles to the Scottish border, then on to Edinburgh and the beginning of negotiations with Henrietta's relatives. Once back in the North East, the main difficulty, as expected, proved to be Huntly. But his endless haverings did lead in the end to agreement that the girl should go to France – provided that no one be told of this. Further complications followed. Henrietta was staying in Edinburgh with the Countess of Haddington, a staunch Protestant, and only reluctantly did she agree to surrender the girl. Then it turned out that Henrietta had converted to Protestantism!

Blakhal was no doubt dismayed – but not deterred. He continued with his planning. It was thought impossible to smuggle Henrietta out of the country through a port in the strongly Protestant south. Arrangements were therefore made to bring her north to Aberdeen, but at the last

minute she panicked, fearing that once in France she would be shut away
in a nunnery. However, Blakhal had no scruples about tricking the girl (he
was, after all, trying to save her soul). She was duped into setting off by
being promised by Blakhal that she was being taken to visit her ferociously
Protestant aunt, the Countess of Mar, at Stirling, and then found herself
carried north.

However, she proved cooperative when it came to going on board ship
in Aberdeen – luckily, because though the authorities did not dare to stop
her as she was the Marquis of Huntly's niece, intensive searches were being
carried out for Blakhal. His relief when they were safely on board ship was
expressed by his singing (no doubt with alcoholic assistance) 'with a loud
voice many songs, amongst others, Ulysses and the Siren' – which sounds
distinctly smutty. With luck Henrietta was out of earshot.

Some perils remained, and were survived by good fortune. An order to
arrest their ship arrived just after they had sailed. Ships of the English
parliament's navy, instructed to stop the ship and remove the priest and
the lady he had stolen, failed to act. The notorious pirates of Dunkirk
were deterred by a warship which provided an escort. At Dieppe the
captain of the ship was reduced to furious indignation when he found
he had been carrying a priest – Blakhal had travelled as 'Lieutenant Hay'.
Even if he had been told there was a priest on board, the captain fumed
that 'I would never have suspected him [Blakhal], he was so merry and
jovial, ever singing, or making sport to the company'. It was all part
of the devilish cunning of priests! Indeed Blakhal begins to sound like a
Protestant caricature of a Catholic priest, drunken, fiendishly kidnapping
innocent girls and smuggling them abroad to popish slavery.

Then off to Paris, deck Henrietta out in the latest fashions in mourning
clothes, for Louis XIII had indeed died (and Huntly had indicated that he
would not have acted on the letter of a dead king, so Blakhal's back-up
letter from a live queen had come in useful). Henrietta, it was decided
by the queen, should temporarily go into a nunnery. There she could
learn French. Until she could speak the language, the maids of honour
at court would tease her, 'and she appears to be one who will not suffer
it patiently'. Moreover, suggested Anne of Austria, she would learn piety.
It was something that it was necessary to have at court, but court was
not a place where you would ever learn it. Henrietta agreed – provided
it was clear that her stay in the nunnery was only to be temporary: a
display of spirit that the queen appreciated. Henrietta's brief venture into
Protestantism was clearly over, but she still wasn't keen on nunneries.

The mother superior of the chosen nunnery was less tolerant of the girl's outspokenness. When, after a year, Henrietta could speak French and wanted to return to court, the reverend mother begged the queen to remove the unsettling presence of the stroppy young Scot. Henrietta was then sent on a sort of training course for maids of honour, but it became clear that she was not just spirited but insufferable. Her rudeness and lack of consideration quickly led to complaints. Unfit for court was the verdict. She was instead, like her aunt Lady Isabelle, offered a place as a canoness in a suitable order. First, however, she was sent to learn 'to sing the canonical hours'. Here she met her match in a strict mother superior, and was soon begging for another move.

Time in two other nunneries followed, as Blakhal struggled to find some secure base for her, the problems of her thrawn nature complicated by the disruptions of the wars of the Fronde. Eventually she arrived back at the court of St Germain to pester the queen. Offered a place in the household of Princesse de Condé, she spurned it as beneath her. The patience of the queen, struggling to rule a disintegrating France in name of her young son, Louis XIV, with the pretensions of this spoilt brat is remarkable.

Henrietta might be dependent on charity, but she had a high opinion of what her blood entitled her to. Soon she was being shunted around various lords and ladies, all of whom quickly decided that they wanted nothing more to do with her. And yet, luck and persistence prevailing over merit, eventually she got settled at court.

Blakhal was now superfluous, spoken of by her as a silly old man, neglected financially, ignored in the sicknesses of his old age. We have only his versions of events, and no doubt his descriptions of his deservings are exaggerated:

> you [Henrietta] cannot be excused from ingratitude towards me, who have deserved at your hands more, both of love and honour, nor [than] any other man or woman ever did, without exception of your father or mother of blessed memory.

In Henrietta's defence, it can be argued that she did not have an easy childhood. Her father had been killed while she was an infant. Her mother seems to have taken thereafter to perpetual mourning, and was weak and indecisive. Her mother's relatives appear to have specialised in neglect and indifference to their plight. Perhaps indeed her own selfishness reflects theirs. Brought up a Catholic, pushed into Protestantism after her mother's death, then pushed back to her first religion by a semi-willing kidnap to France, it is hardly surprising that she may have concluded that looking after herself came first – even if she was pretty unsuccessful in the first years in France. Her determination may be admired, but little else.

Gilbert Blakhal signed off his narration by bidding Henrietta farewell for ever. He had worked off his spleen on paper – though she never read his work, which was completed in the mid- 1660s. This is the last that is known of the man. What is to be made of him? Difficulties of interpretation are considerable. Not only is virtually everything that is known about him contained in his narration, but that narrative was compiled for a very specific purpose: to prove that he merited the gratitude of three women. He presents himself as a man of honour, a man of his word who carries out his missions with dedication, skill and bravery. Whether confronting highwaymen or royalty, he is bold and resolute. He is a man who can be merry, and can pass himself off successfully in whatever disguise he chooses (he assumed so many aliases that remembering who he was supposed to be at any given time was an achievement in itself). The piety of the priest is there, sincere enough to motivate him to take great risks, but other aspects of character are frequently dominant in the narration – often not to his credit. Pride is one of them: it is implicit through much of the narrative. Though often playing humble roles, he is aware of status, determined to be treated right. He loses his temper too easily, he is boastful, he can be insulting. He is often drunk. He harbours grievances, nursing them for years, choosing to give his time and energy in the 1660s to compiling a narrative concerning events of long ago, injustices which there was no hope of remedying.

It seems probable that much of Blakhal's 'official version' of his life is valid, though lacking self-understanding: not as near-infallible as he presents himself but able, energetic and bold. And yet an emotional man, who wept over the problems facing his three ladies. He took his responsibilities seriously, perhaps too seriously where his ladies were concerned. He was emotionally involved with them. He defined what he wanted from them as gratitude and thankfulness, but whether or not he realised it, he probably wanted more. He was devoted to their wellbeing, and wanted devotion from them. He was embittered when two of his ladies failed to provide this. Were they ungrateful? Or did he seem to be trying to take over their lives with an obsessive concern which was stifling? Perhaps breaking away from him completely, earning his wrath, was the only way they could free themselves.

Whatever the answer to that, it is notable that of the twelve men studied in this book, this celibate priest is the only one (with the equally surprising exception of Johnston of Wariston) to write much about women and their characters.

FURTHER READING

G. Blakhal, *A Breiffe Narration of the services done to Three Noble Ladyes*, ed. J. Stuart (Spalding Club, 1844).
A.F.B. Roberts, 'The Role of Women in Scottish Catholic Survival', *Scottish Historical Review*, 1xx (1991), 129–50.

THE HAUNTS OF MAJOR WEIR.   One of the most notorious figures in Edinburgh
legend, Major Weir lived in the West Bow in his later years, lamenting the
betrayal by Scotland of the covenants until, at the dramatic end of his life,
guilt at his own sins overwhelmed him. The Bow is portrayed here in the mid-
nineteenth century by Daniel Wilson. *By courtesy of Edinburgh City Libraries.*

FIVE

INCEST AND PIETY

Major Thomas Weir

SOMETIMES NAMES, BY the associations they conjure up, seem to fit particular individuals. Weir: cold, dark, smooth-running water, already menacing, falling suddenly into black swirling whirlpools with the power to drag one down to death. Fanciful, but the cap fits Major Thomas Weir.

In nineteenth-century Edinburgh the name of Major Weir was familiar among those with a taste for the supernatural. Popular stories depicted him as a great warlock, wielding a staff with magical powers, riding through the streets in a fiery coach. After his execution, it was alleged, his house was haunted for many years. Tales of the wicked major fascinated adults and children alike.

Yet though Major Weir was indeed executed, and was regarded with great horror at the time for his sins, the crimes of which he was accused and convicted were nothing to do with the supernatural. Name, execution and wickedness are the only things the real Major Weir and the later popular legends of his life have in common. Reality and myths had diverged dramatically, because though his wickedness made a lasting impact on popular and literary imaginations, his real crimes were regarded as too repellent to specify. The horrors related about him in the nineteenth century were bowdlerisations designed to hide the truth while preserving an aura of unparalleled evil.

Literary commentators at least were often aware of this. 'I decline publishing the particulars of this case,' noted Hugo Arnot in 1785, for Weir had 'exceeded the common depravity of mankind.' Walter Scott in 1798 was intrigued by the major and rather surprisingly indicated that if he 'were ever to become a writer of prose romances' he might well cast Weir as a hero, or at least as a leading character in a novel. A friend bluntly retorted that Weir was 'a disgusting fellow ... I could never look at his history a second time. A most ungentlemanlike character' – a staggering understatement. Scott at first stood up for Weir: all that was known about him was what his enemies had reported, and a novelist could create a different character for him. But when Scott did indeed become a writer of prose romances, he evidently decided that even an imaginative attempt to rescue Weir from his detractors would be meat too strong for his readers. In his writings, therefore, Major Weir is consigned in his bowdlerised form to a non-fictional discussion of witchcraft – though Scott did mention in passing allegations of one of his real crimes.

Robert Louis Stevenson could not come even this close to the truth, describing Weir's real crimes as 'happily beyond the reach of our intention', and even in the early twentieth century William Roughead lamented the difficulties of dealing in print with a 'veritable monster' like Weir. He therefore treated his case with 'nice discretion' – which turned out to mean hinting delicately at some of the major's crimes through obscure literary allusions, and ignoring his worse offences altogether.

The dark crimes of Thomas Weir, too horrible to lay before the genteel reader, were incest and bestiality. Authors who dared not publish their knowledge of the truth nonetheless talked and speculated about it privately – and one was inspired by him to doggerel verse. Charles Kirkpatrick Sharpe was fascinated by Scottish witchcraft, but was discriminating enough to leave the supposed magic powers of the Major Weir of legend entirely out of his writings on the subject. But he knew all about the real Weir, and when Lord Byron's *Manfred* appeared in 1817, containing hints at incest, he jumped to the conclusion that the poet had been inspired by the exploits of Major Weir. Sharpe was provoked into providing his own – unpublishable – mock prologue to Byron's work:

> Most gentle Readers, 'twill appear
> Our Author fills this scene,
> With what betided Major Weir
> And his frail sister Jean.
>
> He freely here his fault avows
> In bringing not before us,
> The Major's Cat, and Mares, and Cows,
> Assembled in a Chorus
>
> But by and by he'll mend his Play,
> And then the World shall see
> That Incest only paves the way
> For Bestiality.

Convention might require discretion in print, but informally more robust attitudes prevailed.

Thomas Weir was the son of a small Clydesdale laird, Weir of Kirkton, whose land lay in the parish of Carluke. The family claimed noble connections through kinship with Lord Somerville, but was itself evidently fairly humble in its circumstances. In 1636 Thomas gave his consent to the sale of the estate by his parents, and he settled in Edinburgh. There in 1642 he married Isobel Mein, the widow of an Edinburgh merchant, John Bourdoun. The marriage brought him free admission as a burgess and guild brother of Edinburgh – the customary reward for marrying the widow of a burgess and thus providing for her. But it was a call to arms rather than trade that first attracted Weir, for he is recorded as an officer in the Scottish army which crossed to Ireland to fight the rebel Catholic Irish.

Weir was captain-lieutenant in the regiment of Colonel Robert Home. Thus he was lieutenant of the company commanded by the regiment's colonel. This gave him seniority among the lieutenants of the regiment and greater responsibility than most, as he would often in effect be captain of the company through the colonel's preoccupation with regimental affairs. The regiment had originally been raised in 1640, and had seen service against royalists in south-west Scotland in the Second Bishops' War, and Weir may well have already been serving in it then.

The regiment sailed to Ulster in March 1642, the month after Thomas's marriage, but he did not remain long in Ireland. In May 1643 he was back in Edinburgh, and made a modest contribution to a loan raised to support the army in which he had just been serving. But he still had military ambitions, and evidently the skills – or a mixture of skills and good connections – necessary to gain promotion. In June 1644 he appears as a major, second-in-command of the regiment raised by the Earl of Lanark and serving with the Scottish army which had intervened in England to help the English parliament in the civil war against Charles I. The regiment was largely raised in Lanarkshire, and Thomas's connections with the area doubtless helped him secure his position. His career in this regiment also proved short. In August, while it was taking part in the siege of Newcastle-upon-Tyne, he was captured during a sortie by the royalist garrison. He was doubtless freed when the Scots stormed Newcastle in October and returned to his regiment, but evidently left it in 1645. In later claims for arrears of pay he was credited with nineteen months' service in the army in Ireland, and twelve months' with Lanark's regiment. But it sounds as though for Weir service often meant being entitled to pay rather than being with his men.

Thomas Weir may have been recalled to Scotland by the burgh of Edinburgh, because late in 1645 he was appointed to command the guard which was raised to police and defend the burgh in these troubled times. His reputation was presumably that of a reliable officer and a committed covenanter. The strength of his sympathy for the cause was demonstrated late in 1648 when the extreme Kirk Party regime came to power on the fall of the Engagers. Weir proved an ardent supporter, and he was rewarded for his services in guarding the fledgling government while it was establishing itself. In 1650, when the captured Marquis of Montrose was imprisoned in Edinburgh before his execution, Major Weir of the town guard was responsible for his security – and is said to have been harsh and unsympathetic in his treatment of the great royalist general.

The extremist presbyterian cause that Thomas supported soon disintegrated. When the church of Scotland split into two warring factions in 1650–1, he predictably supported the more radical party, the Remonstrants or Protesters. The remaining two decades of his life brought repeated disappointments where public events were concerned: first rule by the republican English, then restoration of episcopacy under Charles II. He remained loyal to his lost cause. By the 1660s he was living in a house in the West Bow, an area in which a number of disappointed covenanter activists were evidently concentrated, earning the sarcastic nickname of the 'Bowhead Saints'. He must have retained some friends in positions of authority, for in 1669 the burgh council, to reward his former services as captain of the town guard, authorised him to collect a duty on goods imported from England.

In this, his outward career and character, there is nothing very distinctive about Major Thomas Weir. The son of a struggling landed family, he had found in the profession of arms an 'honourable' means of making a modest living. But he was no mercenary: he believed in the covenanting cause that he fought for, perhaps influenced by his family background in the Western Lowlands where support for the cause was very widespread and enduring, and where popular extremism often had the support of small landowners. He experienced heady days of success and optimism in the 1640s, followed by long and bitter disappointment, endured through the strength of belief that eventually the cause of the Lord would triumph. Thus far, the major's life could be paralleled many times over.

What distinguished Thomas Weir only emerged in 1670. The obscure retired junior officer, now in his old age, noted in his own circle for his piety, suddenly began to show terror at the word 'burn', as if terrified of hellfire. Then he broke down completely and began to confess terrible crimes to his friends. At first it was assumed he had gone mad, and when word of his rantings reached the provost of Edinburgh, Lord Abbotshall, he sent physicians to examine the distracted Bowhead Saint. It was assumed that medical rather than legal intervention was appropriate. But the doctors reported that he was sane, and investigation soon proved that there was corroborative evidence to support his confessions. A new Major Weir emerged as the facade that had concealed the reality for so many years crumbled away.

The specific instances of crime – or sin, or perversion – recorded in the case of Major Weir are partly based on his own confessions, but sometimes the authority for allegations is unknown. Moreover in addition to the common tendency for exaggeration and invention in such instances of sordid notoriety, there was a political interest in making the most of his offences. A regime which had rejected the covenants and presbyterianism, and which had got bogged down in efforts to repress those still loyal to these causes, naturally saw good propaganda value in the case. The religious dissidents had presented themselves as pious folk seeking to live a godly life, persecuted by a corrupt establishment. Now a man long known as a sympathiser with the dissidents could be shown to have used the cloak of godliness to conceal a life of unparalleled debauchery. Who were dissidents to complain about a bit of honest fornication at court when one of their own number had vastly worse sexual misdeeds to answer for?

Yet the incidents of illicit sexual gratification ascribed to the major by the sources do not read like the inventions of fevered propagandists. The sad thing about them is that they are all so mundane and plausible.

Thomas Weir had a younger sister, Jean. When she was about sixteen their sister Margaret discovered that they were having an incestuous affair. She reported this to their parents, and the liaison was broken up by sending Jean away from home. Her sex and age surely indicate that she was the less guilty, if indeed not entirely a victim; but she was doubtless sacrificed to the need to maintain the reputation of the son and heir of the family. The next dateable incident was many years later. In 1651 it was reported to a horrified parish minister that a man travelling through the parish had been seen committing an act of bestiality. Soldiers were sent to apprehend him, but when he turned out to be the godly Major Weir his indignant denials were believed – and, it is said, the unfortunate woman who had reported him was whipped in the streets of Lanark for making up so dreadful an allegation. Other events cannot be dated. Thomas was evidently guilty of incest with his step-daughter, Margaret Bourdoun, and is said to have married her off to an Englishman when she became pregnant. In 1649 he was referred to as tutor and curator of the bairns of John Bourdoun, but they are likely to have received little protection from him. For twenty-two years Thomas had an adulterous relationship with a servant, Bessie Wemyss, and he evidently revived his incestuous affair with his sister Jean. At all events, Jean, who had been keeping a school in Dalkeith, came to live with Thomas in Edinburgh after his wife's death.

These are the specific allegations against the major, but they evidently represent merely the tip of a very muddy iceberg. There is only one hint of the supernatural in Thomas's case. When asked (not surprisingly, given the age and circumstances) if he had seen the devil, he said he had not, but had often felt his presence in the dark. At his trial he was found guilty of the lesser offences of fornication and adultery by majority verdicts, but on incest and bestiality the jury was unanimous as to his guilt. He was sentenced to death by burning. His attitude remained one of utter despair, as it had been since he had begun to confess. He refused to pray, or to let ministers pray for him. He was convinced of his damnation and therefore that no prayers could help him:

> Trouble me no more with your beseechings of me to repent, for I know my sentence of damnation is already sealed in Heaven; and I feel myself so hardened within that I could not even wish to be pardoned if such a wish could save me ... I find nothing within me but blackness and darkness, Brimstone and burning to the bottom of Hell.

Too weak to walk, he was dragged on a sledge to the place of execution, and there strangled at the stake before being burnt. He died still in his terrible despair, declaring he had no hope of mercy.

His sister Jean was hanged the following day. The crimes of which she

---

Right: Scottish armies invaded England four times in eleven years – 1640, 1644, 1648, 1651. Each time they claimed that they were trying to help the English and serve God. Not all south of the border were convinced, and this print, A CLOAK FOR KNAVERY OR THE SCOTTISH RELIGION WORN OUT, was a propaganda piece denouncing the Engagers' invasion of 1648. The Scot, standing in the centre, is recognisable by his bonnet and by the standard of St Andrew (marked 'persecution') that he carries. Written on his clothes are discord, murder, theft, cruelty, plunder, intrusion, invasion, fornication, whoredoms, etc. He has disguised these qualities under a long cloak marked religion. But the disguise has worn out, and it is being removed by time (on the left). *By permission of the British Library* (E. 652 (13)).

Religion is made a Covering
For every wicked and Rebelious thing ,
Errors are hid heer on the right and left ,
Rebelion, Idolitry, and Theft ,
Plunders, and Rapins, Whordoms, Fornications ,
Dissimulations, Flateries, and Invasions ,
By Time, this Cloake is worn fro of their Back
So, their's discover'd many a Knavish Knack .

had been accused were incest and sorcery. At last the supernatural takes a central place, as in the later legends. It was perhaps inevitable that a woman accused of a crime regarded with such horror as incest should also be accused of witchcraft, but she herself evidently confessed her guilt of several points of witchcraft, some implicating her brother. It seems likely that looking back at events, torn by guilt at her conduct, she interpreted some things, and especially her brother's power over her, in supernatural terms. Indeed her confessions are more concerned with her being bewitched than with her own conduct. Two of her confessions have nothing to do with her brother, referring to incidents which had taken place while she was living in Dalkeith. She had in retrospect come to see a call by a mysterious stranger as a visitation by the devil; and she had spun so much yarn she must have had the devil's help. As evidence of her career as a witch this is hardly impressive – and though she confessed at first, at one point later she rejected the charge of supernatural aid at the spinning wheel, claiming to be just remarkably good at spinning!

All Jean's other confessions relating to the supernatural concerned her brother the major. She had found the devil's mark on his shoulder. She knew that he had had dealings with the devil, and was jealous of them. Once she and her brother had driven with the devil in a fiery coach drawn by six horses to Musselburgh, and the devil had then foretold a defeat of the Scottish army which had followed soon afterwards. The source of all the major's magical powers had been the staff he always carried, according to Jean, and this staff quickly became a central item in the legend of Major Weir. In the light of his sexual hold over his sister the phallic symbolism of the staff which empowered him seems obvious. Such an interpretation would, however, have horrified Sir Walter and Lady Scott generations later. Lady Scott, with her husband's approval, nicknamed his walking stick 'Major Weir' as it had a tendency to get lost, as if it possessed a life of its own!

Jean's confessions could have served as evidence for charges of witchcraft against the major, but such charges were not brought. Moreover Jean herself, though accused of both incest and sorcery, was convicted on the former charge only. The legal authorities and the justiciary court evidently had little taste for wild tales of the supernatural, and concentrated on securing convictions for sexual offences. Thomas showed frantic despair in prison. Jean was calmer. She claimed to be penitent, but failed to convince onlookers by showing conventional signs of it. She believed she deserved a worse death than the one she had been condemned to, and said she intended to die with all possible shame. On the scaffold she made a short speech abusing the crowd for not lamenting breeches of the covenant – according to the propagandists of the day. She then tried to throw off her clothes so as to die naked, but was restrained, pushed off the ladder and hanged before she could do so. The contemporary interpretation seems to have been that this was an act of defiance, a gesture of how she despised convention. More probably it was a frantic gesture of penitence, a willingness to embrace, as merited, a shame beyond that being inflicted on her by others.

Once Thomas Weir is deprived of the exciting aura of the supernatural legends, and attributed merely squalid sexual gratification in their place as a cause for notoriety, is it worth pursuing the disgraced major any further? At the very least he may be held up as an example – indeed an extreme one – of the holy hypocrite. Not content merely to hide his sins and crimes behind a screen of conventional behaviour, he constructed an outward appearance of a man of outstanding piety – though piety of a sort which, by his later years, had gone 'down market', out of fashion with the country's ruling élites. But, on this interpretation, conventional conscience broke through the pretence in old age, the strains between his secret sins and outward morality thus destroying him.

There may well have been much more to Major Weir than this. The duality of his life may not reflect mere hypocrisy, but a coherent theology. Was he an early believer in Scotland in antinomianism, a bizarre heresy within Calvinism? Was he, in his own mind, a justified sinner?

From the squalid life and death of one obscure Scot the argument leaps to theoretical speculation about a matter central to mankind within a Christian framework. What are the rules which settle the destination of the individual soul for eternity? What decides whether it will burn in hell or enjoy the eternal bliss of heaven? Free will doctrines stressed individual responsibility: it was the extent to which the lives led by individuals on earth were in accordance with God's will, with moral law, that was decisive. A good and godly life would bring eternal happiness. By contrast determinist thinking stressed that the decision was God's alone: His omnipotence could not be limited by His accepting that individuals had the automatic right to enter heaven if they met certain conditions. Largely in opposition to popular practices in late medieval Catholicism whereby corruptions of free-will doctrines indicated that entry to heaven could virtually be purchased even by those whose regard for morality in their own lives was not evident in their conduct, Calvinist theology went to the opposite, determinist extreme.

No individual's conduct on earth could influence his eternal destiny. An omnipotent God had determined the fate of all before they were even born. In justice, their inherent sinfulness meant that all deserved damnation. But out of His mercy God had chosen or elected a minority for salvation.

A stark creed, but one that could bring individuals great comfort if they could persuade themselves that they were among the elect – often through a major psychological crisis, the conversion experience. Though God's predestined decision in such matters could not be influenced by individual conduct, it was natural to suppose that those who lived pious and godly lives, adhering to strict moral codes, were most likely to be among the elect. And, indeed, the concept developed that God's grace in granting election could not fail to influence the elect individual, making him the better able to approximate to true godliness in spite of innate human sinfulness, providing a further spur to godly behaviour. Individuals might have their tickets to heaven already issued, but they could only gain conviction that the tickets were valid by identifying the grace of the elect within themselves.

Thus the concept of predestination in Calvinist theology provided a powerful sanction in favour of moral and godly behaviour. Only those who strove to obey God's law would turn out to be among those chosen in advance for salvation. The very fact that they were chosen gave them an added responsibility, beyond that imposed on all men, to obey the God who thus had granted them unmerited mercy.

Yet almost inevitably a few drew different conclusions from predestination. At a crude level this could take the form of practical cynicism. If an individual was predestined to salvation, then even the most immoral conduct could not harm him eternally: eat, drink and be merry, for there are no sanctions. Antinomian – 'against the law' – heresy added theoretical justification to such hedonism. By being picked out by God for election, the elect became exempt from moral law. Grace from on high made them virtually part of the divine, beyond all restraints. Nothing they could do was evil. A just God would punish sin, but the elect had the assurance through their election that God would not punish them. So all they did was acceptable to Him.

The great majority of antinomians nonetheless in practice sought to conform to conventional morality, claiming that the divine grace which had been granted to them guided them to do so. In theory they were not bound to obey moral law, but nonetheless they strove to obey. Their theology carried obvious dangers, however. Impulses inspired by divine grace dictated their conduct. Generally these impulses, governed by habit, inhibition and the conventions of their society might steer them to conventional morality. The problem was, how did you distinguish impulses which were to be confidently followed as they stemmed from divine grace, from those deriving from human instincts and desires? Most antinomians clearly weeded their impulses, separating those taken to come through grace from the unacceptable. Nonetheless, it was possible to conclude that all impulses felt were divine and therefore not only could but should be obeyed.

The early history of antinomian ideas in Scotland is obscure, but controversy was active among puritans in England and the American colonies in the early seventeenth century. The danger of antinomian tendencies arising from predestinarian theology was well recognised in Calvinist circles. Thus such ideas were almost certainly being discussed in Scotland – though the earliest identification of an individual holding antinomian beliefs in Scotland has been dated 1647, and in that case the heretical beliefs arose through contact with English puritans.

Was Major Weir an antinomian, not in the mainline tradition of the heresy which produced earnest and moral (if unorthodox) puritans, but in the deviant tradition which produced a scattering of individuals who believed themselves free to – indeed bound to – follow their impulses and whims uncritically? It would explain much in his life. What others would have seen as sins and crimes were no such things, as he had internal impulses – which must be divinely inspired – to justify them. Outward godliness and devotion to the covenants were not hollow hypocrisy, but obedience to impulses of sensible expediency in a real world in which his secret conduct would be harshly punished if revealed. Moreover genuine belief in the cause he fought for as that of God was entirely compatible with belief that his secret conduct was justified in the eyes of the same God – even if the rest of the godly were too blinkered by orthodox Calvinist belief to see this. Godly obeyers of moral law who could be counted among the elect were his allies, even if they refused to realise the full freedom of action that the privilege of election gave them.

That Major Weir was indeed an extreme antinomian cannot be proved conclusively. But the supposition that he was makes sense of his career, reconciling the outward and the inward in a compelling way. The seemingly unendurable tension between his – and indeed his sister Jean's – public and private lives may not have existed for them: the two could be easily reconciled. Robert Louis Stevenson wrote of Weir as 'the outcome and fine flower of dark and vehement religion'. Quite what he meant is not clear, though the phrases are striking. Probably he believed that the inhuman moral codes of Calvinism, impossible for anyone to conform to fully, encouraged hypocrisy; perhaps also that once hypocrisy was thus induced, all restraints on behaviour might vanish. If Weir was an antinomian, however, Stevenson was nearer the dark centre of the paradox of the major than he realised, for it was not reaction against Calvinism's doctrines that explains his life, but extending them in logical but destructive ways. To the sorcerer of legend, the inward sinner, and the outward saint can be added a fourth aspect of the man, the heretic in action.

If Major Weir was an antinomian rather than merely a run-of-the-mill hypocrite, what happened in 1670 was the most terrible thing that could befall any Calvinist. He lost conviction of his own election. This would explain the extremity of his despair. If he was not one of the elect, he was one of the reprobate, those whose inescapable fate was eternal damnation. Previously no amount of what the conventional would have regarded as evil-doing on his part could have harmed him. Now no amount of virtue or repentance, no expiation of his actions however extreme, could save him. Prayer was pointless, because it could change nothing. Indeed, he confessed that his previous skill in extempore prayer had always been a sham. While this does not make him an antinomian, it does at least hint at the fact that he had taken predestinarian views to unorthodox extremes. If all was preordained by God, then prayer could have no efficacy. Moreover, though his sudden confession might simply be the result of inability to control the despair that came from sudden conviction of his own damnation, it might also relate to the logic of his own belief-system. As one of the elect he had been free from moral constraints on his behaviour; as one of the reprobate obedience to moral law was due from him. He could not undo what he now recognised as sins, he could not escape his fate in eternity; and he was duty bound to confess to his sins.

In 1824 James Hogg's novel, *Private Memoirs and Confessions of a Justified Sinner* was published, the story of an extreme antinomian who followed out the logic of his beliefs by sinning greatly under a cloak of godliness. There is no reason to suppose that Hogg's remarkable psychological drama, with its supernatural overtones, was influenced by the saga of Major Weir. All that can be said is that Hogg developed the concept of perversions of extreme Calvinism in Scotland leading to the emergence of a 'justified sinner'. But it looks as though reality may well have been a century and a half ahead of fiction.

FURTHER READING

D. Stevenson, 'Major Weir: a Justified Sinner?', *Scottish Studies*, 16 (1972), 161–73.

Portrait of SIR JAMES TURNER, from his *Pallas Armata* (1683). His armour refers to his military career and to the military topic of his book. The engraver has been kind: Turner does not look his age (about 68), and his mild gaze seems to contradict his reputation in his later years for frequent drunkenness and furious rages. *By Courtesy of St Andrews University Library.*

SIX

THE LITERARY MERCENARY:

Sir James Turner

LIKE SIR ANDREW MELVILL, his fellow mercenary, James Turner was a son of the manse, his father Patrick being minister of Borthwick and later Dalkeith. Turner made no claims to nobility for his family, but his mother was well-connected, being the daughter of Archbishop James Law of Glasgow. Unlike Melvill, he confidently assumed gentility, and felt no need to assert it. Different men, but also different audiences. Melvill wrote for German princes and courtiers, who would have thought a parish minister as a father something of a lapse of taste. For his colleague in the military trade, writing for – well, it's not clear quite who for, but a more general imaginary audience – parish minister was quite acceptable.

Turner attended Glasgow University, where having 'lightly passed' through the four-year arts course, he wanted to leave without graduating 'as never intending to make use of that title [Master of Arts] which undeservedly was bestowed upon me, as it was on many others before me, and hath been on too many since'. This may be interpreted as a youthful mixture of modesty and arrogance: on the one hand he was not worthy; on the other, he had no use for Mickey Mouse letters after his name.

For students not to graduate after completing their studies was very common at the time, nothing of a disgrace. But Turner's father and grandfather insisted that he take the degree. Their insistence, and his own reluctance, point to a family argument as to his future. A degree was the first step towards qualifying Turner to become a parish minister like his father. He had no wish for such a career, and failing to graduate would have conveniently disqualified him.

In the end, Turner gave way to family pressure by graduating, and he stayed in the family home for a further year, 'applying myself to the study of humane letters and history, in both which I always took delight'. Knowing that he was partly writing to redeem his reputation for being a particularly brutal and drunken officer, a first reaction is likely to be cynicism, but in fact his memoirs provide a good deal of evidence to support this claim of academic interests. He gave careful attention in his reading to controversies between Protestants and Catholics, to strengthen his Protestant beliefs 'that

79

so I might not, in traversing the world, be carried away with every wind of doctrine'. His father doubtless hoped further study would reconcile the youth to entering the ministry. But Turner himself had it in mind that he was preparing himself for a wider world. Inevitably he was excited by news of the Thirty Years' War, and when in 1632 Sir James Lumsden levied a Scots regiment to fight in Germany under the great Protestant champion King Gustavus Adolphus of Sweden, Turner enlisted as an ensign.

Turner doubtless dreamed of serving under Gustavus in battle. Action, glory and the defence of Protestantism formed a tempting package. Instead he found himself engaged in north Germany in far less glamorous work, much more typical of a soldier's life. He was ordered to help 'to reduce some obstinate countries to order, and force them to submit to the Swedish yoke'.

The death rate among soldiers new to the wars was very high even without fighting, with far more dying of hunger, exposure and illness than wounds. Turner long afterwards recalled the hardship of these early days:

> This proved a hard and severe winter to me and all of us, who knew not before what it was not to have two or three meals a day, and go to bed at a seasonable hour at night.

To personal hardship was soon added experience of the more acute horrors of war. In 1633 he was with a Swedish army besieging Hamlym and joined battle with an Imperial army attempting to relieve the city. 'This was a battle wherein so much blood was shed, as was enough to flesh such novices as I was.' When the city surrendered,

> I saw a great many killed in cold blood by the Finns, who profess to give no quarter. The whole time of this siege, my best entertainment was bread and water, abundance of the last, but not so much of the first.

Further sieges and skirmishes followed, and throughout he

> suffered exceeding great want of both meat and clothes, being necessitated to lie constantly in the fields with little or no shelter, to march always a foot, and drink water.

The student from a comfortable background at first longed to be back in Scotland (perhaps even for the life of a minister!). But in time he adapted to his new life:

being inured to toil, I fully resolved to go on in that course of life of which I had made choice, and I thought then I could have lived all my days on a very spare diet, and without a bed too.

The old campaigner who liked his luxuries looked back with amusement at his youthful self who had become almost idealistic about hardship.

Early in 1634 the regiment was reduced to one company, but he was kept on its strength while most officers were 'cashiered, and in great necessity and poverty'. Moreover, though the company was 'badly used, tossed to and fro, in constant danger of an enemy, and without pay', Turner found his own circumstances less hard than before:

I had learned so much cunning, and become so vigilant to lay hold on opportunities, that I wanted for nothing, horses, clothes, meat, nor moneys; and made so good use of what I had learned, that the whole time I served in Germany, I suffered no such misery as I had done the first year and a half that I came to it.

Is it unfair to say this could be summarised as 'I became brutalised in order to survive'? What precise skills he acquired he does not specify. Doubtless he was not altogether proud of them himself. In a devastated land over which starving soldiers swarmed, desperately seeking the necessities of life, Turner would have learned to be ruthless in giving his own interests absolute priority, to lie, steal and cheat, to be brutal in seizing whatever he needed from the peasantry, and feel no guilt when they starved. He had not invented the conventions of the ghastly game in which he was a very minor player, but had to conform to them or die. Yet, like Andrew Melvill, he considered the life he led an honourable one.

A break came when news of his father's death brought him back to Scotland in 1634 to visit his mother, but he had no hesitation in returning to Germany the following year. In search of employment, he resolved to join a party of German and English officers being recruited to train Persian troops to fight the Turks. This exotic plan fell through, and Turner was soon back in Swedish service under the old Scottish field-marshal, Alexander Leslie. In campaigns of confused sieges and encounters he thrived modestly, rising from ensign to lieutenant, to captain-lieutenant, to captain. But in 1639 a quarrel with his colonel led him to resign, and as he had heard that forces were being raised in Scotland to help the Elector Palatine, Charles I's brother-in-law, regain his lost territories, he returned home. However, he found Scotland itself in turmoil, with the regime of Charles I collapsing and talk of civil war rather than of recruiting for foreign service. Returning disappointed to Germany, he was cheated by a colonel in Swedish employment under whom he enlisted. On travelling to Sweden he was unsuccessful in an attempt to gain redress. But he found the Swedes ready to help him return to fight in his native land in a new war.

It is at this point that a major tension in James Turner's autobiography emerges. When he was writing, he was a staunch royalist. But for most of the 1640s he had served the covenanters against the king. The change of allegiance was one made by many men, who opposed the king initially but were later to swing round to support him as the covenanting movement disintegrated, so Turner was far from alone. Nonetheless, he felt that explanations were necessary, and provided them by references to circumstances and the conventions of his mercenary profession. The impression given is that he would really have preferred to serve his king all along. He may well exaggerate, but much of the rest of what he says has a ring of honesty to it, for he was ready to take some blame upon himself.

The Swedes were willing to encourage Scots mercenaries in their employment to return to their homeland in 1640 for two reasons. They had less need of their services than in the past; and they sympathised with the cause of the rebel covenanters in Scotland, because of their commitment to Protestantism and their rejection of what they saw as the pro-Catholic proclivities of Charles I. Alexander Leslie had returned to Scotland and been appointed general of the covenanting armies, and was about to invade England. Former mercenaries, many of them veterans of the Swedish service, formed the backbone of his officer corps. Turner was giving way to one of many simplistic royalist conspiracy theories when he stated that there was 'no doubt' that the Scottish rebellion had been plotted by the Swedes and the French, but the Swedes were certainly ready to help the rebels.

At Gothenburg Turner had the choice of an English ship bound for Hull, or a Danish one sailing for Leith. By his own account he was indifferent as to whether he sailed to England or Scotland. With a civil war in progress he could hope to find employment in either, and which side he fought on was secondary:

> I had swallowed without chewing, in Germany, a very dangerous maxim, which military men there too much follow: which was, that so we serve our masters honestly, it is no matter what master we serve; so, without examination of the justice of the quarrel, or regard of my duty to either prince or country, I resolved to go with that ship I first encountered.

The English ship was on the point of sailing, and would not wait until Turner's baggage arrived. 'This only hindered me to present my endeavours to serve the King against the Covenanters' – though 'endeavour' seems to mean merely a slight preference, for he immediately shipped for Scotland instead, 'resolving to serve either the one or the other without any reluctance of mind; so deeply was that base maxim rooted in my heart'.

The 'base maxim' that honour lay exclusively in obeying orders obviously has terrible echoes in our own century. It is interesting to find it attributed so long ago to Germany. Doubtless its centre lay there because the wars fought there were so dominated by mercenaries and their codes. They were men who had thrown off allegiance to their 'natural masters or lords or sovereigns', and set off to sell their allegiance. Their exclusive allegiance was due to the leader who had bought them, their only loyalty obeying orders. Such unthinking obedience had been formed into a code of honour to ennoble the mercenary trade. At least Turner came in the end to question it.

On landing in Scotland, Turner made his way to the rebel army, which by this time had occupied Newcastle. There he got the post of major in Lord Kirkcudbright's regiment. It was assumed he must already have signed the National Covenant, so he was not asked to do so. To Turner the fact that he did not sign was clearly important, though he was honest enough to admit that

> I would have made no bones to take, swear and sign it, and observe it too; for I had then a principle, having not yet studied a better one, that I wronged not my conscience in doing anything I was commanded to do by these whom I served.

– the principle learned in Germany.

Turner served ten months in England before the army returned to Scotland and disbanded in the summer of 1641. New employment soon offered. Early in 1642 a new Scottish army began to cross to Ulster, employed by the English parliament to join local Protestant forces in fighting the Catholic Irish rebels. The war was a brutal one, with prisoners usually being killed. Newry being surrendered by the rebels, the prisoners along with many merchants and tradesmen were massacred – shot, hanged or drowned. A further 'unofficial' massacre of the women of the town by the soldiers was, according to Turner, stopped by his personal intervention after 'about a dozen' had died. Killing of prisoners was, in Turner's eyes, both unnecessarily cruel, and inexpedient. But, he observed philosophically, soldiers are often cruel simply because of man's wicked nature, as shown by the 'Discourse on Cruelty' which he himself

had compiled. The literary pretensions of the former university student
are beginning to show.

Stationed in Newry, Turner experienced the hardships and frustrations
of the Irish campaign: indecisive skirmishes with the elusive but persistent
Irish, shortage of food and other supplies, exposure and sickness. Eventually,
late in 1643, suffering 'extreme want of all manner of provisions, both for back
and belly' – clothes and food – the Newry garrison made a truce with the local
Irish, and Turner set off for Scotland to get permission to withdraw from the
town. But if Newry brought him hardship, it also brought some consolation.
He found some leisure time in which to indulge his literary impulses, and
began to compile a treatise entitled 'Buchanan Revised'. This is clear
evidence that Turner's convictions were swinging away from indifference
as to the cause he served and towards royalist commitment, for his work
was designed to contradict the political philosophy of George Buchanan,
whose ideas justifying rebellion by subjects in certain circumstances were
central to the covenanters' legitimisations of their actions.

Turner's second consolation in Newry was more personal: he fell in
love, and thus gained in the end something which was in his estimation
worth more than the worldly riches that he had hoped service in Ireland
would bring him. Mary White was of good family, and 'thought by others,
much more by me, to be of a good beauty'. Her qualities of mind 'have
rendered me happy amidst all the afflictions [which] hath befallen me since'.
But there were complications. Turner had not the means to support her
adequately, and she was a Catholic. An officer trying to make a career in
the covenanting army could hardly expect favour if he married a papist.

Early in 1644 Sinclair's regiment (in which Turner served), in more
or less open mutiny through neglect and lack of supplies, sailed back
to Scotland. Turner's newly emerging conscience could justify his
having fought 'the bloody rebels in Ireland'. But the covenanting regime in Scotland had now allied itself with the English parliament
in the Solemn League and Covenant and invaded England to help
parliament in its civil war against the king. Turner and other officers
of the forces from Ireland, disillusioned by their experiences – it had
been the English parliament which had promised to supply them and
failed to do so – now plotted to declare for the king in alliance
with Scots royalists. But the opportunity was missed, and Sinclair's
regiment became part of a supplementary force being sent into England
under the Earl of Callander. The earl's assurances that he himself
hoped eventually to help the king reconciled Turner to his new

Opinions in Europe of the SCOTTISH MERCENARY SOLDIER may be gauged by
this German caricature (*c.* 1630) condemning the recruitment of barbarians by
the Swedish army occupying large parts of Germany, and ending with a plea to
God to protect the fatherland. The 'barbarians' are a Laplander (accompanied by a
most unlikely-looking reindeer), a Livonian and (on the right) a 'Schotländter' – a
Scot. See also p.134. As James Turner freely admitted, he was employed 'to reduce
some obstinate countries to order, and force them to submit to the Swedish yoke'.
The Swedish army largely supported itself by preying on the peasantry.

employment. He swore the new covenant, hoping that this would in time the better enable him to serve the king. Looking back, he reflected that the act was dishonest and sinful. More to the point, no good came of it.

Late in 1644 Turner was one of the first into Newcastle when the city was stormed by the Scots. Further campaigning followed up to the end of the English civil war, culminating in the surrender of the king to the Scots army in 1646. Turner managed for the first time to speak to his sovereign, offering to help Charles escape. But his royalist tendencies were suspected, and he was kept away from the king.

With the war in England over, and being out of favour with his employers, Turner thought he might have to return to the Continent. He therefore sent to Newry, and Mary White came to marry him – evidently conforming to Protestantism. She found him recovering from wounds incurred in a drunken brawl – the first time in all his campaigns that his blood had ever been shed. 'This was an effect of drinking, which I confess, beside the sin against God, hath brought me in many inconveniences.'

Sinclair's regiment was disbanded, but Turner found employment as adjutant-general in the army that Lieutenant-General David Leslie led in 1647 against Alasdair MacColla and the remnants of the Irish and Highland forces which had served the royalist cause under the Marquis of Montrose. Turner as usual found a way to justify himself for serving the covenanters: the rebels he was fighting had first deserted Montrose, and had then refused to lay down their arms on the king's instructions. Thus even though he was serving with the king's enemies against them, he was doing his royalist duty. In Kintyre he witnessed the massacre of the garrison of Dunaverty, several hundred strong, after it had surrendered. He tried to prevent the slaughter, but he had to admit that the killing was not against the accepted conventions of warfare, as no terms of surrender had been agreed – though mercy would have been more honourable and Christian.

This campaign was followed by a brief lull in Scotland's wars, but the following year a new conflict emerged, with the rise to supremacy in Scotland of the Engagers, dedicated to helping the king against his English enemies. At last Turner found himself serving the king he had so long protested his loyalty to. Sent to Glasgow to stifle opposition to the Engagement, he did his work with the thoroughness of a veteran:

> I found my work not very difficult; for I shortly learned to know, that the quartering of two or three troopers, and half a dozen musketeers, was an argument strong enough, in two or three nights time, to make the hardest headed covenanters in the town to forsake the kirk.

Having soldiers, who were no doubt encouraged to be demanding and offensive, quartered in a man's household with his family was a powerful persuader, and soon the Glasgow men grew 'pretty tame'. An attempt to the south, at Mauchline in Ayrshire, to resist the regime in name of the church, was easily dispersed by Turner's and other troops. The 'slashing communicants' fled the field, and their leaders were sentenced to be hanged or shot – though they were soon pardoned, with Turner's support as president of the 'court of war' which had condemned them.

Less success attended Turner once the army, straggling and poor led, entered England. His first problem – a little matter of rats keeping stealing his stockings while he was billeted near Appleby – was soon sorted out. However, it led the literary soldier off into a disquisition on the sagacity of rats and on whether they could foresee the future. Rats gnawing clothes was held to be an omen of misfortune about to overwhelm the owner. Of course he himself did not believe such nonsense, he asserted: nonetheless, it so happened that disaster quickly followed.

Taken by surprise by Cromwell near Preston, the Scottish army scattered. Turner tried to make a stand at night with a brigade of foot, the rearguard of the retreating infantry. But in the confusion of the night, 'my pikemen being demented (as I think we were all)', Turner was mistaken for an enemy and attacked by two of his own men. One pike he managed to turn aside, but the other wounded him in the thigh: 'this was an unseasonable wound, for it made me after that night unserviceable'. Unfortunately, he was not rendered unserviceable immediately. Furious at his wound, forgetting 'all rules of modesty, prudence and discretion', he ordered a regiment of Scots horse to charge his own infantry. Having scattered his own men and thereby worked off his fury at being attacked by them, he took some thought as to the real enemy, the English, and ordered drums to beat to reassemble the infantry he had just forced into flight. The only honour Turner emerges with is that he admitted to the incident. There could hardly be a better illustration of the shameful chaos into which the Scots army disintegrated.

After a few days of further confusion, Turner surrendered with the bedraggled remnants of the army. His first attempt to serve his king had led him to rat-foretold disaster, and was to lead his king to the scaffold. As Turner realised, 'what we intended for the king's relief and restoration, posted him to his grave'.

Turner was sent to a fairly easy imprisonment in Hull, alleviated by a nuptial visit from his wife, 'and having the use of books, paper, pen and ink, I deceived the longness of the time with reading and writing'. Here he finished his treatise 'Buchanan Revised' and exercised his literary inclinations with other writings — essays and discourses, and papers on the state of Europe since 1618, the year 'that the dreadful comet appeared', an omen of the wars to come. All his papers were to be destroyed when Dundee, to which they had been sent for safekeeping, was stormed by the English in 1651. In later years he doggedly rewrote at least the Buchanan treatise.

At the end of 1649 the order for his release came, and he took the first ship available that was sailing to the Continent. Scotland, now in the hands of the presbyterian extremist Kirk Party regime, would not have welcomed him home. At Hamburg he met up with other royalist exiles, and missed involvement in Montrose's disastrous 1650 landing in Scotland only because he lacked the money to equip himself. In Holland he had another visit from his long-suffering wife, bringing him money. He joined the exiled Charles II in Breda, but was left behind when the latter sailed for Scotland. Turner seems to have been uncertain what to do next. He set out for Sweden to try to get arrears of pay from many years before, but evidently lost heart in Denmark, and after some sightseeing returned to the Netherlands intending to seek his fortune in France. Persuaded to return to Scotland instead, he landed in September 1650 near Aberdeen — the day before Cromwell routed the Scots army at the battle of Dunbar.

Life was difficult for a while, for the Kirk Party was still demanding punishment of and repentance from Engagers. Turner kept a low profile. In time, however, the consequences of Dunbar worked in his favour: facing military defeat by the English, the regime had to give way to pressure to accept the services of former Scots enemies. Eventually Turner was forgiven for his harsh dealings with the godly of Glasgow, and appointed adjutant-general of the foot:

Behold a fearful sin! The ministry of the Gospel received all our repentances as unfained, though they knew well enough they were but counterfeit; and we on the other hand made no scruple to declare that Engagement to be unlawful and sinful, deceitfully speaking against the dictates of our own consciences and judgements. If this was not mocking the all-seeing and all-knowing God to his face, then I declare myself not to know what a fearful sin hypocrisy is.

The burden does not seem to have weighed too heavily on him, however.

On the march again, he moved south with Charles II's army, 'with a great deal of mischief to all these poor Scotch people by whose dwellings we marched, robbing and plundering being used by the soldiers, even to admiration and inhumanity'. Turner gives no details of the Worcester campaign, simply stating that he was one of the many thousands of Scots captured in the battle who were marched towards London. Presumably expecting severe treatment on being captured by the English for a second time, he resolved to escape. Climbing out of a house he was billeted in on the march, he made his way into an empty building next door, 'not without obstructions and some merry passages, the memory whereof was afterwards pleasant, though then I ran twice the near hazard of breaking my neck'. Hiding in the empty house until the search for him was over and the other prisoners had been moved on, Turner set off for London in disguise, accompanying some watermen. His feet giving out through lack of suitable shoes, he ended up being carried by the watermen on condition that he bought them a drink at every alehouse they passed. The arrangement sounds as though he was as much in peril of his neck as during his initial escape. Hidden by London royalists, he heard of the sack of Dundee, where his wife had fled with their possessions as the English advanced. Not for several weeks did he receive confirmation that she was still alive.

Eventually Turner made good his escape, through Dover, and found his way to Paris. There he brushed up his French (which luckily he had begun to learn while a prisoner in Hull), though interrupted by the confused advances and retreats of the forces engaged in the civil wars of the Fronde. In the years that followed, Turner travelled widely, seeking support for the royalist cause. In Bremen in 1653 he met up with his wife, and the following year he was back in Scotland to take part in a royalist rising against the occupying English forces. But a few profitless adventures and skirmishes, and no sign of concerted action, soon disheartened him and he took ship to Ostend, admitting that he was glad to get out. At Bremen

> I had the comfort to find my sweet wife in good health, having myself passed
> the year 1654 with as much trouble and anxiety of mind, fatigue of body,
> and danger both at land and sea, as any year I ever passed in my life.

He lived quietly with his wife until 1656, but then lack of money forced
him to seek a living. Rejoining royalist exiles, he was employed on a mission
to Poland. This proving abortive, he sought employment in Denmark. He
was sent to raise a regiment in the Netherlands, but the project collapsed
when the Swedes invaded Denmark across the ice of the frozen Sound
in 1658. However, prospects nearer home were looking brighter as the
republican regime collapsed after Cromwell's death. Once Charles II was
established back in London in 1660, Turner hastened to court, flocking like
so many others to seek reward for his services. Luckier – or more deserving
– than Andrew Melvill, Turner gained a knighthood and appointment as
sergeant-major of the king's footguards in Scotland – a modest appointment,
but enough to persuade him to return to his native land.

Turner probably assumed that his life as an active soldier was now over
and his duties would be largely ceremonial. In fact a spell of duty lay before
him which was to bring him far greater celebrity – or rather notoriety –
than any of his past exploits. Open opposition to the religious settlement
made after the Restoration in Scotland soon emerged, centred in the western
Lowlands, and Turner was sent to quarter troops on dissidents and generally
enforce obedience to the law by sending out parties of soldiers. According
to covenanting legend, he was a harsh oppressor, a brutal military veteran
harassing poor peasants. By his own account, his error was that, if anything,
he was too lenient, his mildness encouraging further trouble. That, however,
has been the opinion of many a failed persecutor on his lack of success.

In November 1666 Turner and a small party of soldiers were surrounded and
captured by a body of 'fanatics', who then broke out in open rebellion, carrying
round the unfortunate Sir James Turner as a symbol of their success and of the
repression which had provoked their rebellion. Turner, who had been sick at the
time of his capture, was humiliated. He consoled himself that 'towns, castles,
citadels, strong forts, well garrisoned, yea and some armies too, have been
surprised in our own days', even though they had expected to be attacked. Why,
then, should he be blamed for allowing himself to be captured, when there had not
even been a war on at the time? The military expert was indignant at irregulars
who broke the rules, who had failed to let him know a war was beginning. He had
hopefully told them at the time of his capture that he could not be a prisoner of
war as there was no war, but they were deaf to this piece of military logic.

Hauled around the countryside by rebels who seemed to have little organisation and not much idea of what they were trying to do, beyond serving God, Turner often feared for his life as he was reviled as the greatest persecutor of Christians in history, a man hardened in wickedness. Hundreds of horsemen with swords and pistols, footmen with anything from muskets, pikes and swords to scythes, pitchforks and even 'great and long' staves, rallied to the cause as Turner was taken north and east. The tumultuous band approached Edinburgh, but then realised that the cause was not receiving the support in the capital and the Lothians that had been hoped for. A retreat began. At Rullion Green the forces of the king caught up with them, and after hard fighting the rebels were dispersed. Turner anxiously waited on the fringes of the encounter until his guards made off to seek safety.

Thus Turner regained

> my well near despaired of liberty; which was very refreshing to me, after
> a short but sad trial of the vissisitudes and instability of human affairs;
> for all which I give to God the praise and the glory.

But soon he was to observe that though his imprisonment was over, his misfortunes were not. For both sides he became the scapegoat for the rebellion. The government was happy to blame it on his severity, rather than on a now discredited official policy of persecution. Since the policy had provoked rebellion instead of preventing it as intended, it was convenient to pretend it was not the policy that had been at fault, but the man implementing it in the field. By 1668 Turner's conduct had been investigated, and he had been stripped of his commissions – while moves were made to change the policy which had caused the trouble in the first place.

He was a convenient victim. He had no powerful friends or noble kin who would be offended by his disgrace, and there appears to have been a feeling that he had discredited himself by allowing himself to be captured by the rebels, and to be led about by them without attempting to escape.

Sorting out myth from reality is difficult. The treatment of dissidents had undoubtedly been harsh, even brutal, though by the standards of the day their treatment was not extreme. Turner's own demeanour undoubtedly counted against him. As his own account of his life admits, he was prone to violent bad temper, and a heavy drinker who often got himself into trouble while intoxicated. Others bore out his recognition of his faults. Gilbert Burnet described him as 'naturally fierce, but very mad when he was drunk, and that was very often . . . he knew no rule but to obey orders.' Thus while it is true that, in spite of accusations to the contrary, he always acted within his orders, that does little to redeem his reputation.

On the other hand, he was not merely the brutal, drunken, bloodthirsty oppressor of exaggerated legends. In his memoirs he shows that there were other, more attractive, aspects of his personality: his literary interests, his love for the wife who stood by him through many difficult times, his wry sense of humour at times as he reflects on his life, his readiness to admit to his faults (late in the day, perhaps, but better than never). Nonetheless, it is the furious drunk who gets remembered.

Enforced retirement gave Turner time to take up again his literary inclinations. It was in these years that his memoirs were compiled, covering his life up to 1670, basically honest though inspired by the need he felt to justify himself – the long final section is devoted to explaining his part in the events of 1666. When he completed the memoirs he was fifty-six years old,

> being in indifferent good health; my body, considering the fatigue of my life, not very crazy [damaged, broken-down]; the intellectuals which God hath bestowed upon me, sound enough; and my memory so good, that though I never used to keep notes in writing, and that I have written within these last four months, the introduction to my Discourses, and the introduction to this long narration with the narration itself, in which are comprehended the most remarkable passages of my life; yet all and every one of them represented themselves as freshly to my remembrance as if they had been but the occurrences of yesterday.

As well as defending himself in his memoirs, Turner strove to uphold the reputations of others who had struggled in the morass of the troubles. He sprang to the defence of James, Duke of Hamilton, whom he had served under in the army of the Engagement in 1648. Henry Guthry, a former covenanting minister who had become a royalist and was made Bishop of Dunkeld in 1665, had circulated 'observations' on the troubles in Scotland which at many points cast doubts on Hamilton's loyalty to his king. Turner prepared a paper bitterly refuting the bishop point by point, ending venomously:

> assuredly when he [Guthry] wrote this paper, he might have spent his time better to have written a homily. And now, good bishop, I am so perfectly weary of this most malicious and lying pamphlet of yours, that I am ready to swear never to read any of your sermons after it.

In Turner's manuscript of his own works, sections of his memoirs of his life and copies of various discourses he had written on religious and political matters, are all mixed up together. The discourses are largely concerned with political theory — the duties of sovereigns and subjects; supreme power; monarchy, aristocracy and democracy — but also stray into essays on other subjects that caught his fancy: the Jews' Cabal; magic; and friendship. The discourses end with a group of topics which were evidently inspired by his own experiences and personality: misfortunes; imprisonment; anger; revenge; duels; cruelty. For good measure, he added in a few verses and elegies, and a miscellany of biographical essays ranging from Petrarch to Mary Queen of Scots, Wallenstein to Queen Christina of Sweden. Turner then devoted his attention in 1670–1 to the composition of *Pallas Armata. Military Essayes of the Ancient Grecian, Roman and Modern Arts of War*, which was eventually published in 1683.

His writings may lack originality, but they indicate a lively, well-informed mind at work, musing on his own life, political controversy and literary and historical subjects. Whatever else Turner was, he was a man of energy. As soon as he was deprived of military action — in lulls in fighting in Ireland in 1643, in prison in Hull in 1648–9, in retirement after 1668 — he seized the pen as an alternative to the sword as a source of activity and satisfaction.

In his last years his fortunes improved. The publication of *Pallas Armata* (dedicated to James, Duke of York, the heir to the throne) doubtless drew attention to the old soldier, and his failure to deal effectively with the religious dissidents in the south-west in the 1660s was evidently forgiven after the passing of time — especially as others in succeeding years had also failed to solve the problem. Presumably through the prestige brought by his book he was hauled out of retirement and given a command in 1683. But the old man was soon allowed to lapse back into retirement, his past loyalty rewarded by a pension in 1685. Soon thereafter, Turner died in quiet obscurity — and thus avoided seeing the Stuart dynasty he had served driven from its thrones for a second time, in 1688. His beloved wife Mary White lived on through the trauma of that revolution, the 1707 union of parliaments and the 1715 Jacobite rising, dying about 1716.

Sir James Turner would have been out of place in the new century. Very much, he was a figure of the great age of Scots mercenary soldiers in the seventeenth century, and of the Restoration era of often drunken reaction against the covenanting piety which had brought the country to disaster. In history he tends to figure as one of the ogres of the Restoration. Turner would have been much happier to learn that his life was later to help to inspire a literary genius. Sir Walter Scott, in the creation of his character Dugald Dalgetty, is said to have drawn on Turner for inspiration. Thus Turner has won a sort of literary immortality by contributing to the character which came to be regarded as typifying the tough old Scots campaigner of the era. Highly appropriately, military and literary themes thus combine, as they had done in his own life.

FURTHER READING

Sir James Turner, *Memoirs of his own Life and Times* (Edinburgh, 1819).

SEVEN

THE SECRETIVE CHRONICLER:

Mr John Spalding

THE NAME OF John Spalding is well known to Scottish historians through the account which he compiled of 'the troubles', largely concentrating on events in north-east Scotland. His name is also commemorated by three Aberdeen-based historical publishing clubs named after him in the nineteenth and twentieth centuries. Yet very little has been known about the man himself. From his writings it is clear that his sympathies were strongly royalist and episcopalian, and a few references in his chronicle make it clear he was resident in Old Aberdeen, the little burgh huddled between the cathedral and King's College just north of Aberdeen itself. Since the eighteenth century it has been assumed (rather than proved) that John was the son of Alexander Spalding, a lawyer in Old Aberdeen. But beyond this, his life has in the past remained a mystery.

Why did a man who recorded in such detail events in Aberdeen and Old Aberdeen say nothing about his family, and only mention himself (very occasionally) as a witness to events? Clearly he was a man deeply interested in his community – yet he was highly reticent about his family's place in it. Such self-effacement in a man so closely concerned with recording for posterity events in his own community seems strange.

Fragmentary information from other sources pieced together makes it possible to reconstruct at least the skeleton of his story, and the picture that emerges strongly suggests the reasons for his self-effacement. His family was not so much famous in Old Aberdeen as notorious, and his own life was one of disappointment and lost causes – with a great culminating irony which seemed to sum up his experiences. He would probably be distressed at the idea of historians rattling his bones, but he brought it on himself. By writing his chronicle, he made himself of some historical interest.

John Spalding's father was indeed the Old Aberdeen lawyer Alexander Spalding, and Alexander married Christian Hervie in 1608. So far John's background sounds solid and respectable. But among the earliest surviving minutes of the kirk session of Old Machar (the parish in which Old Aberdeen

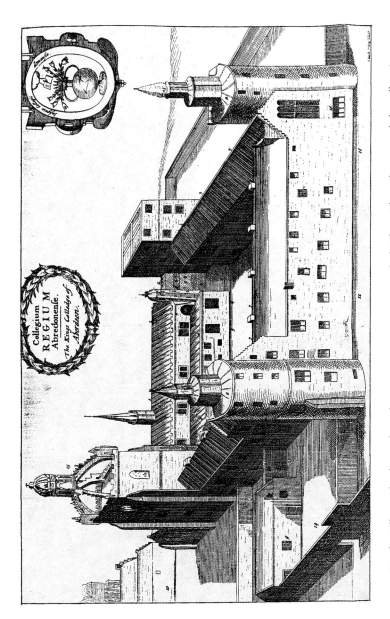

King's College, Aberdeen, where the young JOHN SPALDING studied. The avid royalist entered the college in 1640, just after its royalist staff were thrown out and replaced by covenanters. The engraving of the college is an inset on James Gordon's map of Old and New Aberdeen, 1661. James Gordon, *Aberdoniae Vtriusque Descriptio* (Spalding Club, 1842), opp. p. xxviii.

was situated) is evidence that contradicts this. In 1621 Alexander was convicted of adultery, being the father of a son born to Margaret Hervie. Whether Margaret was a relative of Alexander's wife Christian is not clear, but the identity of their surnames suggests as much.

The severity of the punishment inflicted on Alexander – being repeatedly admonished and prayed for before the congregation, and finally appearing in sackcloth – suggests this may not have been his first offence. Certainly it was not his last. Late in 1623 Euphame ('Effie') Lillie was reported to be pregnant, and was summoned to explain her condition. She named Alexander as the father, confessing to having an affair with him. Moreover, she said that when she had told him she was pregnant, he had promised to provide a remedy, and had given her a drink intended to induce an abortion. Penance in sackcloth was ordered for both sinners: they were to stand at the door of the cathedral (now used as the parish church) before services, as the congregation filed in, and were to sit on the stool of repentance during services. This was to continue until they showed signs of repentance. Alexander's repeated appearances are recorded early in 1624, but Effie may have been spared as the end of her pregnancy was approaching.

Alexander's wife Christian must still have been alive in 1624, because his offence was adultery, not fornication, but she predeceased him. By 1649 (and probably long before) Alexander was married to Effie Lillie, and he had two daughters by her. After his disgrace in 1624 there is a twenty-year gap in Alexander's life. There is no record of his presence in Old Aberdeen, suggesting that he may have moved away for a period, perhaps in the aftermath of the 1623–4 scandal. Already one motive for the reticence on the part of John Spalding about his family is clear. Mention of the family name might revive prurient recollections of his father's past. But it seems probable that John the chronicler had a far greater and more bitter family legacy to conceal.

A diversion is necessary here on the question of when John was born. His chronicle or *Memorialls* begins its coverage of events in 1624, and it has always been assumed that Spalding was an adult by that date, writing of events as they happened. But even cursory examination of the *Memorialls* makes it clear that this is not the case. He was born much later than previously thought. It is true that his chronicle begins in 1624, but all the early entries are derivative, being copied from other sources. Only in the late 1630s at the earliest do entries begin to appear that are evidently original. Why, then, does the derivative section of the chronicle begin in 1624? The date seems at first sight entirely arbitrary – especially when the first entries concern Highland feuds with little or no relevance to the later Aberdeen emphasis of the work. The problem is solved by the suggestion that John Spalding was born in 1624. He regarded himself as writing not memorials of the troubles, though that has been the title his work has acquired from editors, but memorials of his own times – though definitely not of his own life. That seems the only sensible reason for the 1624 starting date – but he had to resort to Highland material as he lacked sources about what had been going on in Old Aberdeen at the time of his birth. Moreover, he became a student at King's College in 1640. This fits in quite well with a man born in 1624 (though he would have been rather older than most first-year students), but would have been a nonsense for a man a generation older. Middle-aged men simply did not become students.

One child fathered by Alexander Spalding is known to have been due to be born in 1624: the child carried by Effie Lillie, the child that developed from the foetus that Alexander had tried to destroy by illegal abortion. That this was John Spalding cannot be proved, but the circumstantial evidence is persuasive. Was John born illegitimate (though legitimised by his father's subsequent marriage to Effie) and brought up surrounded by lingering whispers of gossip about his father's adulteries, sniggers about the fact that, had his parents had their way, John would never have been born at all? A boy growing up in these circumstances would have plenty of motive to maintain a deep silence about his family, even if fascinated by recording the details of events in his community.

Much later events involving his family would have confirmed such a desire for silence. In 1646 his sister or half-sister Jean appeared before the kirk session accused of whoredom with a soldier, Corporal Groser. She confessed to having been 'in the naked bed several nights' with the corporal, but denied any carnal dealing. This she offered to swear, but the session refused to let her take an oath. This seeming harshness in not allowing her to defend herself was probably motivated by humanity and intended to benefit the unfortunate girl. The session was so convinced of her guilt that her oath would change nothing – except make her guilty of an additional serious offence, perjury. Elders appointed to interrogate Jean failed to win any further admission from her, so it was decided she should be regarded as a fornicator though not punished until the corporal had been traced and his version of events discovered. He could not be found, and Jean fled from Old Aberdeen to escape her pious persecutors. Eventually the long arm of the kirk located her in Edinburgh, but efforts to have her returned evidently failed.

There Jean Spalding's story ends, so far as surviving records are concerned. John's embarrassment at her downfall must have increased his tendency to be taciturn about his family: that her partner in sin was a covenanting soldier doubtless added to the anguish of her royalist brother.

Later examples of the weakness of Spalding girls for military men can have been no more acceptable to him. In 1654 an English soldier, a member of the Cromwellian army of occupation in Scotland, married Elspeth Spalding in Old Aberdeen. Her relationship to John is uncertain, but it is likely that she was a sister or half-sister. Certainly Marie Spalding was – and in 1655 she married another English soldier, Sergeant Philip Sheylds. English republican conquerors as brothers-in-law were unlikely to be congenial to a chronicler who believed that it was a secret conspiracy of English traitors with discontented Scots which had led to the seizure of power by the covenanters at the outbreak of the troubles. (Conspiracy theories were very fashionable: recall that James Turner had seen a French-Swedish conspiracy behind the troubles.)

In family affairs life seemed to conspire to embarrass John Spalding, and public events affecting his life contrived to disappoint him as well. In 1638 he signed the King's Covenant, the royalist rival to the National Covenant; but soon the covenanters established their supremacy. Entering King's College in Old Aberdeen in 1640, he was just too late to experience the university as he would have liked it – as the intellectual heart of episcopalian and royalist resistance to these rebels – since shortly before his studies began the college was purged and covenanting staff took over control. That he had to study under such auspices was another secret to be concealed. The chronicler is loud in his denunciations of the actions of the new principal imposed on the college in 1640, William Guild, but Spalding never even hints that he was Guild's student at the time.

John Spalding graduated in 1644 – an inauspicious time for a young man of royalist persuasion to embark on a career, as vicious civil war disrupted the North-East. He sought to make his living as a clerk. Already while still a student he had done some work in this line for the kirk session. His life is obscure until 1648, when there is recorded the only known instance of his activities matching his royalist convictions. He had, it appears, no inclination to act for the king in a military capacity, but did serve the Engager regime as a clerk. There is no evidence that he worked with the Engagers during their early success in raising an army of moderate covenanters and royalists, but he appears after invasion of England ended in disaster and the regime collapsed in the face of its Scottish enemies backed by the English army. In the last days of the regime he acted as its clerk as it negotiated surrender to its enemies.

The next fourteen years are again a blank in Spalding's life, though it was probably in this period that he compiled most of his chronicle. Unfortunately the text is lost after June 1645, and there is no way of knowing how far beyond that he carried his narrative – though there is a reference to a summary of his work up to 1650 having once existed.

In the early 1660s events brought the loyal if obscure royalist some reward. Once monarchy was restored and episcopacy re-established, Mr John Spalding was admitted an honorary burgess of Edinburgh, as a servant of the new Bishop of Aberdeen, and burgess-ship of Aberdeen soon followed. After such minor honours came office, for the bishop's patronage brought Spalding the post of clerk of the commissary court of Aberdeen. His father had once been clerk-depute of the same court – which dealt mainly with matters concerning marriage law and testaments (wills).

Most of the life of John Spalding is so hazy that the records of these modest events of the early 1660s provide what seems a blaze of light. But, typically, he soon vanishes back into the darkness. In 1665 he resigned office, and already by that time he had abandoned Old Aberdeen and was living in Edinburgh. Again, darkness. A brief flicker in 1669 confirms that he was still alive, but then nothing for twenty-one years. He seems to be a man with a talent for obscurity. One last time he emerges, in 1690, to play a role in helping to bring about a new – and in his eyes, abhorrent – religious revolution.

In 1688 James VII and II was overthrown, being replaced on his thrones by his son-in-law and his daughter, William of Orange and Mary, as joint sovereigns. Uncertainty about the religious consequences of this revolution in Scotland was prolonged, but at last in 1690 it was decided by the new regime that presbyterianism should be restored. To initiate this process it was arranged that the general assembly should meet – for the first time for nearly forty years – on 16 October. In the weeks before this, presbyterian ministers gathered in Edinburgh and held meetings to discuss what should be done in the assembly. The clerk who kept records of their deliberations was Mr John Spalding. How he came to occupy this position is unknown, but the ministers were evidently well satisfied with his services, for at the last of these meetings they appointed him 'to attend the opening up of this General Assembly'. This he did, but on the very first day of the meeting, he 'did lay down his charge, and desired the Assembly might proceed to the choice of a Clerk'. His request was refused:

the Assembly nemine contra dicente [without anyone speaking to the contrary] did continue the said Mr John Spalding Clerk for the time, till the Committee for Overtures, to be chosen by the Assembly, should have their thoughts of choosing one fit to be their Clerk.

There was, however, to be no escape even after the committee had deliberated, as an account of the assembly indicates:

Having chosen a Moderator, the next thing most requisite was a Clerk, they appointed Mr. *John Spalding*, who had been Clerk to the General Meeting, to officiate in the interim till they should choose one, but he continued all the time of the Assembly, for there were so many competitors for the Clerkship, and each of them had such Interest by their Friends in the Assembly, that they durst never put it to the hazard of a Vote, for fear of dividing the Assembly.

Spalding had the frustration of being forced to carry out functions he found repugnant even though there were others clamouring for the job, for fear of a contest between candidates causing dangerous quarrels.

Thus John Spalding, staunch royalist and episcopalian, who had sadly chronicled the collapse of both causes in the years after 1637, was now compelled to prepare the official records narrating the renewed triumph of presbyterianism in 1690, the last act of a second revolution destroying what he held dear.

How convincing is the evidence that the Mr John Spalding who was clerk of the presbyterian general assembly in 1690 was the same man as the episcopalian historian of the 1640s? It cannot just be assumed that the same name means the same man, especially after so many years had passed. As might be expected with a man so elusive as Spalding, an element of doubt must remain, for the evidence is circumstantial. Nonetheless, it is strong and persuasive. The name Spalding is an uncommon one, and Spalding the chronicler and Spalding the 1690 clerk have in common in addition their Christian names; their possession of a university degree (indicated by the prefix 'Mr'); and the profession of clerk. There is no evidence of the existence of more than one John Spalding holding a degree or working as a clerk.

The obvious place to look to settle any remaining doubt is handwriting – a particularly appropriate way, surely, to settle the identity of a clerk. But the very fact that we are dealing with a clerk gives rise to a problem. A man whose profession was writing usually developed a number of hands, as different styles were appropriate for different documents, depending on their formality and importance, or as they would appeal to different clients. Moreover, a professional writer might vary his hand simply for the sake of variety. Thus in the surviving papers of the 1690 assembly, a note of an act of 12 November is in a very different style – and bears a very different version of the clerk's signature – from two papers dated 13 November. If just the two signatures survived, isolated from their contexts, they might well be judged those of different men. Similarly there are wide variations between the hands used by Spalding the chronicler in the 1640s and in the 1660s, yet they are indubitably the work of the same man. Thus evidence of handwriting cannot be conclusive – though the 12 November 1690 signature does bear a number of striking resemblances to that of the John Spalding who acted as clerk for the Engagers in 1648.

At first it might seem surprising that the distinctive name of the 1690 assembly clerk, John Spalding, has not provoked comment and speculation previously. But while it was assumed that Spalding the chronicler was already an adult in 1624, when his *Memorialls* open, anyone struck by the same name appearing in 1690 would have immediately dismissed the idea that the same man was involved. It was hardly credible to think of the chronicler acting as assembly clerk sixty-six years after starting to write his historical work. But if he was *born* in 1624 this problem disappears: he would only have been sixty-six or so when the general assembly met. And, by some trick of fate, he was picked upon as the most suitable clerk available to act in a role which must have been deeply distasteful to him.

Reconstructing the life of Mr John Spalding is a fascinating exercise in historical detective work. He presents a challenge not only because of his undistinguished life but because of his evident concern to maintain a low profile. In doing so he has been greatly helped by a single false assumption concerning his date of birth. Investigators searched for him in the wrong place, chronologically.

One question remains. Why did the man who so shunned publicity draw attention to himself in the first place by writing his chronicle? It is surely far too elaborate a production – compilation must have been very time-consuming – to have been simply for his own use. Sometimes he addresses a reader, 'you', but this could be interpreted simply as a rhetorical device. In all probability at some time during the early stages of the troubles, the young John Spalding realised that he was living in momentous times, with rebellion and war not distant events but matters disrupting his own community and destroying much that he valued. As a clerk whose vocation was recording, he felt bound to chronicle what was happening, if only to deplore it. Probably he contemplated his record at a future date circulating (in manuscript) among men sympathetic to his outlook, a memorial to a time of catastrophe. But during his lifetime it would seem that he kept his work to himself. It was for posterity, and publicity would only have drawn unwanted attention to the author.

Spalding has achieved posthumous fame through his work. He presents us with the most detailed provincial account of the troubles of any Scottish author of the age, an unrivalled richness of incident. He has little of value to say about national events, but provides an interesting provincial perspective on what was happening. His conspiracy theories of the origins of the troubles, for example, are useless as evidence of what had really happened; but they give insight into what royalists in the North-East believed.

Modest Mr Spalding probably would not have been hurt by criticisms that his work is unsophisticated, that he merely narrates what he saw and heard with a royalist and episcopalian bias. He was not a man of intellectual pretensions, and to those who claim he was not a historian but 'merely' a chronicler he would probably have quietly responded that he never aspired to be a historian, that he merely tried to record meticulously. In this way his modesty of ambition is central to his achievement, for it is his day-to-day detail of events that makes his work of interest to historians.

FURTHER READING

J. Spalding, *Memorialls of the Trubles in Scotland and in England*, ed. J. Stuart (2 vols., Spalding Club, 1850–1). Earlier editions were published in Edinburgh in 1792 (reprinted 1829) and (under the title *The History of the Troubles*) by the Bannatyne Club in 1828–9.

D. Stevenson, 'Who was John Spalding?', *Aberdeen University Review*, li (1985), 102–115.

D. Stevenson, 'The Inappropriate Fate of John Spalding', *Scottish Historical Review*, lxxv (1996), 98–100.

SIR THOMAS HOPE OF CRAIGHALL, by George Jamesone (1627). Hope had just reached the status which made it appropriate to have his portrait painted, having been appointed joint lord advocate the previous year. His setting is stark, with only a fairly plain chair and an empty table visible. The book he holds symbolises his legal interests.

EIGHT

A LAWYER AND HIS LOYALTIES:

Sir Thomas Hope of Craighall

SIR THOMAS HOPE of Craighall never intended to write a diary. He set out simply to keep a log of the correspondence he received and dispatched, both private and official, the latter concerning his duties as lord advocate. This log in itself is of interest, charting the wide range of contacts he had at court and elsewhere, the very varied matters he was involved in as the crown's leading legal adviser in Scotland, and the mechanics of sending and receiving letters. But soon the dry log expands. Notes on the subject matter of correspondence grow more detailed, and entries which have nothing to do with his correspondence begin to appear and to give indications of Craighall's opinions and emotions. But he never makes a comprehensive attempt to justify and explain his actions – largely, perhaps, because he regarded himself as writing as an aid to his own memory rather than for others.

Thomas Hope was the son of a successful merchant, and was admitted to the faculty of advocates in 1605. He almost immediately won recognition as an outstanding lawyer, through his role in a show trial in 1606. A number of parish ministers opposed to the creeping takeover of control of the Church of Scotland by the king made a stand on principle by refusing to accept the jurisdiction of the privy council over them. It was a civil court: they were only answerable to ecclesiastical ones. The ministers were brought to trial, and four lawyers were appointed to represent them, Hope being one of them. All recommended that their clients submit. It was an open and shut case, with the law clearly supporting the crown. But the ministers refused to accept their lawyers' advice, whereupon the two senior lawyers refused to act any further for them. This gave Hope, still a raw young advocate, a far greater prominence at the trial than he would otherwise have had, and he took full advantage of it. He knew the case was lost, but nonetheless his defence of his clients was regarded as brilliant and this, in so widely publicised a case, made his reputation overnight. His career was thus initially not based on success, but on losing well.

He quickly built up a thriving practice – and a profitable one, leading him to invest widely in land, including the estate of Craighall in Fife.

He was a workaholic, and in addition to all his work in the courts Craighall found time to compile his *Major Practicks*, a substantial legal treatise; compilation was eased by using references to his own cases in many instances as examples of recent judgements. If the work fails to be either systematic or comprehensive, this was partly because it was compiled piecemeal over many years (1608–33) as the author jotted down decisions on his return from court. Added to this work are the *Minor Practicks*, and translations into Latin of the Psalms and the Song of Solomon.

After Charles I came to the throne in 1625 the emphasis of Craighall's work quickly switched from private to public. He began to be employed by the crown, in the first instance to draft documents relating to the Act of Revocation, the disastrous piece of legislation which made many members of the landed classes of Scotland bitter towards the king by threatening their rights to large amounts of former church property which had been granted to them. However, whatever the long-term results of Craighall's actions, the king was more than satisfied, and in 1626 he was rewarded with the office of lord advocate. The job was at first held jointly with Sir William Oliphant (1626–8), after which Craighall became sole holder of the post and was granted a baronetcy.

In 1634 Craighall again had a central part in an event which played a major role in undermining the regime of Charles I. He acted as prosecutor in the trial of Lord Balmerino, another show trial, designed to demonstrate that even peaceable opposition to Charles's religious policies was life-threatening. Balmerino was condemned to death, though later pardoned. At the end of 1636 as a member of the privy council Craighall was present when the order imposing a new prayer book on the church was issued.

Thus, right up to the eve of the outbreak of the troubles Craighall was closely associated with the king's unpopular policies, very much a king's man in the public eye. But though in his actions as lord advocate he stood for the king's interest, privately he was deeply unhappy at Charles's religious inclinations. Only one hint of this appears in his diary before the outbreak of the troubles. He went to the parish of Pencaitland to take communion in April 1637 – and received subsequently a letter complaining about his action from William Laud, Archbishop of Canterbury. The English archbishop's intervention is, incidentally, typical of his meddling in the affairs of a church over which he had no jurisdiction. That Laud seemed to think he was Archbishop of Great Britain increased Scottish opposition to official policies.

Craighall had evidently gone to Pencaitland as there he could take communion without submitting to 'novations', such as kneeling to receive the elements, which had been imposed on the church. There is another intriguing possibility. It is said to have been a secret meeting in April, attended by Craighall, which discussed how to oppose the prayer book after it was imposed. The source for this story – Bishop Henry Guthry – is frequently unreliable (as James Turner was later to point out so abusively), but maybe the meeting at Pencaitland was more than a communion service.

On 23 July 1637 Craighall baldly records that the new prayer book had started to be read in the Edinburgh churches, but was interrupted by women and others. In his diary in the months that followed Craighall's reaction to the mounting disorder in Scotland was to ignore it: 'no comment'. But in reality he was torn by incompatible loyalties. He was the king's servant and loyal subject but he was convinced that the king's opponents were justified in resisting his ungodly innovations in religion. He continued to be consulted on legal matters by the regime, but the advice he gave was generally unwelcome and unhelpful to the royal cause. Moreover he was simultaneously in contact with the leaders of the regime's opponents, also giving them legal advice.

Craighall's legal rulings were a major obstacle to the regime. When in November its opponents organised meetings to elect commissioners to join the protests in Edinburgh, Craighall declined to declare that this was illegal. His ruling was that lairds had a right to choose commissioners for any public business. He refused to sign a proclamation denouncing the opposition in February 1638. When the National Covenant appeared he would not sign it – but he joined other lawyers in declaring it justifiable and legal. When the King's Covenant was produced as a counter to the National Covenant he signed it – but then ruled that those who signed it, as the king ordered, by doing so in fact bound themselves to oppose religious innovations! Thus all the covenanters should sign it, and then could proceed in the king's name to destroy the hated innovations that the king was fighting to preserve.

This ingenious plan for the king's opponents to hijack his covenant was largely a failure, because the covenanters decided not to sign the new covenant. Nonetheless it was deeply embarrassing to the regime that its own legal adviser declared that all royalists who had signed the King's Covenant had, by doing so, sworn to abolish episcopacy. Not surprisingly, Craighall was denounced by royalists as 'a bad and most wicked instrument'. But he remained lord advocate. Evidently it was thought it would be too damaging to the reputation of the regime to deprive him of office: he would become a martyr symbolising a regime which found the law inconvenient.

The only action taken for the moment was to forbid him to attend the Glasgow Assembly of 1638 – and that was done only after he refused an order to attend and defend episcopacy.

Craighall continued to undermine royal policy, and greeted the abolition of episcopacy as being 'to the unspeakable joy of all them that fears the Lord, and waits for his salvation'. Yet nothing was done to limit the damage he was doing until January 1640, when he was confined in his own house at Craighall on the excuse of some minor offence. It was action that would have been more effective if it had been taken two and a half years earlier. Among Charles I's faults was a tendency to continue to employ people though he knew they disagreed with him. This might sound a benign tolerance, but seems to have been based on an arrogant assumption that it didn't matter what his servants thought. The point was that they would obey because he was king, God's representative.

Craighall's conduct was an outstanding example of how wrong the king was. Even now the lord advocate was only being slapped on the wrist, by exile from Edinburgh. A strangely ambivalent attitude to him prevailed in the king's mind. The Second Bishops' War was approaching, and Charles decided that a planned meeting of the Scottish parliament, dominated by the covenanters, should be delayed. Incredibly, Craighall was chosen to implement the prorogation. It might be a task appropriate for the lord advocate, but that Craighall would find some way of thwarting it was predictable. Sure enough, Craighall appears to have taken advantage of some confusion as to what commission he and others were acting under to create a situation in which it was impossible to proceed with the prorogation. Thus when parliament met it was able to claim that it had royal approval – and it proceeded to sweeping constitutional reforms largely destroying royal power.

This was one of Craighall's greatest services to the covenanting cause, but by no means his last. He continued to be almost as much legal adviser to the covenanters as to the king. It is true that in 1641–2 he refused to act as a prosecutor in the trials of royalist 'incendiaries', because the king had told him not to, but he still felt justified in privately drafting papers for and giving advice to the prosecution. In 1643 he played a similarly equivocal role over the summoning of a convention of estates (identical in membership to parliament, but with more limited powers). Craighall objected as king's advocate to the summons as a breach of royal prerogative, but privately he encouraged the covenanters to proceed.

His dubious actions seemed to win him reward rather than punishment,

THE SCOTS HOLDING THEIR YOVNG KINGES NOSE TO Y GRINSTO

Come to the Grinstone Charles tis now to late :
To Recolect tis presbiterian fate :

You Covinant pretenders must Sbee
The subiect of your Tradgie Comedie

Jockie

Stoope Charles

THE SCOTS HOLDING THEIR YOUNG KINGES NOSE TO THE GRINDSTONE. In 1650 the covenanters allowed Charles II to return from exile, but only after he had signed away most of his authority. At first he was almost powerless. Here an English caricature shows a presbyterian minister forcing the king to stoop with his nose to the grindstone, while 'Jockie' – the Scots – turns the stone. By the time the print appeared (July 1651) it was out of date: the collapse of the covenanters had allowed the king to regain power. Jockie's bonnet is coloured blue, the 'blue bonnet' of the Scots.

for royalist nobles agreed that he should be appointed king's commissioner to the 1643 general assembly. It was, however, an appointment which was intended as a trap. The assembly, it was almost certain, would ratify the Solemn League and Covenant, allying the covenanters to the king's English enemies. No commissioner would be able to stop this, but whoever acted would get the blame for not stopping it. So: make Craighall commissioner – and perhaps at last his acts would bring the full wrath of the king down on him.

In the event Craighall entered token protests against the new covenant when the assembly met, but made no sustained attempt to get it rejected.

Still no action was taken against him by King Charles – even when Craighall had the nerve to send him a bill for £1,680 sterling, a huge sum, for his work in the assembly.

Something of the religious zeal which inspired Craighall's desertion of the king's interests creeps into his diary sporadically after the troubles began, and from April 1639 he confided instances in which mysterious voices spoke to him when he was in prayer:

> I fell in an earnest incalling of the Lord, that His Majesty would pity his people, and vindicate them from the power and rage of their adversaries, and would establish the glory of His blessed truth in the land. And while I was praying, these words were spoken, but whether by me or some other I dare not say, but the words were, 'I will preserve and save my people.' Whereupon I woke out of my drowsiness; for I was not sleeping, but as it were oppressed with grief and tears, until these words were spoken and certainly heard by me.

His wife had heard nothing, and Craighall was shaken by the experience. Even in the privacy of his diary he could not make explicit his suspicion that God had spoken to him. Six weeks later the voice came again. Early in the morning Craighall was lying in bed, pouring out his heart to the Lord, asking Him to pity His poor kirk. 'I will pity it' came the response – and this time Craighall accepted that the voice was divine. For the second time God had assured him that the cause of the covenanters would prevail. Further instances followed over a period of months, but then the voice disappeared – or at least Craighall makes no further mention of it.

Words reassured him, but dreams frequently troubled him as he usually saw ominous implications in them. Two in particular shook him in January 1641 – and when recording them he concealed what he was writing in Latin. In one he was lost in a dense mist or darkness. The other was far more specific. In this 'terrible' nightmare he was accused of treason and was to be imprisoned. Ever since 1637 this was something he must have feared – with good reason. But in his dream all was well in the end. He managed to run away and escape: 'to God be all the glory'. Whatever his fears, Craighall was ultimately confident that the God he served would rescue him.

To an early nineteenth-century editor the voice, and the attempts Craighall made to interpret his dreams, were signs that his religious beliefs were 'degraded ... by strange and humiliating indications of weakness and credulity'. The modern reader is likely to have more tolerance and understanding of these manifestations as psychological symptoms explicable in a man so deeply torn by conflicting loyalties and justifiable worries about his future.

Very occasionally in the diary Craighall writes in Latin. Even more rarely he produces a few words of Greek or Hebrew. The nosey historian is likely to jump to the conclusion that this must be intended to conceal more than ordinarily confidential material – which would therefore be more than usually interesting. Alas in reality it is hard to see why he sometimes used these languages. It cannot even have been to impress with his erudition, since this was a private diary – and his grasp of Greek and Hebrew was sufficiently dubious for it to be clear why he never ventured beyond a few words. Hebrew is used almost exclusively for Biblical quotations indicating that Yahweh (God) will help him. On a couple of occasions Greek records a paroxysm: some form of fit, presumably, that he was keen to keep secret.

On 13 October 1643 Craighall was present in St Giles Church when the new Solemn League and Covenant was first sworn and signed. Legal scruples made him declare that he could not swear to one clause in it. This would have bound him to maintain the privileges of the parliament of England: and as a subject of Scotland he maintained that he could not be bound to maintain the privileges of another kingdom's parliament. Perhaps this niggle salved the royalist side of his conscience.

Craighall's private practice had declined ever since he became lord advocate, and in the 1640s his public business also declined rapidly, as the covenanters' takeover of government disrupted legal routines. Moreover both sides in the political conflict now marginalised him most of the time through exasperation at his ambiguities. And he was aging. He had probably been born about 1580, and so was now in his sixties. Increasingly his diary is dominated by personal and family affairs, and by notes on public events which he played no part in. The campaigns against the Marquis of Montrose in the north in 1644–5 receive worried attention. The battle of Tippermuir: 'our people was inhumanly defeat by the Irish'. The battle of Aberdeen: 'taken by the Irish, and our forces defeated'. The battle of Inverlochy:

word came of a defeat given by the Irish and the Earl Montrose to that part of our army which was led by the Laird of Auchinbreck in Lochaber. God be merciful to us.

Thereafter the word came that . . . the whole body of our army was there, and the Marquis of Argyll in person, and that there was killed and taken of our army one thousand and five hundred men . . . The Lord be merciful to this poor kirk and kingdom, for this is a sad and heavy stroke.

The battle of Auldearn:

This day a general bruit [rumour] came of a bloody conflict between Montrose and Major Hurry, near to Spynie in Moray, wherein was great slaughter on both sides. But Montrose keeps the fields and Hurry fled to the castle of Spynie. The Lord be merciful to us . . . The certainty came of the conflict, which was worse nor [than] the first report.

Craighall's records of the battles are typical of covenanter reports: he was clear that the covenanting armies were 'us'. It was also 'our army' which won the battle of Marston Moor in England – a combination of Scots covenanters and English parliamentarians. Craighall was also typical in at first regarding the enemy in the north of Scotland in 1644–5 as 'the Irish'. Essentially it was an Irish expeditionary force which had to be crushed. Only later does Montrose begin to be mentioned, as his climb to fame as one of Scotland's greatest heroes – or villains – began.

Craighall notes no more battles. The 20 May 1645 entry which includes information on Auldearn is the last in his diary. Increasing infirmity probably led to his giving up the note-keeping that he had maintained for over twenty years. Appropriately, the very last words take the diary back to its original purpose: 'Item, a letter to my Lord Wariston, anent [concerning] my Lord Chancellor his answer'. He died the following year.

Sir Thomas Hope of Craighall could regard his life as a success. He was acknowledged as an outstanding member of his profession. He had held high public office for many years. He was a rich man. Of his four sons who reached adulthood, three became senators of the college of justice (judges on the court of session) – perhaps with the help of a little nepotism – and one became cupbearer to the king. Of two daughters, one married a lord, the other a knight. Set against this was the disapproval of both sides in Scotland's conflicts of his seemingly indecisive stance as divisions increased, positions hardened, and it became difficult not to be an avowed covenanter or an avowed royalist.

What are we to make of Craighall's divided loyalties? Was he just unable to make up his mind finally in a conflict which left many confused, uncertain and inconsistent in their actions? Or was he a calculating, unscrupulous lawyer, performing a careful balancing act, keeping a foot in each camp so that, whatever the outcome, he would be on the winning side?

Craighall's reply would almost certainly have been an indignant rejection of such interpretations, and an argument that it was in fact the very strength of his commitment to principle that led to his seeming inconsistency of actions and to accusations against him. In religious matters the covenanters were basically correct. Resistance to the king could be − should be − justified in the name of a higher authority, the Lord. But the political actions the covenanters took to enforce their religious views on the king, their defying his authority, were a different matter. In such civil matters the authority of the king was supreme, and as lord advocate, Craighall had a particular responsibility to uphold royal sovereignty. He is said to have told one of the covenanter leaders, the Earl of Rothes, in 1640, 'For civil points, never look to have me go with you'. Thus, Craighall would have claimed, he was both a good royalist and a good covenanter. Others, in his view, veered too far to one side or the other. For example his son Sir Alexander, cupbearer to Charles I, needed to 'fear his Lord in an other sort nor [than] as yet he has done' and change his attitude to the king 'whom he idolit [idolised] as his god'. Craighall himself might serve his king: but he would not make an idol of him, and even in civil matters he would stand by his interpretations of constitutional law rather than obey the king.

Ultimately, when he was forced to choose between them, the interests of true religion came before those of the king, even to the point of opposing the king in battle − or rather, in the conventional disclaimer, opposing not the king himself but the evil advisers who had led the king astray. The king came to regard him as a paid servant who betrayed his trust, a lawyer who betrayed his profession by not pleading his client's case. Craighall's stance was that even as a lawyer he could not be made to act against his conscience. He would not become one of the evil advisers. In effect, he claimed the right to judge the dispute in which he was employed as advocate. His balancing act was not always consistent, hardly glorious. Yet the maxim that the king was not an idol was a worthy one. Craighall struggled to act within the law of the land, of the king, but God's law had to come first.

No wonder he had nightmares.

FURTHER READING

A Diary of the Public Correspondence of Sir Thomas Hope of Craighall, Bart., 1633–1645 (Bannatyne Club, 1843).

J.A. Clyde (ed.), *Hope's Major Practicks, 1608–1633* (2 vols., Stair Society, 1937–8).

G.W.T. Omond, *The Lord Advocates of Scotland* (2 vols., Edinburgh, 1883), i, 93–147.

R. Paul (ed.), 'Twenty-Four Letters of Sir Thomas Hope, Bart., of Craighall, Lord Advocate of Scotland, 1626–1646', *Miscellany* (Scottish History Society, 1893), 71–139.

My thanks to Professor Harry Hine for translations of the short passages in Greek and Latin in the *Diary*, and to the Rev. Mary Shields for similar help with the Hebrew.

NINE

ERUDITION IMPENETRABLE:

Sir Thomas Urquhart of Cromarty

IF THE PEOPLE studied in this book were to be assembled together, Sir Thomas Urquhart of Cromarty would be the one to be noticed first. He would be in front. He would be making extravagant gestures and talking non-stop in a loud voice. His bursting self-importance and manic elation would be as evident as his flashy, attention-attracting clothes.

Sir Thomas Urquhart's self-image can be seen in two engravings of himself that he had prepared for his publications. In the first, dated 1641, he looks out proudly from beneath his long curly locks. He is dressed in the most extravagant of outfits, bedecked with lace wherever possible. On a table lie a rich coat and hat to complete the ensemble. Though he looks straight at the viewer, he stretches out his right hand to take a laurel wreath proffered to him which is labelled 'for arms and arts'.

In the second engraving, in one sense Urquhart himself is less prominent, but this is because he is now surrounded by a bevy of other figures, as muses and other mythological creations crowd round to honour him. This time at least six wreaths are being offered. Some carry inscriptions: 'For Judgment, Learning'; 'Wit'; 'For Invention, sweetness, Style'. The subject of this adulation points to his head as the proper destination of the wreaths, while other appropriate mythological themes jostle for attention. The flying horse, Pegasus, happens to be passing overhead, and feathers are plucked from his wings, no doubt to make quills for Urquhart to write with. Urquhart is sitting on Mount Parnassus, and is again in full lace-chocked sartorial splendour.

Whether Urquhart ever actually dressed as he appears in the engravings is unknown. Perhaps his outfits were merely figments of his outrageously fertile imagination. But they are nonetheless significant. These images are how he would like to be seen, an ideal of a man who loved display to draw attention to himself, and whose belief in his own genius was overwhelming.

Thomas Urquhart was born in 1611, the eldest son of another Thomas, who was knighted in 1617. The family dominated the shire of Cromarty, and indeed a wider area, holding a number of offices (including that of sheriff of

SIR THOMAS URQUHART OF CROMARTY in his full foppish finery. This is the earlier of the two prints of Urquhart which survive, being dated 1641. The knight is being handed a laurel wreath symbolising both success in arms and in the arts. The print, by George Glover, forms the frontispiece of Urquhart's earliest published work, the *Epigrams*.

Cromarty) and rights, as well as estates sufficient for the Urquharts to be regarded as prosperous though not outstandingly wealthy. Thus Urquhart was born a member of a major gentry family, and his early life reflects this background. He went to Aberdeen University (King's College), but didn't bother graduating – what use was a degree to a gentleman such as himself? But his academic interests had already developed, and he evidently made good use of the opportunities available to him, studying far beyond the requirements of the curriculum. His time at Aberdeen probably also reinforced the younger Urquhart's episcopalianism. Until recently the family had remained Roman Catholic, but his father had converted, and episcopalianism was to have a central part in determining Urquhart's royalist allegiance during the troubles.

Another prominent characteristic was patriotism. After university he set off on his travels to broaden his experiences. Very little is known of his itinerary, but it evidently included France, Italy and Spain, and he records that in three different kingdoms he fought duels to defend Scotland's honour – triumphing in all of them (but of course), and then sparing his opponents' lives on their admitting their errors.

Probably he wandered in Europe for some years (nothing certain is known of him for a decade), most of his time spent in a mixture of socialising and study, building up the vast range of learning he was to exhibit haphazardly in his later publications. The long silence was ended by a dramatic incident – aptly enough, given his taste for ostentation. Urquhart and one of his younger brothers were accused of illegally imprisoning their father for several days. That the family crisis was serious is indicated not only by the imprisonment, but by the fact that old Sir Thomas was prepared to make the scandal public by bringing charges against his sons. Disaster faced the family at this point, in the form of bankruptcy, and it is likely that the family quarrel centred on this.

The elder Sir Thomas had inherited a prosperous, debt-free estate in 1607. Thirty years later he was hugely in debt, having to sell off land but even so with no way of fully meeting his commitments. Had his sons locked him up in fury on learning how bad the situation was? Or to stop him entering into some new, damaging financial transactions? There can be little doubt that the financial situation was largely Sir Thomas's fault, and that he had managed his affairs with folly and neglect. This was partly at least because in his pride (like father, like son) he deemed it beneath him to take much interest in financial dealings. His servants had systematically cheated him for years, and his distaste at having to deal with merchants had led him to accept without proper scrutiny many contracts which were seriously damaging to him. He borrowed money on the security of his land whenever he needed it, without thought for the future.

The timing of his main land sales – in 1634 and 1636 – increases the likelihood that his financial troubles were connected with his brief incarceration, for the latter took place at the end of 1636. However, before assuming that all the blame for the decline of the family fortunes was Sir Thomas's, it is worth noting that when the crown granted him a protection from his creditors for a year, the blame for his problems was placed on the behaviour of his undutiful children. Sir Thomas had about seven sons and seven daughters. Had their demands for the means to live proudly as independent gentlemen and ladies led an over-generous father into trouble? His heir, the young Thomas, was to blame his father's downfall on particularly rapacious creditors (but how had he acquired them in the first place?) and on his father being too honest in his financial dealings. But this reads like family piety rather than convincing explanation – and presumably father had financed the young man's long travels.

To private was soon added public conflict – the two being linked by the fact that as allegiances to king and covenant became clear, the royalist Urquharts found their demanding creditors were all covenanters. When in 1639 the two sides began to mobilise in the North-East, the area of Lowland Scotland in which royalism was strongest, it was young Thomas Urquhart who represented his family in arms (his father was now in his fifties). He was present in the royalist raid on a covenanter castle in Aberdeenshire which has the gloomy distinction of being the first occasion in the civil wars in which a life was lost, the precursor of so many in the three kingdoms in the years ahead. The royalists managed to advance and seize Aberdeen, but in the face of covenanting attack the leaders of the king's forces – including Urquhart – hastily sailed for safety in England.

There Urquhart evidently attached himself to the royal court, and won royal attention in 1641 when he was knighted. Presumably his supporting himself at court for several years was a further drain on family resources. Still, the stay allowed him to launch himself as a literary figure, producing a volume of 134 *Epigrams: Divine and Moral* (London, 1641).

Commentators have usually vied with each other in their denunciations of these little verses. They have been regarded as consistently banal, dull and pointless, indeed in some cases scorned as remarkably bad verse. Some defence has been made: the sentiments of the epigrams are generally unexcitingly sensible, and that was what the seventeenth century expected from an epigram. Wit in the modern sense was not required. Nonetheless, this was a most undistinguished start to establishing himself as a man of letters – and perhaps it was the reception of the book that led to a further 1103 further epigrams mercifully remaining unpublished. Typically, he boasted he had written them in thirteen weeks, as if speed of composition was a guarantee of quality. But he had not yet developed the obsessive self-praise that was later to become his trademark: all he claimed for the epigrams was that 'they be but flashes of wit'. Whether he was sincere or merely conforming to conventions of authorial modesty may of course be questioned.

In August 1642 Urquhart left London to return to Cromarty. He indicates that he went north on his father's death. Other evidence shows that his father was already dead by June, so it seems that he was in no hurry to return home. Indeed, death in the family was probably a convenient excuse – strangely conventional for Urquhart – for the journey. London had lost part of its attraction to Urquhart when early in the year Charles I and his court had withdrawn as Charles's quarrel with the English parliament grew. In view of one of his later obsessions, it seems likely that Urquhart had stayed on as he was more interested in finding publishers than in serving his king, but by August London was becoming potentially dangerous. The king declared war on parliament and began an advance on London. What was the royalist Urquhart to do? If he stayed in London he was in effect in an enemy-held city which was likely to come under attack. He could himself have joined royalist forces advancing southwards, displaying the gallantry about which he boasted so much. Instead, however (perhaps arguing that as a Scot it was not really his war), he decided on a hasty retreat to Scotland – and the death of his father provided a good excuse for leaving the battlefield.

At Cromarty the financial situation was desperate. His father had left twelve or thirteen thousand pounds sterling in debts, a vast sum, and almost exactly twenty times the total income of the estate. In addition to supporting himself, Urquhart had to give his mother her due; he had five adult brothers who expected something; and two sisters approaching marriageable age who would need settlements to attract socially appropriate husbands. At least one other brother and five sisters had already been provided for!

The new laird's solution for crushing financial problems at least had the virtue of simplicity. All revenue except that due to his mother would be applied to paying off debts. Administration of all revenue would be placed in the hands of local friends, who would act as trustees. Urquhart himself would remove the burden of his own support from the estate by leaving to travel on the Continent.

Urquhart shared something of the financial naivety (a kindly word for stupidity) which had beset his father. He had dreamt up a painless way of sorting out his problems. He would go off travelling (which he loved doing), and while he was absent his debts would melt away, and he could then return to take up the proper life of a gentleman. He admitted later that his extensive travels had required some money from home, but argued that the cost had not been 'considerable'. What 'not considerable' meant to this man of frequently bizarre judgements is difficult to tell. If he lived in the style to which he believed himself entitled as a lace-encrusted fop, life on the Continent must have been expensive – and while there he bought a considerable library of books to bring home with him. Anyway, the best way to restore a mismanaged and neglected estate was hardly to hand it over to others to look after for him while he went away to play. One suspects that Urquhart, so much the gentleman, the dandy, the intellectual with grandiose ideas to develop, was horrified at the thought of being stuck indefinitely at the back of beyond in the far north of Scotland. Grubbing about with rents and bills and bonds and charters, dealing with farmers and merchants and ministers, with debtors and resentfully poverty-stricken relatives, was not for him. Far better to take off hastily for the intellectual centres of the Continent, in pursuit of learning, of fashion, of the exotic.

Urquhart's debt-escaping travels lasted until 1645, though his claim to have visited (in his earlier and present travels) sixteen kingdoms may be his usual hyperbole; and as there is convincing evidence that in 1644 he was living in London, his definition of foreign travels may be a little elastic. What he was doing in London, seat of the rebel parliamentary regime (now allied to the hated Scots covenanters), may be explained by the publication there in 1645 of *The Trissotetras: or, a Most Exquisite Table for Resolving all manner of Triangles*. Finding a publisher was one practical task he took seriously.

In the 1641 *Epigrams* Urquhart had displayed his abilities (or lack of them) in the arts. Now he turned his attention to the sciences with an elaborate treatise on mathematics, claiming to apply logarithms to trigonometry, greatly simplifying many calculations and rendering the teaching of arcane mathematical matters easy.

Introductory matter to the work includes a section addressed 'To all Philomathets' (lovers of mathematics) by one 'J.A.' This is clearly Urquhart himself, hiding under an alias so he can praise himself the more freely. Urquhart, thus disguised, praises his former *Epigrams* for 'the transcendent faculties of his [the author's] mind'. The muses had never 'inspired sublimer conceptions in a more refined style than is to be found in the accurate strain of his most ingenious Epigrams'. Hope of a literary reputation clearly had not yet been abandoned. Turning to mathematics, 'J.A.' insists that millions in gold and 'several rich territories of a great and vast extent' would have been worth less than the author's 'sublime and divine invention'. Everything Urquhart says in his mathematical work about the genius of Napier of Merchison (the inventor of logarithms) applied equally to Urquhart himself, it is claimed. As Napier had just been hailed as one whom the great ancient philosophers would have regarded as a god, whose invention rendered the philosophers' stone 'trash' and was more important than the discovery of America, greater self-praise is hardly conceivable.

One of the problems in discussing the *Trissotetras* and the later works of Urquhart is that the claims they make for themselves are so fantastical that the books cannot possibly live up to them. Another problem is simply understanding them. Among the qualities of his writings which he tends to praise (or sometimes to apologise for) are simplicity and brevity. But the realities are the opposite, with immense complexities in construction and vastly obscure vocabulary. Most authors when stuck for a word will usually avoid Urquhart's audacious solution: invent one – or, in his case, hundreds. Often their meaning can be worked out, as they are derived from existing words, but with the many derived from Greek the result for most readers is simply incomprehension. In all, it is not surprising that one distinction that Urquhart can validly claim is to belong to that exclusive band of authors who are more written about than read. And, it may be, is one of the authors who is sometimes over-praised by critics who feel that if they can't understand something it must be a work of genius.

Why did Urquhart work so hard to hide what he had to say from his reader – presumably unintentionally? Partly it was an aspect of the same character trait that assumed that the most elaborate of dress was the clothing which would display him to best advantage in engravings. His costumes were the visual equivalent of his convoluted language and verbal flourishes. Like the clothes, the language was intended to impress, to proclaim how learned he was.

In the same year that he published *Trissotetras*, 1645, Urquhart returned to Cromarty. It seems surprising he did not await in London the reception of his treatise, but it may be that as the English civil war approached its climax he found life as a royalist increasingly difficult in London. Or it may be that he could no longer escape giving personal attention to financial problems. But one of his priorities once back at his ancestral seat was installing the most substantial product of his journeyings – a library of books purchased in spite of his great debts. Needless to say, he found that his money problems had not evaporated in his absence, and possibly his return made things worse as creditors, exasperated by his not being available to harry personally, moved in for the kill now that he was present. In 1647 the estate of Cromarty itself and the hereditary right to the sheriffship of Cromarty were awarded to his main creditor, Sir Robert Farquhar of Mounie – a leading Aberdeen merchant who was establishing himself as a laird. Farquhar was a committed covenanter, and political tensions no doubt complicated an already difficult situation.

The same is true of Urquhart's problems with local ministers. He was responsible for the stipends of three ministers – who may well have been finding it difficult to get them paid for years. They greeted his return with demands for increases in stipends and necessary repairs to churches and manses. The beleaguered Urquhart fought back with the only asset he had: his genius. When threatened with the loss of his lands, he had responded by claiming to have moveable goods of such value they could settle his debts. 'I do promise shortly to display before the world wares of greater value than ever from the East Indies were brought in ship to Europe'. These incredible riches, alas, turned out to be confined to his head. They were marvellous inventions he was prepared to reveal to the world, of incredible value in monetary terms. Elsewhere he complained that he could have produced 500 'treatises of inventions' if not constantly interrupted by the bother of creditors and their business. Thus, like Oscar Wilde, Urquhart declared only his genius. Like the New York customs authority, his creditors assigned no value to this commodity. At some point even his library, one of his most prized possessions, was seized.

Military complications added to distractions from his wonderful inventions. In 1648 he supported the royalist-covenanter alliance of the Engagement, and helped raise forces locally for it. He took no part in the Engagers' failed invasion of England, but once the extremist Kirk Party regime took over in Scotland he could expect punishment for his activities. In the despair of financial ruin, likelihood of persecution, and news of the king's execution, Urquhart joined a hopeless local rising against the new regime. Led by Thomas Mackenzie of Pluscardine, the rebels seized Inverness and demolished its fortifications, but seem to have had no further ambitions, and most were soon captured. Urquhart escaped – but was declared a rebel and traitor. Endeavours to make his peace were overtaken by a new war: that against Cromwell's invading army in 1650–1. Nothing is known of Urquhart's part in the war except for its dramatic ending. His royalism

SIR THOMAS URQUHART OF CROMARTY. He would have found it entirely
appropriate that he has two portraits in this book, while the rest of its subjects
are lucky to get one. This print of the great genius being virtually worshipped by
the muses was intended for a second volume of epigrams in 1646, but the work
was never published. The print was substantially altered later, and appeared in
some copies of *Logopandecteison*. It is this revision that is reproduced here.

would have meant that at first he would not have been allowed to fight, but as the English seemed to be unstoppable, principle gave way to expediency. Indeed Urquhart was (he says) colonel of a regiment by the time the desperate march into England ended in catastrophe at Worcester.

Andrew Melvill described graphically what happened to him in the chaotic street fighting of the battle of Worcester. James Turner merely states that he was captured. Urquhart's approach is similar. He says nothing of how he was captured. What did inspire him to write was that he lost his luggage. He had set out for war with seven large portmanteaux or cases, and after the battle he was 'plundered, pillaged, pilfered, robbed and rifled' five times. In horses, arms, clothes and money, he reckoned he lost over £500 sterling. These losses he lamented — perhaps especially his 'scarlet cloaks' and buff suits. Worst of all, however, was the loss of the papers that had filled three of the portmanteaux, worth, by his estimate, over 10,000 crowns. He hadn't managed to sell his genius to his creditors. Instead he lost the proceeds of it in battle.

The English soldiers looting Urquhart's lodgings at first threw the papers aside as worthless, but later returned and seized them. They could be used by soldiers for all sorts of purposes such as wrapping up food. Many were abandoned, and collected by shopkeepers of all sorts, always on the lookout for paper to wrap their goods in. Urquhart was outraged by the thought of his inspired work being destroyed for such mundane purposes, but his full horror was reserved for the fact that some of his papers were put to 'posterior uses'.

Why had he marched into battle accompanied by a virtual baggage train? Why had he brought his almost priceless contributions to the knowledge of mankind, his various treatises, on such a hazardous venture? He provides two reasons. The first makes a good deal of sense: to ensure their safety it seemed best to keep them with him. However, the second reason was probably dominant. He took the treatises with him so he could have them published in London. Most of those with any understanding of the military situation regarded the 1651 Scots invasion of England as a despairing gesture of defiance, with failure almost inevitable. Urquhart, however, assumed the army would triumphantly enter London. The Scots fought for a mixture of national pride, the covenants, and King Charles II. The laird of Cromarty seems to have done battle to find a good publisher.

With a few exceptions, his intellectual riches were lost. Only a few were in time restored to him, having been found under a pile of twenty-seven corpses in a Worcester street. He himself, like many other Scots officers, was imprisoned, spending a few days in the Tower of London before being transferred to Windsor Castle. Typically, he immediately bounced back from disaster with elaborate new plans.

The battle was fought on 3 September 1651. Already by 25 September the council of state in London was instructing a committee to examine Urquhart and find out what he had to offer for the advantage of the nation. Within three weeks of the battle, and the following chaos as the English tried to deal with 10,000 Scots prisoners, he had made his voice heard at the highest levels of the regime, and it was ready at least to listen to him. He had done this by renewing his claims that he had genius to offer, treatises to write that would be of great benefit to mankind. Cromwell's troops might have destroyed virtually all the works of genius he had committed to paper, but he was now ready to rewrite them for the English regime. But whereas *Trissotetras* had been given to the world freely, Urquhart now wanted a return on his intellectual investment. He would only reveal his discoveries fully in return for his freedom, and restoration of his property in Scotland.

He got some of what he wanted. He was very soon freed on parole. Orders were given that any papers found in the House of Cromarty were to be kept safe, and in 1652–3 he was allowed to visit his (former) home in another vain attempt to sort out his affairs. Meanwhile he was busy writing again. His first offering in seeking the patronage of the republican regime might seem typically eccentric, but there was a simple practical reason for it to be the first treatise to appear. It had survived the disaster at Worcester, and with a bit of ingenuity a preface could be quickly provided to make it seem (in his own eyes at least) that family history was relevant to his purposes.

Pantochronochanon. Or a peculiar promptuary of time ... (London, 1652) presented the world with a history of the descent of the Urquharts of Cromarty since the creation of the world. Again, as with *Trissotetras*, the work is prefaced by a fictional writer, this time one G.P. In this guise G.P. explained that the manuscript of the book had been rescued by 'a surpassingly honest and civil officer' of the English army, from soldiers who had been intending to use the pages for lighting their pipes. It had come into G.P.'s hands and he, finding it 'exceedingly useful and ingenious', had decided to publish it, especially as the author was already

> highly esteemed of for his literature and other qualifications; whereof by treatises long ago evulged [divulged], and actions of more than ordinary virtue, he hath at several occasions given many ample testimonies.

G.P. also felt it necessary 'to speak a word or two' on behalf of the author as he was a prisoner of war (technically speaking: he was in fact on parole). Providence had always been highly favourable to the Urquharts, through innumerable political and military upheavals. Surely even the greatest state in the world (England of course: he was working hard on the flattery) would not now cut the thread, the unbroken succession of the family? Quite what the prisoner was to be saved from is not clear: presumably from losing his land. Perhaps from execution, though in reality there was no danger of that. The progress of 'all former ages' would be destroyed in 'the person of him whose inward abilities are like to produce effects conducible to the State of as long continuance for the future'. Thus in ways which would endure until the end of time, Urquhart would continue to be what he already had shown himself: a benefactor of the scholar; a patron of the soldier; a favourer of the merchant; a protector of the artificer; and an upholder of the yeoman. This must be the only place in which Urquhart has anything favourable to say of merchants and their like. In reality he despised them.

The genealogy which followed began with God creating Adam in 3948 B.C., and confidently proceeded to chart the descent of the Urquharts for 143 generations to Urquhart himself. A postscript by the supposed editor explained how the author could 'finish' the genealogy already sketched out if he was freed: and do 'other things of greater importance'. Why on earth the council of state should think further elaboration of an already tedious family tree should be to the public good is hard to understand.

Ridicule has been heaped on the tree itself by most subsequent commentators, and is quite justifiable from a factual point of view. The great majority of it is pure invention, and has been taken as yet more evidence of the eccentricity, if not absurdity, of its author. But just as the *Epigrams* are not so bad as they might appear when viewed in the context of what was expected when they were written, so the *Pantochronochanon* proves far from unique if other sixteenth- and seventeenth-century genealogies are examined. Plenty of noble and gentle families made what are, to the modern reader, silly and fabulous claims about their ancestries, tracing them back to ancient and biblical times. Royal families often took the lead. It was the sort of thing to be expected in the important game of genteel one-upmanship.

Yet, Urquhart does carry a fashion to an extreme. And the last words in the pamphlet noted how he intended to extend his work which, if carried out, would have made it truly unique. He would have added notes on families all over Europe which had been descended from the Urquharts or had connections with them, and on how many places had been named after the family. Why was it that the shire of Cromarty, alone of all areas of Britain, had placenames which were pure Greek? All such matter, and supporting evidence for the existing genealogy, would prove the truth of what he had to say as certainly as Euclid's *Elements* were provable. With his usual over-confidence, he thus promised mathematical certainty for his work.

Did the council of state ever see the *Pantochronochanon*? It would no doubt have been best for the credibility of the author's claims to have great inventions to offer if it had not – though if it persuaded the council that he was not worth supporting, it might have simultaneously convinced them that he was a harmless eccentric who could safely be allowed his freedom.

Urquhart followed up his genealogy with a work specifically written for his circumstances, carefully crafted (in his opinion) to demonstrate that he had great inventions to offer the regime. Instead, it might well be regarded as an exercise in demonstrating how *not* to go about winning respect and influence, of how to hide instead of highlight your message. It has its own logic, but can seem a rambling chaos of a book. *Ekskybalauron: Or, the Discovery of a most exquisite Jewel, more precious then Diamonds inchased in Gold . . . to frontal a Vindication of the honour of Scotland . . .* (London, 1652) at first claims that the author is unknown, then hints at his authorship, then advertises his genealogy of the Urquharts at great length, then indicates that the purpose of the work is to gain him his liberty and lands in return for his priceless 'jewel'. None of this is the workings of a convoluted genius. It is inconsistent nonsense. That the work was, as it claims written at immense speed, the author passing the text a page at a time, as it was written, direct to the printer, rings true. Here is an author failing to remember what he has already written and sent to the publisher. It is frenzied, self-defeating activity.

What was the great jewel Urquhart had to offer, far more valuable than the cash and land merchants had taken from him? It was a universal language, constructed on rational principles to replace all existing languages. One reaction may be this was a scheme typically eccentric, vastly inflated, an intellectual silliness of a fantastical mind. But in reality Urquhart was addressing an issue regarded as of central importance by many intellectuals. Latin had long been in decline as an international language in the western world, and the increasing reliance on national languages even for academic works was fragmenting the intellectual community. A truly universal language seemed the answer – and a number of major figures drafted proposals for new tongues. Urquhart was thus in the mainstream, however eccentrically. His lengthy exposition of his new language combines the logical, the sensible and the useful with the the irrelevant, the trivial, the terrifyingly over-complicated, and the absurd. Take proposition 88, whereby every noun or verb could begin or end either with a vowel or a consonant as 'shall seem most expedient' to the person concerned? Or 93, which asserted that every word in the new language if spelt backwards produced another word? Even Urquhart, had he read over what he had written, could have seen that he was talking nonsense.

The language's principles expounded, its outstanding advantages detailed, the *Jewel* plunges off into its secondary subject, the matter of rescuing the reputation of the Scots from the harm done by presbyterians and merchants. First comes the naming of many dozens of Scots officers who had won renown and promotion in wars all over Europe, and in some cases descriptions of their achievements. This includes perhaps the best-known passage in all Urquhart's writings – the extended sketch of the life of the Admirable Crichton, the perfect gentleman. Unrivalled in bravery and skill as a swordsman; awe-inspiring in the breadth of his scholarship; traveller; lover; outstanding actor. Doubtless this fairly obscure figure receives such attention because he represented so much that Urquhart saw – or wanted – in himself.

Next comes a rambling roll of Scots scholars whose achievements honoured their country – with some bias towards those from the north of Scotland, and particularly the author's own University of Aberdeen. A little further wandering brings the text to a disquisition on what a splendid, reliable chap Sir Thomas Urquhart was and a prolonged denunciation of the greed and ambition of presbyterian ministers – the book was supposedly edited (would that it had been edited!) by 'Christianus Presbyteromastix', or 'the Christian scourge of presbyterians'. Merchants come in for a bashing too: they had 'abused [the] simplicity of the gentry', ruining such honest, simple folk as Urquhart.

Is all this relevant to the universal language? Of course it is. Persuade the English that the Scots are basically a decent lot and they will be more likely to treat one particular Scots prisoner of war well. Show them that the few nasty Scots (merchants and ministers) are making life hard for Urquhart, and they will see that they should help him – because only then will he be able to devote attention to perfecting his great new language which will be so valuable to England.

The *Jewel* meanders to a conclusion with support for the parliamentary union of Scotland and England, and then a plea for Urquhart's land and liberty.

There is a logic in the book, but as a work of propaganda it must be in the running for the title of the world's worst. The message is delivered with awe-inspiring obscurity, only being made clear in the closing passage. Yet of all Urquhart's publications it is in parts the most readable, entertaining – and even useful – as it provides (chaotically) a good deal of the autobiographical material from which his life can be reconstructed. Moreover, in trying to write propaganda, Urquhart to his credit pulls his punches. He does not renounce his beliefs to gain favour. He regarded himself as a man of honour. In his family tree he gave himself the nickname 'Parresiastes', one of his cheerfully invented words, which to him denoted honesty and fair dealing. Thus he may be trying to win the support of a republican regime for something he regards as of immense importance (himself), but he never denounces Charles I or disowns the monarchy. He never indicates that he had been mistaken in fighting for the Scots at Worcester (though he does go so far as pointing out that he did not take part in the Engagers' invasion of England, and didn't fight at Dunbar). So far as is known, the *Jewel* had no effect whatever. The jewel of a new language was ignored. Never give up. He tried again, with a new book for 'his own utility, and that of all pregnant and ingenious Spirits'. This time his own name appears on the title page, and the motto

To grant him his demands were it not just?
Who craves no more, than reason says he must.

At last, the message is clear from the start. *Logopandecteision, or an Introduction to the Universal Language* (London, 1653) begins with a cheerfully bitter 'Epistle Dedicatory to Nobody' on the ground that this 'Sovereign master of contradictions', Nobody, had greatly helped him develop the new language, just as Nobody had helped him in all his other troubles. Having worked off his frustrations by denouncing Nobody, the work (which is divided into six 'books') launches into its main subject – with a reprint of what had been said on language in the *Jewel*. The second 'book' veers off, inevitably, into dealing with 'Impious Dealings of Creditors', pleading for the removal by his creditors of 'impediments' which prevent him from producing various inventions for the good of the country, which of course include his new language. Book three pleads for the author's ancient inheritance. Next 'The Covetous Preacher' is denounced, the ministers who had persecuted him for both financial and political reasons. Book five turns its wrath on 'The Pitiless

Judge', while its successor at least ends the work on a more positive note: 'Furtherance of Industry', designed to prove that if the author's problems were sorted out, the country would benefit from not just the universal language and 'other kinds of literature' but from 'all manner of virtuous undertakings whatsoever'.

Anyone who bought *Logopandecteision* eager to hear more about the new language would rightly have felt cheated at finding the work crammed with details, expressed with great elaboration, at absurd length, of the financial and other problems of an obscure Scots laird. This seemed to occur even to Urquhart, who added a sort of postscript, not apologising, but explaining their relevance: until these problems were sorted out, the language could not be developed.

In his final work, also published in 1653, Urquhart at last escaped from his obsessions, and in doing so produced something which would attract the admiration, rather than the bewilderment, of posterity. To do so, however, he had to surrender his independence as to subject matter, and base what he did on another author's genius. He undertook a translation of Rabelais' *Gargantua and Pantagruel*. No work could be conceived of which was more suitable for Urquhart to translate, for like his own writings it was an extreme extravaganza of prose. Its wild comedy suited Urquhart's fevered mind, its florid language his unstoppable pen. In parts Rabelais was making fun of the foolishly pretentious language of the learned. Did the translator ever realised this, that he was aiding and abetting the mocking of his own chosen style, winning lasting fame by ridiculing himself?

Certainly he joined in with gusto. He outdid Rabelais himself in adding flourishes and embellishments of his own. In a list of games the author only offered 108; the translator managed 238. The 1653 edition was a translation of the first two books of Rabelais only, and publication of the third book of the translation did not follow until 1693, long after the translator's death. The fourth and fifth books Urquhart did not translate.

Hardly anything is known of the last few years of Urquhart's life. He set off to travel abroad again sometime in the mid or late 1650s. In 1658 he can be found writing to his relative and supplanter as owner of the family estates, Sir John Urquhart, calling him an overgrown mushroom and arranging for a duel. His local difficulties at home clearly remained as acute as ever. In 1660, before he was able to return north, Sir Thomas Urquhart of Cromarty died, his family property and offices already dispersed, his great discoveries and inventions undeveloped. If there was much to be bitter about, however, the legend of his death suggests that he could still boast a sense of humour

– and as might be expected, an extreme one. He died of excessive laughter on hearing of the Restoration of King Charles II. Unfortunately the story does not appear until over a century later, and it is hardly plausible. The Restoration didn't come as such a surprise that it was likely to provoke such a reaction (it was well known that negotiations were in progress). Hugh MacDiarmid, deciding that abuse was the best form of argument, announced that 'Dullards have doubted the truth of this story'. Perhaps dullards are more interested in trying to assess what is most likely to have actually happened, while MacDiarmid was more concerned with the defence of a good story. Still, certainty is impossible, and it has been earnestly suggested that Urquhart could already have been in such an intensely emotional state as he awaited an event he had hoped for, that when the event actually took place it proved too much for him. After all, he was above all a man of obsessions and extremes. Sadly, the anecdote comes into the category of too appropriate to be true. But he would have loved the legend of his own Rabelaisian death.

Of all those whose lives during the troubles are examined in this book, Urquhart was probably the least affected by personal involvement in public events (except for John Spalding). With brief exceptions they were, indeed, a sideshow as far as he was concerned. They were distractions from the insoluble financial problems of his Cromarty dynasty. And these, in turn, were distractions from his learned pursuits of literature and invention. He was an unswerving royalist, but so far as taking an active role was concerned he might be described as an occasional royalist. His foreign travels apart, much of his life was one of frustration. He had so much that was marvellous to offer the world. But not only was he hindered by domestic poverty and public conflict; when he did manage to present his gems, whether poetic, mathematical or linguistic, the world proved utterly indifferent. All he had, as he bitterly pointed out, was the support of 'Nobody'.

Was Urquhart a genius, or a self-publicising charlatan with grandiose opinions of himself? Was he, indeed, mad? Certainly he was hugely eccentric, fantastical, impractical. He carried normal human egotism to insane lengths. He seems to have believed whatever he said was automatically of great importance. Manic, paranoid, but with flashes of genius. It is hardly surprising that he never married, in spite of his obsession with family continuity. He had no room for anything outside his own mind and the impression he made (or more usually, failed to make) on others.

But that would be an unfair note to end on, however much Urquhart exasperates the reader much of the time. He was genuinely remarkably learned in a great range of subjects. His mathematical treatise can be sneered at; his universal language can be derided as ridiculous. But while impractical, his mathematical work is regarded as impressive and logical. If it is complex and hard to understand, this is only partly the result of his talent for complication: it also reflects the complexity of the material. His choice of subjects (apart from himself) was not so eccentric as has often been assumed. Prosaic epigrams and mathematics were fashionable. So were fabulous genealogies and universal languages. His contributions to such things were certainly original – but mainly through being obscure and nonsensical, almost using language for its own sake rather than meaning.

He is remembered as an eccentric: unreadable – but memorably, epically, stylishly unreadable. And as a translator of genius for a single work, though it is highly doubtful if any other work would have been able to inspire him to such heights.

FURTHER READING

H. MacDiarmid, 'Sir Thomas Urquhart, the Knight of Cromarty', *Scottish Eccentrics* (London, 1936, reprinted New York 1972), 26–56.

H. Tayler, *History of the Family of Urquhart* (Aberdeen, 1946), 29–103.

Sir T. Urquhart, *The Admirable Urquhart. Selected Writings*, ed. R. Boston (London, 1975).

Sir T. Urquhart, *The Jewel*, ed. R.D.S. Jack and R.J. Lyall (Edinburgh, 1983).

The Works of Sir Thomas Urquhart of Cromarty, Knight [ed. Thomas Maitland] (Maitland Club, 1834).

Selections from Sir Thomas Urquhart of Cromarty, ed. J. Purves (Edinburgh, 1942).

J. Willcock, *Sir Thomas Urquhart of Cromartie, Knight* (Edinburgh, 1899).

TEN

THE WAY OF THE WARRIOR:

Alasdair MacColla

TAKEN PRISONER IN battle, Sir Duncan Campbell of Auchinbreck, commander of the covenanting army, was given a choice as to his fate. The choice was not generous but grimly sadistic. Did he want to be made longer or shorter? In other words, did he want to be stretched by the hangman's rope, or shortened by the headsman's sword? He prevaricated, protesting in Gaelic that it was a choice that was no choice. Impatiently Alasdair MacColla, second-in-command of the enemy army, settled the matter by removing Auchinbreck's head (or, by one grisly account, the top of it) with one stroke of his sword.

Alasdair himself was to experience equally crude dispatch when his time came. Three years later he was captured, in Ireland. Though promised quarter, he too was killed almost immediately, either shot or stabbed to death in cold blood.

These merciless events tell something about the aspects of the 'wars of the three kingdoms' in which Alasdair MacColla was involved, the wars in Ireland and the Highlands. They had levels of bitterness, depths of hatred, not found nearly so commonly elsewhere.

Alasdair was a man fighting on the boundary which both linked and separated two cultures. His very name, or rather names, proclaim it. To his own people, the Gaels, he was simply Alasdair MacColla. He needed no rank or title. The fame of name alone identified him. To the English speakers with whom he fought in uneasy alliance he was, at the time of his death, Lieutenant-General Sir Alexander MacDonald – or MacDonnell. Thus the Gaelic Alasdair is 'civilised' with a mainstream Scots Christian name, and for 'son of Coll' is substituted a fixed surname, the name of his clan. Then military rank and the title of a knighthood are added. An officer and a gentleman.

English-speaking enemies, on the other hand, demonised him with the name 'Colkitto', a name that soon struck terror into the hearts of Scots. A barbarous, alien name for a barbarian enemy. In fact it was not his name at all. His world was so little understood that in this name he was confused with his father, Coll Ciotach, who had

133

HIGHLAND SOLDIERS, serving with the Swedish army at Stettin in North
Germany in 1630 or 1631. The top print describes them as 'Irrländer' – Irish.
Highlanders were often called 'Irish' at the time, and on the Continent it was
probably assumed that all Gaelic troops in Gaelic dress came from Ireland. The
bottom print is a crude copy of the top one, and inserts a Laplander among
the Highlanders. To Germans, Highlanders and Laplanders were weirdly dressed
barbarians from distant parts.

been a notable warrior in his day. His lingering reputation led to his son being mistaken for him.

In the troubles many put the interests of themselves, their families or their localities before the great national causes of covenanter or royalist that dominate history. Alasdair MacColla went further than most – or rather, perhaps, he displayed the fierce particularism which was a central feature of Gaelic culture. Family came first, followed by clan. His wider 'patriotism' related to Gaeldom, not to Ireland or Scotland specifically, for he was both Irish and Scottish – and doubtless thought the distinction meaningless. He achieved fame as a royalist, but that was a flag of convenience rather than a matter of conviction.

Alasdair came of what had once been the greatest clan in the Highlands. The MacDonalds had been Lords of the Isles, providing the only approximation to a central authority in the Western Highlands and Isles. But the great day of the clan had long gone. The branch which had settled in Ulster, the MacDonnells of Antrim, had asserted its independence. Other internal feuds rent the clan, while lesser clans took advantage of its misfortunes to encroach on its authority and lands. The most powerful branch of the now fragmented MacDonalds had been based on Kintyre and Islay. In the 1590s the clan became involved in a war with neighbours over land in Islay. After that it won itself a unique degree of official hostility when its chief reacted to royal intervention with provocative stupidity. He and his son then proceeded to virtual warfare with each other in a bitter family feud. A final element in this disastrous combination of circumstances was provided by the presence in the background of the Campbells, a remarkably successful up-and-coming clan always on the lookout for opportunities to benefit from the misfortunes of others. Royal favour brought them the MacDonald clan lands of Kintyre and (later) Islay. The downfall of the clan was complete, and in the final episode, two disastrous MacDonald rebellions in 1614–15, Coll Ciotach had played a leading part. Many of those involved were executed after the rebellions, but Coll made a dramatic escape to Ireland after the first – and bought his own life after the second by handing over a number of his own men to the enemy, who executed some of them.

That Coll's reputation did not, it seems, suffer by this callous treachery suggests a respect for self-preservation at all costs. And Coll had soon re-established himself back in Scotland, on the island of Colonsay, where he had spent his early life. A dispute developed with the owner of the island, and Coll solved it in the sort of way one might expect from his past. The owner was murdered, then, with grim economy, his murderers dug the musket balls out of his corpse so they could be used again. Recycling? Environmentally friendly?

Coll maintained possession of his ill-gotten gains, though he had to accept that he was not owner of Colonsay, but a tenant of the Campbells. Still, he had a base providing economic security and social status. There most of the childhood of Alasdair MacColla was spent. Of his birth, all that can be said is that it must have been sometime in the first two decades of the century. It seems likely that he was seized as a hostage by government forces in 1615, when he must have been very young. He may also have spent some time fostered in a Campbell household, in an attempt to reconcile the son of Coll Ciotach to Campbell domination. All else that is known of Alasdair's childhood consists of material which is more legend than fact. Still, it is useful, for much of it narrates childhood happenings which indicate the great strength of the boy or predict a heroic future for him. The legends are an impressive tribute to the stature Alasdair was to achieve later, mythology creating a suitable childhood framework for his epic deeds to grow from.

A quiet life for the MacDonalds of Colonsay, keeping a low profile and not offending the Campbells, must have seemed the best that could be hoped for in the 1630s. No doubt tales were told of the great days of the MacDonalds in the past, and dreams were dreamt of the revival of their power and the slaughter of Campbells. But few could have had any real expectation of such developments. Then the world changed: if not overnight, certainly with bewildering speed. First the defiance of the crown and then the open revolt of the covenanters rendered central government powerless. A few months later came what must have seemed in the Highlands an even more stunning development. Lord Lorne (soon to be Earl of Argyll) led the Campbells into support for the covenanters – and indeed became the most prominent of the leaders of the latter. The Campbells had risen to greatness as agents of the crown. Now they were rebels.

If Cambells were covenanters, MacDonalds were likely to discover that they were royalists, whatever the crown might have done to them in the past. But they were royalists with their own specific agenda. Their priority in the wars of the three kingdoms was to be the recovery of lost MacDonald lands, particularly Kintyre and Islay. Soon Coll Ciotach and others were deep in plots with the Earl of Antrim, chief of the MacDonnells of Antrim, for an invasion of Campbell-held lands by the latter, with the help of anti-Campbell clans. The plan remained a dream, and in 1639 the Campbells easily mopped up resistance by their Highland enemies. Coll Ciotach and two of his sons were captured, and were to spend several years in prison. Colonsay itself was raided and subdued. But Coll's other two sons escaped, one being Alasdair.

The brothers fled to their kinsmen in Ireland. Late in 1640 they raided Islay with eighty men, evidently with the intention of kidnapping prominent Campbells who might be exchanged for their imprisoned father and brothers. The expedition was a failure, however, and Alasdair had to flee back to Ireland. This, so far as is known, was his first involvement in military action. Then came a complication – a huge complication – for MacDonald/Macdonnell plots and plans. The Irish rebellion (or rising, to be neutral) broke out in October 1641, as native Irish Catholics copied the covenanters – who had shown that revolt could gain concessions. But if the Irish followed the example of the covenanters, they also acted out of fear of them, terrified by the ferocity of their anti-Catholic propaganda and its adoption by Scots protestant colonists in Ulster.

On Antrim's estates there was confusion (Antrim himself was absent – probably deliberately) but the resolution was taken to oppose the rebels, and to do so by raising a joint Catholic/Protestant regiment. Among the captains of companies appointed were Alasdair and his brother. That the regiment held together and kept the peace locally for just two months may not seem impressive. Given the bitterness of sectarian hatreds, it was in fact quite an achievement. But increasingly the Protestants in the regiment, embittered by stories (frequently exaggerated) of atrocities by the rebels, began to retaliate against local Catholics. The Catholic companies in the regiment naturally feared that their Protestant colleagues, who were already taunting them, would turn on them next. There was, indeed, evidence of a plot against them, they claimed. They decided on a pre-emptive strike – led, evidently, by Alasdair MacColla. The Protestant companies were quartered separately from their Catholic colleagues, and were taken by surprise in a dawn raid. Many of them were killed, most fled. Alasdair and his men then joined up with the rebels, and soon overran north Antrim, with a good deal of indiscriminate killing in the process. But though guilty of much, Alasdair was not the most bloodthirsty of those involved in these events. He opposed the burning of the town of Dunluce, withdrawing his company; and he opposed an Irish order that anyone speaking English was to be executed. Not much to present in extenuation, perhaps, but interesting.

Bloodshed continued, however – and Alasdair remained allied to the Irish. On 11 February 1641 occurred the battle of the Laney, between 600 and 900 Protestants, the majority of their force, being killed. It was an event of great local significance, but pretty unimpressive in scale as battles go. Only tiny numbers, in the brutal accountancy of war, were involved. Yet the battle has a much wider significance than this suggests. It was the first occasion on which the tactic which was to become known as the Highland Charge was used, a tactic which was to bring repeated victory to Highland armies for a century. It was not to be countered successfully until Culloden in 1746.

So the Highland Charge, it seems, originated in Ireland, and was first used by Alasdair MacColla. The charge was a tactic at once sophisticated and simple. It was based on recognition of opportunities presented by recent changes in weaponry in the Gaelic world. In place of the old two-handed sword, Highlanders had adopted the single-handed basket-hilted sword combined with the targe or target, a small, round wooden shield covered with leather and studded with nails to reinforce it. In addition, the musket was now almost universal – though occasional references to bows and arrows still occur. The infantry opposing Highlanders would usually be armed either with musket and sword, or pike – a long wooden pole with an iron tip – and sword.

When rival forces drew up opposite each other for battle, the Highlanders would take the initiative and fire a volley with their muskets, and the enemy would reply with their volley. So far, entirely conventional. But then came innovation. The enemy would proceed as was usual, and start reloading their muskets. The Highlanders, however, would immediately drop their muskets and charge with sword and targe. The genius of the tactic lay in its exploitation of the fact that the musket took a long time to reload, and while reloading the musketeer was frequently defenceless. The musket itself was virtually useless while unloaded – unless used as a club – as bayonets had not yet been introduced. Struggling to reload, the musketeer had to decide when to abandon that weapon and draw his sword. But the conflict would then be between sword alone, and sword and shield, giving the Highlander a huge advantage. It might seem paradoxical that it was the most sophisticated weapon employed on the battlefield, the musket, that proved to have the weakness that allowed Highlanders to win battles, but the latest technology often has teething problems. Often the enemy simply fled before the charge hit them.

As for pikemen, the Highland technique was to catch a pike thrust on the targe. The tip would embed itself in the wooden shield, and before the pikeman could wrestle it free his Highland opponent would hack the pike in two with his sword, leaving the pikeman with a fairly innocuous wooden pole – or his sword as a last resort.

GOLD CORONATION MEDAL OF CHARLES II, commemorating the ceremony at
Scone on 1 January 1651.

The evidence that Alasdair MacColla employed the Highland Charge at
the Laney is not entirely conclusive. All we have is the statement that he
got his men to put down their guns at the start of the battle. But why else
would they do this unless to proceed with the charge? And when Alasdair
was, a few years later, second-in-command in battles in which the charge
was employed, the laying down of muskets being a central feature of it,
then the circumstantial evidence may be said to be very strong.

Victory at the Laney. But within a few months a Scots covenanter army
began to land to protect Protestant interests. County Antrim was occupied
– and by a regiment commanded (*in absentia*) by the Marquis of Argyll –
as the earl had now become. Fleeing to western Ulster, Alasdair and his men

joined the main Irish army, only to be defeated in battle after misguidedly insisting on offensive action. He was also wounded, shot in the thigh, and only escaped the rout with the help of friends.

Alasdair was probably pretty demoralised at this point. The Irish rebel cause seemed lost. The dreams of regaining the MacDonald lands in Scotland had turned into the nightmare reality of the entire loss of the MacDonnell lands in Antrim. He had been defeated, with the loss of many of his men, and wounded. But as a military leader his reputation among his enemies was high. He was feared enough to be worth buying off. The Scottish army of occupation offered him terms. He, his brother and all his men would be pardoned. His father, his other brothers, and friends held prisoner by Argyll would be freed. Coll and his family would have their lands restored – or be given compensation. But there was a price to be paid. Alasdair and his brother would have to recruit and lead a company of men against the Irish. Further, as evidence of good faith Alasdair must take part in killing and plundering Irish forces before he formally changed sides. He agreed.

The only plea in mitigation of this treachery was that he evidently evaded the killing of any Irish. But he and his men plundered their Irish kinsmen and hosts extensively to provide a peace offering to the Scots army.

Within weeks, Alasdair and his brother deserted again – back to the Irish. Two explanations are given: that Alasdair found that luring him into the Scots army in Ireland was the first stage of a plot to assassinate him, and that Argyll refused to keep his part of the deal and release Alasdair's father and brothers. These are perhaps equally plausible. The Irish were surprisingly merciful in not punishing Alasdair harshly for his treachery, but he does seem to have been ostracised. It was hard to see how his military career could recover.

Yet very soon a new path, this one leading to glory and notoriety, opened before him. The English civil war had begun, and complex reshufflings of alliances and possibilities throughout Britain followed. The Earl of Antrim schemed to rally support for Charles I in both Ireland and Scotland. The price – there was always a price – was the restoration of his own Irish lands, and of Kintyre and Islay to the MacDonalds. Alasdair MacColla and his relatives were one component of Antrim's complicated plottings, and in the end the only component to achieve anything. Antrim undertook to aid the king through a typically grandiose scheme. He would send a large army to England to tip the military balance there decisively. A smaller force would be sent to the West Highlands, which would link up with a royalist army raised elsewhere in Scotland by the royalist Earl (soon to be Marquis) of Montrose.

Alasdair was appointed commander of the Irish-Scottish dimension of this venture. As one commentator asserted, he was the man for the job

> because he was not only experienced in military discipline and endowed with special greatness of soul, but also he had long been well loved by and well known to his most noble fellow tribesmen . . . and so he was very well suited to raise them in a warlike alliance.

In addition, he had led a prolonged raid on the Western Isles in 1643–4 and so had recent experience of conditions there.

Antrim's grand scheme for sending an army to England came to nothing, but the force destined for Scotland eventually sailed. Something approaching 2,000 men were involved, mainly Irish but including many MacDonnells from Antrim, and a few Highlanders. Omens and prodigies occurred which, if properly interpreted, would have given warning of horrors to come: above all, a great explosion was heard throughout Scotland at the moment when Alasdair first set foot on the Scottish mainland. Thus folklore again confirms his status – as hero or ogre.

The campaign of the Irish expeditionary force started well. Alasdair's men captured two castles. But his fortunes soon changed for the worse. Most of his ships were captured or destroyed. Approaches to many supposedly royalist chiefs, on whom he had relied for reinforcements, were rejected. As far as they were concerned, he was facing almost certain defeat, and it was best not to get involved. Alasdair lacked credibility: noted as a leader of rebel bands, perhaps, but distinctly dubious as commander of an army, as a major royalist leader. And then, salvation. When Alasdair reached Atholl, he was met by the Marquis of Montrose, the king's lieutenant-general in Scotland. At last the expeditionary force had a leader – for Alasdair seems to have been quite content, perhaps even relieved, to hand over command – who had the status and direct contact with the king that meant that many would take him seriously.

Admittedly Montrose's own reputation was somewhat tarnished. He had formerly been a zealous covenanter. His attempt at an incursion into Scotland earlier in 1644 had been a complete failure. And his attempts to recruit royalists to bring to join Alasdair had been totally unsuccessful. His journey north to join the Irish force in Atholl was a last, almost despairing, attempt to achieve something for the king. The gamble paid off astoundingly well. Critical mass was achieved. Montrose provided an inspiring general, status and respectability. He frequently had the sense to follow the advice of Alasdair MacColla, his second-in-command, in managing the Gaelic-speaking Irish and Highland troops who made up the majority of his army. Above all Alasdair provided the Highland Charge, the key to success in most of Montrose's victories. Finally the Irish expeditionary force provided the core of the army, soldiers already in action whose presence would give other royalists encouragement to rise in arms (though on the other hand the fact that most were both Irish and Catholic alienated many).

Alasdair had leading roles in the victories of Tippermuir and Aberdeen. He then returned west with some of his men to relieve the castle of Mingary (besieged by the Campbells) and see if Highland royalists would now join him, two victories having enhanced his credibility. There may also have begun to emerge a tension between Alasdair and Montrose. They had different priorities, though they overlapped. So far as Montrose was concerned, the whole point of his campaign was to overthrow the covenanting regime in Edinburgh and march into England to help Charles I in the civil war there. Alasdair probably didn't give a damn about the king – except insofar as alliance with him might advance his own cause. He was fighting for a far more limited end – the revival of the fortunes of his family and clan, a fiercely enjoyable aspect of this being the killing of as many of the Campbells as possible. At first sight some of Alasdair's actions in life are seen as involving treachery, changes of direction, and inconsistency. His response to such charges would undoubtedly have been that he had always been consistent in pursuing what he saw as the interests of the MacDonalds/MacDonnells. Just as nations gave priority to their own interests, making and breaking alliances, so in the fragmented Gaelic world, with its narrower political foci, similarly cynical conduct was justifiable. Alasdair pursued self-interest, but his morality was the same as that of a king or a state.

Thus Alasdair's going west in September 1644 may have partly been the result of his putting pressure on Montrose to let him get back to slaughtering Campbells. But it was a successful expedition from the point of view of both men. Mingary was relieved, considerable numbers of Highlanders agreed to join Montrose's army (though most of the major chiefs still held back) – and, most satisfyingly, the Campbells fled or shut themselves up in castles whenever the now-feared Alasdair's men approached.

In November Alasdair rejoined Montrose in the Eastern Highlands with his reinforcements. Soon a dispute arose between them. Montrose believed it impossible to winter his army in the Highlands, and proposed therefore to find somewhere in the Lowlands where they could defend themselves and benefit from the milder climate. Alasdair, the Irish and the Highlanders objected. Exposing themselves in the Lowlands would be hazardous, and it would be perfectly possible to subsist in the Western Highlands, with a milder climate than the east. Gaels wanted to winter among Gaels. Alasdair argued that there was now a great opportunity to defeat the Campbells on their home ground. That would be a devastating blow not just to them but to the covenanting regime as a whole. Their chief, Argyll, was the leading figure among covenanter politicians and was believed to have invincible military power through his clan. His reputation would be shattered by defeat. And, of course, the cause of the MacDonalds would simultaneously benefit. Montrose, to his credit, in the end agreed to the change of plan.

Predictably, the invasion of Argyll was a brutal affair – not through royalist/covenanter hostility, but MacDonald/Campbell clan hatreds. Complete surprise was achieved, and large areas were overrun with little fighting. Nonetheless, there was much bloodshed. All Campbell men captured were killed. One account – a gleeful Gaelic one – records nearly 900 deaths without any fighting. All houses were burnt, food and other possessions plundered. How the Campbell womenfolk and children fared through the winter may be imagined. But as well as savage vengeance there was a terrible logic at work. These were territories the MacDonalds intended to occupy for themselves after final victory. Before they could take over, the existing inhabitants had to be disposed of to free the *lebensraum.*

By now covenanting armies were gathering to counter Montrose. But he retained the initiative by attack, and no doubt under pressure from his men he gave priority to dealing with a mainly Campbell army. At Inverlochy in February 1645 perhaps half of the 3,000 covenanters present were killed, a great many of them Campbells. That many were killed trying to surrender or escape after the defeat is indicated by Montrose's comment that he would have prevented the slaughter if possible. Alasdair MacColla would have expressed no such sentiment, as his summary dispatching of Duncan of Auchinbreck after the battle indicated. On a day of exultation he must have had only one regret: the Marquis of Argyll escaped in his galley. To have killed him would have been sweet indeed. Still, the Campbells had been totally humiliated. Gaelic poets gloated sickeningly – and made Alasdair rather than Montrose the hero of the day. Well-congealed Campbell blood made excellent manure. The ground was littered with mutilated naked corpses, hacked and slashed. As for their families' mourning, 'the howling of the women of Argyll', a poet had no sympathy: 'To Hell with you if I care for your plight'. A woman poet on the other side lamented the death of her husband, all three of her sons, her four brothers, and her nine foster brothers. After the battle Alasdair is said to have mused that though sixteen Campbell lairds had been killed, what was the good of that? There were doubtless wives at home with sixteen Campbells in their wombs. The logical conclusion of such a line of thought is sickening.

The repercussions of Inverlochy, though most intense in Argyll itself, echoed round the three kingdoms. The vast reputation of Campbell military power was shattered – and as this had been a major component of the covenanters' reputation, that too was significantly diminished. Montrose chose not to continue the ravaging of Argyll, and Alasdair and his men had evidently shed the blood of enough Campbells to agree for the moment to give priority to royalist rather than Gaelic priorities. The army moved around the North-East and the south Highlands for several months, plundering widely and tying up enemy resources in the shape of the army shadowing them. Each side was manoeuvring for advantage, for a good opportunity to attack its opponents.

The covenanting Major General John Hurry finally took the initiative. In May 1645 he undertook a sudden night march to surprise Montrose at Auldearn. Interpretation of the battle that followed is difficult, but it was the most remarkable battle of these campaigns. The covenanters greatly outnumbered the royalists. But they did not quite achieve the surprise they planned. Their approach was detected, and there was time for Alasdair MacColla to get a few hundred men wakened, armed, and assembled ready to resist and divert the covenanters from the main royalist camp, where officers led by Montrose struggled to get the army prepared for battle. Astonishingly, Alasdair and his men managed to hold out against overwhelming odds for a considerable time. That the covenanters were tired and somewhat disorganised after a long night march (about eighteen miles) in heavy rain no doubt helped their enemies. Nonetheless, to have stopped the advance of such a force was a remarkable achievement. But eventual defeat for so few men was inevitable. At the critical moment, however, Montrose arrived on the battlefield with the rest of his men. The royalists were still greatly outnumbered, but after hours of intense fighting they were victorious. Virtual massacre followed, with most of the covenanters being trapped on the battlefield and hacked to death.

It was an amazing victory, and soon there was further cause for celebration for Alasdair. His father, Coll Ciotach, and two brothers had at last been freed in an exchange of prisoners. Alasdair was dispatched on a recruiting expedition to the Western Highlands, but it is probable that recruiting was partly a pretext and that he had demanded permission from Montrose to go west to be reunited with his father – and to beat up more Campbells. But the expedition was profitable, Alasdair returning with over 1,000 recruits. In his absence, Montrose had destroyed another covenanting army, at Alford. Five victories in battle in a row, and there was one more to come, at Kilsyth in August. It was by far the biggest of these battles, as success swelled Montrose's ranks. He had something like 5,000 men, the covenanters maybe 2,000 more. A Highland Charge, ordered by Alasdair at what he considered a crucial moment, without waiting for orders from Montrose, had its usual effect. And the usual indiscriminate killing followed.

There was no army left in Scotland to oppose Montrose, and as the covenanting regime temporarily collapsed he set about trying to establish a royalist one. Yet the victory that seemed so overwhelming quickly turned out to be worthless. Montrose was faced by insoluble problems. To 'rule' from the capital, Edinburgh, would bring prestige and credibility, but plague raged there. And there were still covenanting armies in England and Ireland to worry about. He was desperate to hasten into England to overthrow the king's enemies in what he rightly saw as the decisive theatre of the wars tearing the British Isles apart. Many of his men lacked that vision. To some of the Irish and Highlanders it seemed that their services had not been sufficiently rewarded or recognised. Perhaps Montrose's knighting of Alasdair at this point was a token attempt to demonstrate his appreciation of the services of others. If so, the gesture didn't work. Highlanders began to drift away from his army. They wanted to return north and west to fight their own little war on a provincial stage, and Alasdair decided to lead them. Montrose accepted that he could not stop them, and to try to maintain some semblance of control over them he sanctioned their departure and appointed Alasdair to command them.

Alasdair was tired of footling about in the Lowlands in a war he saw as having little to do with his concerns and loyalties. There was still work to be done in Argyll, and he must have been deeply worried by the prospect of Montrose immersing him in an irrelevant war in England, giving the Campbells a chance to revive their strength in the north.

The size of this virtual mutiny in Montrose's army is impossible to assess, but hundreds rather than thousands of Highlanders were involved. A few Irish went with them, and it is significant that there were not more. The Highland war was not so directly their war; and they had a wider perspective of what was going on. The first priority of the war of the three kingdoms for them was not killing Campbells, but serving the interests of the Irish confederates. They could see that this cause would be helped by aiding the king in England – and thus forcing the withdrawal of their enemies from Ireland. The chess game of wars in Britain and Ireland was almost as complex as that of the wars on the Continent.

Montrose found few Lowland recruits, and other sections of his army drifted away. Logic dictated that he withdraw to somewhere safe in the north until he could rebuild his army. Pride, or realisation of how desperately the king now needed help in England, prevented this. Instead he marched towards the Borders, hoping for recruits there. In September, blunders on his part allowed his men to be surprised in his absence by a large (relative to his own little army) body of cavalry from the Scottish army in England. Total destruction of his force followed. Most of the Irish who had survived a year of bloody campaigning were killed during or after the battle of Philiphaugh, the covenanters being no more merciful in victory than Montrose's own men. He himself fled to safety in the north – too late. His attempts to rebuild an army had been hard when he had had a series of stunning victories behind him. Now, discredited by crushing defeat, his task was impossible.

Certainly Alasdair and the Highlanders now had no intention of rejoining Montrose. Relations with him had been difficult from the start, and there seemed no point in returning now that he was on the run. Montrose was to hang on until going into exile in 1646. Alasdair was to fight in Argyll until mid-1647, so the ordeal of the Campbells was to be prolonged for nearly two years after Philiphaugh. The picture that emerges is of the Campbells holding on to their castles, but otherwise engulfed by a sea of enemies, mainly Alasdair's men, but also including clans that joined in for their own motives, including plundering. The routine killing of Campbell men continued, and if women and children died too there was not much concern. On one occasion, indeed, a barn, subsequently known as 'The Barn of the Bones', was evidently filled with women and children and then set alight.

In mid-1646 the Marquis of Antrim arrived with reinforcements: under 2,000 men, but very significant in terms of the very small forces involved in the campaign. But delight must soon have given way to fury. The king, defeated in England, joined the Scottish covenanter army there, hoping to negotiate some desperate form of alliance with the Scots. Naturally enough, they immediately insisted that he order all those fighting in his name in

Scotland to lay down their arms. All that had been gained in Argyll was to be abandoned for reasons of grand strategy. Montrose, a true royalist, obeyed (perhaps with some relief, given his circumstances), Antrim and Alasdair at first refused to stop fighting. However, Antrim was soon persuaded by the king to give up the battle and abandon Kintyre to the Campbells, the persuasion taking the form of a royal promise that Kintyre would be given back to Antrim as soon as possible.

Antrim was out of the war, but most of his men still refused to withdraw to Ireland. To many of the MacDonnells it seemed crazy that, when most of their own territory in Antrim was in Argyll's hands, they should tamely surrender their hard-won bargaining counter of so much Campbell land in Scotland. Perhaps, indeed, Antrim was not too sorry to have men 'disobeying' him and continuing to occupy Kintyre.

They fought under Alasdair's command, but he must have realised that his position was increasingly perilous. He could no longer even claim to be fighting for the king, something which seriously undermined his standing with many clans. Some of them now negotiated pardons for themselves with the covenanters. Alasdair, too, in the end tried to obtain terms for himself and his men. But it had been resolved that he should not be pardoned under any circumstances. He was by this time notorious throughout Britain – or Protestant Britain – as a figure of unparalleled brutality and barbarity, personally responsible for the deaths of many thousands of innocents.

Morale may well have been collapsing, and as the covenanters advanced, Alasdair himself is said to have shown incompetence – explanations ranging from drunkenness to innate stupidity! He was defeated, and though many of his men managed to escape, some hundreds were trapped in the Kintyre peninsula. At Dunaverty Castle, 300 of them were massacred after they surrendered to the covenanter army in which James Turner was serving under David Leslie. In the mopping up that followed one of Alasdair's brothers and his father, Coll Ciotach, were captured, and executed. Alasdair himself, the arch-criminal, managed to escape to Ireland. With him he brought 7–800 men, indicating that though his retreat was precipitate, it was a reasonably orderly affair.

He hoped to be able to regroup and return to the Highlands, with reinforcements that had been promised by the Irish, but their attention was occupied by internal feuding. Far from being sent back north, Alasdair and some hundreds of his men were joined to the confederate army of Munster in south-east Ireland. He was to be lieutenant-general, which was perhaps some consolation. The enemy he was sent into action against was the army of Lord Inchiquin, fighting at this point in alliance with the English parliament. (Please do not demand an explanation of this. It would take too long.) In November 1647 the two armies met at Knocknanuss. The confederates were routed. While they fled, Alasdair and his men carried out the last of their Highland Charges – and triumphed on the wing on which they were fighting. But they were isolated and soon subject to massive counter-attacks. Alasdair was captured and killed.

War criminal? That is certainly one judgement on Alasdair MacColla. He was a major figure not just in what might be regarded as the normal bloodshed of a soldier, but in the widespread killing of those willing to submit, the surrendered, the captured, the innocent. All that can be said in his defence was that he fought according to the conventions of his age and culture. As to his general rating as a military leader, he was a much more significant figure than is usually accepted. He has always been reputed to have been outstandingly courageous, but he has been accused of treachery, and a lack of intelligence led him to folly which could endanger the armies he was fighting for. Worst of all, his desertion made a major contribution to Montrose's disaster at Philiphaugh.

There are, however, answers to these charges. Alasdair has almost always been considered in the context of Montrose the hero, and has tended to become the fall guy. When anything goes wrong for Montrose, it can't be his fault: it must have been that stupid barbarian Alasdair MacColla. On several occasions when Alasdair has been blamed for problems, he had in fact played a key role in avoiding disaster – perhaps, above all, at Auldearn. It is true he could be impetuous, and he could act as he thought fit rather than according to orders – often with happy results.

Charges of disloyalty he would have indignantly denied. Loyalty was complex. As Hope of Craighall and so many others found, they had various loyalties, and they often pulled in different directions. They had to be ranked in an order of priority. His overwhelming loyalty was to the Clan Donald, his greatest ambition the regaining of Kintyre (for Antrim) and Islay (for himself). Next in his list of priorities probably would have been, in 1644–7, allegiance to the confederate Irish, who had employed him, supplied him with men and sent him to Scotland. And commitment to Catholicism has to be fitted in somewhere. Only then came his obligations to Montrose and the royalist cause. In the tribal society of the Gael, his prime loyalty was narrowly focused. Those like Montrose who thought in terms of national issues were understandably exasperated by him.

Consistent even when being inconsistent. Loyal even when changing sides. Betraying some to save others – himself included. These are judgements which have a sort of sense in accounting for the ambiguities of Alasdair MacColla.

The last word on him, however, must concern the Highland Charge. It is here that his claim to a significance beyond his clan lies. Non-Gaels often interpreted the charge as a wild, undisciplined action of disorganised savages. They found it hard to accept it as a planned military tactic. But they had to accept, with bewilderment, that it was successful – and then generate a sort of indignation about it. It wasn't playing according to the rules. It was like the Zulus beating the British army: it didn't really count, because they did it the wrong way.

The charge did win battles, however. It was Alasdair MacColla's most important legacy to the Gaels, and served them well until, after a century of considering the matter, rival armies realised it was a specific tactic, analysed it, and invented their own counter-tactics to destroy the Highland Charge at Culloden.

FURTHER READING

D. Stevenson, *Alasdair MacColla and the Highland Problem in the Seventeenth Century* (Edinburgh, 1980). A reprint of the book was published by the Saltire Society under the title *Highland Warrior. Alasdair MacColla and the Civil Wars* (Edinburgh, 1994).

SIR ARCHIBALD JOHNSTON OF WARISTON.

ELEVEN

DEPRESSION AND SALVATION:

Sir Archibald Johnston of Wariston

AFTER POINTING OUT Wariston's merits, Thomas Carlyle wrote: 'But, alas, will any human soul ever again *love* poor Wariston? . . . the chance seems rather dubious'. Why Carlyle stressed the question of Wariston in this very personal way, in terms of emotion, he does not say, but it suggests recognition that on the one hand Wariston was a deeply unpleasant man, and so would be most unlikely to win sympathy or love from anyone studying him. On the other, perhaps there is also realisation that in Wariston himself there simmered and exploded tremendous intensities of emotion that ultimately destroyed him. Underneath the bombast of Carlyle's rhetoric there is acute perception.

On some aspects of Wariston there is general agreement. He was a man of great ability and energy, of major achievements, a man who played a leading role in the politics – civil and ecclesiastical – of the wars of the three kingdoms. But after this assessments of him diverge dramatically. To a minority, following in his religious tradition, he was a martyr for the cause of God, dying for his faith and setting an example of striving and sacrifice. Presenting that image has required some cosmetic effort, and the sanitised saint thus produced lacks conviction these days. Overwhelmingly, majority opinion is negative. Wariston was a man regarded by many at the time and in subsequent generations with deep distaste at best, more often with deep loathing. He came to be seen as a symbol of religious fanaticism, of extremism, rigidity, mercilessness: an archetype of the grim Calvinist.

The hostile verdict has much to recommend it, but on its own it leaves out so much of the man. To assess the 'real' Wariston, the living man, it is necessary to concentrate on his remarkable personal diaries, into which he poured something of his agony and exaltation, as well as trivia, hypocrisy and sheer nastiness. The diaries don't help to make the reader love Wariston, but are essential to understanding him. No other work of the age is so self-revealing, so intimate. Returning to Carlyle, he knew nothing of the diaries when he made his comment on Wariston, yet he still had the insight to single him out as someone worth examining in terms of emotion as much as public life.

The career of the man who did and felt so much, who experienced so much pain and inflicted so much on others, began hesitantly, for his family was well enough off to make a delay in choice of profession possible for a youth uncertain of his future path. By the time Archibald Johnston had been born in 1611 his father had become one of the leading merchants of Edinburgh. There were also a number of eminent lawyers in the family, so he was very much born into the burgh élite. His mother, Elizabeth Craig, was a leading figure in another (self-defined) local élite: that of the presbyterian-inclined opponents of royal power in the church, of bishops, and of changes in worship. Her eminence in this faction stemmed, it would seem, from two distinctly different factors: recognition of her piety, and of her wealth. Not many of the better-off supported the cause, and when worldly resources were needed to support it, Elizabeth Craig was most useful.

Elizabeth's influence doubtless lay behind the fact that from his youth Wariston was obsessed with religion. He was sent to Glasgow University, and there one of his teachers was Robert Baillie — another relative. After graduation he travelled in France for three months (Baillie must have been envious), seeking out Huguenot congregations with whom to join in communion. His trip was partly just a sign of status, the way richer students completed their education. Often it was useful in helping a youth to make up his mind as to what he wanted to do in life (if that had not already been decided by his family), and this was probably very much so in the case of the indecisive Archibald Johnston. If so, the venture was a failure. Wariston spent his time in religious observances and studies, and seemed to give little thought to a career.

When he returned home priority was, surprisingly, not given to the matter. Instead came marriage, and it may be that his family urged this on him in the hope that it would help settle him. Further, he was the only surviving son of the family, and continuation of the line was required. In principle Archibald was in favour, God not having preserved him from 'temptation' in such matters. What he was worried about was choice of a bride. His temptations might lead him to marry for beauty, being 'deceived by thy [his own] passion for a fair face'. Enigmatic entries in his diary indicate that he had several girls in mind; but nothing came of them. His merits as a prospective partner included the relative wealth of his family: against him may well have been a reputation as intense and grim.

Eventually relatives came up with a candidate for his bride who also had strengths and weaknesses. She was the daughter of one of the most successful lawyers of the time, so the match would join two prominent

legal families. But Jean Stewart was only thirteen years old; she was said
to be bad-tempered; and her face was scarred by smallpox.

On first sight Archibald didn't like the look of his proposed bride. But
though he had 'no hope' of the results of the marriage, he agreed to go
ahead. The match was being urged by his friends, and he had decided that
it was God's providence. It may be that he was also favourably influenced
by the fact that she was ugly, lacking one of those 'fair faces' that could
be a temptation.

In 1632 the twenty-one year old Archibald married Jean, who was
probably by then fourteen. Something of the tensions between the partners
are indicated by an anecdote Wariston himself recorded. It would seem that
each had been infuriated by the behaviour of the other on their wedding day
itself, because they made an agreement the following morning. He promised
'never to gloume nor glunche on hir befor folks'. In other words, he was not
to scowl or glare at her when they were in the company of other people. In
return, she agreed not to disobey him in company, which would humiliate
him by showing that he didn't have full authority over his wife. Through her
age, her sex, her being his wife, Jean was in a weak, subordinate position. But
she had argued the dour Wariston to a draw and negotiated a compromise
within a few hours of marriage. She retained the right to disagree with him
when they were alone together – on which occasions he was entitled to
glare back at her. One visualises the young couple behaving genteelly to
visitors, but seething with impatience to be alone together so they could
exchange disagreements and glares!

How did Jean get concessions from the formidable Archibald? Part of the
answer lay in his reaction to the marriage. He hadn't liked his bride, he
had been gloomy about prospects. But almost immediately he found himself
falling deeply, passionately, in love with Jean. He was to be profoundly happy
in this marriage so inauspiciously arranged. Jean was a seriously religious girl,
and here in spite of their differences in age they could share much. In bed on
the morning of the first Sunday after the wedding he examined her as to
her knowledge of God, and was happy with what he found as a basis for
their religious life. At communion and when praying at other times she
wept copiously, and he thought her face more beautiful when tear-stained
than otherwise. Let psychologists make what they can of that.

Though prayer and piety dominated much of their time together, in
his repeated reveries on the marriage Wariston included mention of 'all
carnal supposed lawful contentments'. Admittedly this is in the context
of recording that as he got into bed with her he assured God that he

preferred a sight of His face to carnal activities! But is there any other Scot of the age who in autobiographical writings gets so close to referring to sex openly? It may seem extraordinary that it was the man who in many ways is seen as a caricature of a puritan fanatic who admitted on paper to such sexual passion. The intensity of his thoughts and emotions seems to have driven him to write them down, whether sexual or religious, as if this gave him some release from pressure. Intensity was his hallmark throughout life. Intensity in emotional, even sensual, religious expression drew on some of the same elements in his make-up as his passionate sexuality. The experience of religious exaltation and sexual orgasm have something in common. This of course was far from being unique to Wariston. Contemporaries, implicitly if not explicitly, accepted a link between sexuality and religion, however much they might separate the two passions and insist on the immense superiority of the latter. Samuel Rutherford, for example, one of the most famous divines of the age, sought to stir up parishioners and others to faith by long letters packed with sexual imagery and sensuality applied to religion.

A marriage of great happiness, founded on sex and religion. And then, less than a year into it, Jean died. 'It pleased God . . . for causes known to himself to separate those souls which he had joined out of his love, and to take the one to eternal glory, and to leave the other plunged in an unspeakable misery.'

All comfort departed from heaven and earth. 'My hope and my strength perished from the Lord.' It was he who was the sufferer: she now had the joys of heaven, he had 'this hell of misery'. He became obsessed with the correct interpretation of what had happened, and about this time began to write his diary or memoir, partly to discuss this, partly to record anecdotes of his religious life and his brief marriage. Jean must not be forgotten. 'Lord strengthen my memory.'

In his diary this emphasis on the past soon gave way to daily records of religious practices – endless hours of prayer, Bible reading and attendance at services – and his own sense of God's continuing wrath, or occasional forgiveness. Solitary, he wandered in a wilderness, 'for my other half and companion' had been 'recalled'.

Something had happened that was devastation for Wariston. The obvious interpretation was that the Lord's wrath against him had led to this punishment. His sins and abominations had to be carefully examined – especially those committed since his marriage. Weeping as part of worship was quite acceptable, at least among the more religious. Indeed, many took it as a sign of outstanding piety. Wariston seems to have been an unusually copious weeper from an early age. It was only to be expected that now, with his wife to mourn, this would intensify. His diary records the process: hours of weeping, especially during prayer or meditation. And it was not a matter of a few decorous tears. It was often a noisy, passionate business. On the anniversary of the day he had first spoken to Jean he 'shouted, mourned, groaned, sobbed beyond all expression'. Many other days, now and later, have similar entries. He always woke very early in the morning, and it was often then that he wept and agonised most. He wrote of near despair – though basically he remained confident that he was destined for salvation, and he had his moments of exaltation.

Did Wariston suffer from manic-depressive illness? The proposition that one of the central aims of a Calvinist upbringing was to induce manic-depression has something to recommend it, and many of the pious displayed some symptoms. But two features of Archibald Johnston make applying the diagnosis to him seem particularly appropriate. Firstly, his early morning waking and it being a time of particularly acute misery. This is an extremely common and distinctive symptom of depressive illness. Secondly, while mood swings from prostration to exaltation in religious experience were regarded as normal, his swings went far beyond the accepted scale. He spent more hours in misery contemplating his worthlessness, in weeping, in self-disgust, than others. And his exaltations reached dizzy heights.

He was an ill man. Though this was not said openly, there was some recognition that he was regarded as sick at this time. Often when people were having a depressive episode in their religious development, friends and relatives would feel sorry for their misery – but also glad for them. It was something positive in their spiritual lives, showing their concern and perception. It might even be a turning point for someone previously careless in religion. But Wariston's family and friends seem to have been worried by the depth of his wretchedness. If the swing of mood went too far in that direction, there was fear of the ultimate horror, despair from which one could not be rescued. Suffering was necessary for godliness, but could go too far. People therefore sought to help him out of his moods of misery and to deal with other problems. Advice ranged from suggesting a change of diet (his sister) so he would sleep better, to getting started on a career, which would give him something to do apart from grieving and thinking of his sins and soul.

His brother-in-law, a lawyer, urged that he become an advocate. He was too impatient to be a parish minister, and as for the religious side of his character, it could be satisfied in law: one could do good as an advocate! Robert Baillie, on the other hand, urged the ministry, which Archibald had once intended as a career. Wariston himself prayed for help in his choice and – which sounds more modern – studied a book on careers guidance (a *Treatise of Callings*). This, and consultations with those he respected, led him to conclude that his talents were not suited for teaching, but arguing. In spite of his intense religiosity, his friends could see that this rather solitary, grim and impatient young man would not be an ideal minister. Moreover, considering his tortured religious life, he realised he could not look after the welfare of other souls as well as his own.

Advocate was the answer, and once he was pushed into the profession he soon proved very successful. From 1636 to 1637 he acquired many clients – among them not only two earls, but ones holding the highest offices in the state, the chancellorship and the treasurership of Scotland. Given his family connections, nepotism was doubtless involved in this startling early progress. Nonetheless, he must have acquired a notable reputation. One can only guess at the qualities that helped him: a quick and well-stocked mind, dedication to work, seriousness, and a passionate conviction that was infectious.

The young lawyer now set himself up as a laird, buying the estate of Wariston in 1637 (probably with family money as well as earnings). He had also acquired a second wife, Helen Hay, the daughter of one of the law lords (judges of the court of session). He combined his proposal to her with a warning: he told her he had 'imperfections of kankeredness [bad-temperedness], silliness [weakness] and profaneness, to the end she might be forewarned of the hazard'. Nonetheless, agreement was reached, and the marriage took place in September 1634. Wariston's beloved Jean had died in June 1633. Given the extremity of his grief, the new marriage seems remarkably quick – and Wariston had started to look for a new wife at least as early as November 1633. The main motive his diary indicates was pretty basic: sex. When he had first married he had been as 'innocent' as Jean herself. Now that he had had experience – and particularly joyful experience at that – he found abstinence much harder to bear than in the past. He felt overwhelmed by temptations. If he was to avoid sin, the sooner he remarried and had access to legitimate sex the better. There was nothing unusual in this. One of the main recognised motives for marriage in men was the avoidance of 'incontinence' (in the sexual sense); and women had defined for them as one of their main functions in marriage the providing of services sufficient to prevent their husbands straying sexually.

Better marry than burn, though Wariston showed rather unseemly haste in obeying this injunction from the Word of God. There is no sign in the diaries of the bliss Wariston had enjoyed with Jean Stewart. He may, indeed, have sought to make sure that it was not part of his relationship with Helen. In 1637 he was to note the many sins of his first marriage. These included 'excess of carnal affection, wantonness in speeches, gestures, superfluities every way, etc.' Too much love for your wife was sinful, perhaps arousing God's jealousy. Wariston had discovered his capacity for passion in a personal relationship, but now held back for fear of his terrible God. Nonetheless, the new marriage was to be long-lasting, and produced more than a dozen children.

Just after his second marriage, there is a gap in the diary until early 1637. When it begins again religion still predominates, and tears are still present. But the atmosphere is different. Even when recording an extreme 'ecstasy' (tears pouring down his cheeks, hair standing on end, hands reaching out as if to embrace the deity, soul leaving the body) Wariston was relatively calm. The pages of self-loathing pleading with the Lord are gone. Law cases are frequently mentioned – though religion is often still present as Wariston craves the Lord's advice about them. A brisk, busy, confident lawyer had emerged.

Very soon all changed. In June he had a long meeting with a leading minister on 'preparation for subsequent trials'. In the past, though his life had been dominated by religion, he had not been involved in religious controversy to any noticeable extent. His presbyterian leanings had meant that there was much in the church of which he disapproved, but like the vast majority of those with similar views, he had lived with such features or avoided the most obnoxious by care as to which churches he attended.

Now, however, things were being imposed on the church which could not be sadly accepted in this way. The book of canons had arrived, the prayer book was due shortly, and of course when it came, it brought riots. Wariston described them – the first time any public event had received much attention in his diary. From the first Wariston was absolutely opposed to the book, and persuaded of God's wrath if he 'licked up this vomit of Romish superstition'. He did nothing in public, but he began to study the legal side of the issues – he had plenty of time, as court business was interrupted by the 'tumults' in Edinburgh.

By the end of the year Wariston had agreed – with much hesitation – to become one of the legal advisers to, and a representative of, the king's opponents. Once involved, his rise was spectacular. Soon he was drafting major papers for the campaign, and giving advice to the nobles and others leading it. He even felt justified in labouring on such work on the Sabbath. It was holy work. By late February 1638 he was involved in the discussions that led to the National Covenant; and he was co-author of the Covenant itself, first signed on 28 February, 'that glorious marriage day of the Kingdom with God'. Wariston had arrived, he was a nationally known figure, significant enough (in a sick measure of such things) to be threatened with assassination.

In these months Wariston continued to record his religious life, and there was plenty of lamenting of sins, a central part of worship. But there were hardly any tears – which seems to have disconcerted him, he having come to regard them as a normal part of prayer. Combining his legal and religious callings, and the excitement of events, had raised his mood. Indeed vanity as to his achievements is clear – even if he was still a filthy worm in the conventions of prayer. The death of his baby son a fortnight after the covenant was signed had no lasting effect. The death of babies was too common to be a very great interruption to life.

Wariston continued his work as the paper contest with the king continued. Whereas in the past he seems to have read nothing but religious works (and presumably legal ones), now he was reading much political theory. The fate of the religious struggle would ultimately (in worldly terms) depend on political power, and he was gathering arguments limiting royal authority. When the crucial Glasgow Assembly met, he was elected clerk, and carried out a theatrical coup which significantly influenced events. The godly magician produced the records of the early assemblies of the reformed church in Scotland. The registers had been lost for many years, leaving much scope for argument as to the practices of the church in its first days, assumed to have been its days of purity. Now the authentic records were available as evidence – and generally supported the arguments of the covenanters rather than those of king and bishops.

Ecclesiastical revolution followed, and Wariston rejoiced. A few weeks after the assembly a second son was born to him and Helen, and named Archibald, not after its father but after the Earl of Argyll, not only the greatest of the covenanting lords but the one in some ways most likely to be found sympathetic by Wariston, through the seriousness of his religious commitment. But the happy event was marred by Helen falling ill. After his experience with his first wife, Wariston seemed determined to be prepared for her death. The obvious diagnosis might seem to be

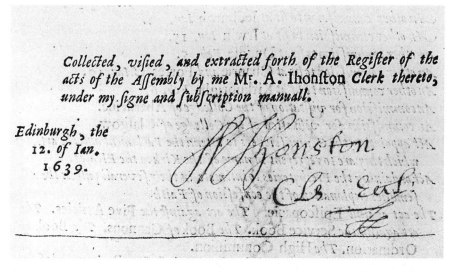

Collected, vised, and extracted forth of the Register of the acts of the Assembly by me Mr. A. Ihonston Clerk thereto, under my signe and subscription manuall.

Edinburgh, the
12. of Ian.
1639.

THE SIGNATURE OF ARCHIBALD JOHNSTON OF WARISTON on a copy of the acts of the General Assembly of 1638. As the assembly was so controversial, Johnston, who was appointed clerk of the church by the assembly, was ordered to sign all copies of the acts to authenticate them. Unfortunately he took this as God offering him financial favour, and sold the acts at such a high price that it caused a scandal. *By Courtesy of St Andrews University Library.*

some complication following childbirth. But there was, it was suggested to him, another likely cause:

> My wife's sickness was thought to proceed from melancholy for the daily decay of my state [wealth]; this I represented to God as a great strait [restriction] both to have my estate to melt away when I expected with submission upon his promise for the increase of it, and to lose my wife of grief of that decay.

Once recruited to the godly cause, Wariston had abandoned his lucrative legal practice, and his other resources were running out. God's work might be glorious, but it didn't pay. Yet Wariston accepted no blame. It was all God's fault, for He had promised him an increase in wealth, and He would keep His promise in His own good time. Whether this was much consolation to poor sick Helen as she lay worrying about her baby's future may be doubted.

Alerted for the moment to the fact that money mattered, Wariston was on the lookout for the ways in which God was going to provide for him and his family. He soon found one. As clerk he was responsible for publishing the acts of the recent assembly. Clearly God intended him to sell them at a price that would allow him to rake off a good profit. The result was scandal, Wariston being denounced for profiteering. The episode must have increased his disinclination to meddle with money matters.

In February 1639, the diary ends, for the infuriatingly trivial reason that Wariston had come to the end of the volume he was writing in. Its immediate successors are lost, but a fragment survives covering May and June 1639. Reading it, it could be by a different author. It is brisk, factual, almost entirely taken up with copies of letters and other official documents, narratives of events in the First Bishops' War and the subsequent negotiations with the king. The author hardly makes a personal appearance at all, there is nothing on his religious life. No historian seems to have thought it necessary to mention this change, or to try to explain it. Perhaps the most likely explanation is that Wariston had decided to separate public and private. What we have surviving is his public, his official, diary recording the events he was involved in and transcribing the main papers exchanged between the king and his Scots rebels. Was there, simultaneously, a parallel private diary for his religious experiences, for the doings of family and friends? This seems plausible.

However, there are a couple of incidents recorded in the fragment which are revealing about Wariston himself. The war having been not so much fought to a finish as staggering bloodlessly to one, negotiations opened at the border between Charles I in person and Scots commissioners. Wariston was one of them. On the second day on which Wariston took part in the negotiations, as the session ended the king allowed the Scots to kiss his hand, and took the opportunity of 'bidding me walk [act] more circumspectly in time coming'. Wariston ignored the warning and continued to behave in his usual way, and as a result at a later session on two occasions when he began to speak 'the king absolutely commanded me to silence'. As in many future negotiations, the involvement of Wariston was regarded as essential. But this was a tribute to his knowledge – of law, of Scottish ecclesiastical history, of political theory – his memory, his tenacity in argument, rather than to his tact. He was intense, abrupt, outspoken, and deferential to no man when the cause of his own Master, the Lord, was at stake. In the presence of Charles I in 1639 the other Scots representatives had in their manners, if not in the matter of what they were demanding, behaved fairly deferentially – though still annoying the king. The young upstart of a lawyer went much further. He seemed to overlook royalty and said what he meant with a sometimes offensive directness. He had taken a major step in singling himself out among enemies as someone particularly insulting, thus taking the first step towards the scaffold a generation later.

Then there is no diary until 1650. It seems Wariston did keep a diary for some at least of this period. He refers to acting to preserve his 'great book' when the English prepared to invade the country in 1650, and that is the last that is ever heard of it. If the 'great book' was indeed a diary of the 1640s as seen by Wariston, it would have been an immensely valuable historical and personal source, for he remained at the heart of national affairs.

Because of his stature his life can be charted easily without the diary. In 1640 he at last gained some regular (in theory at least) income for his work in the public cause, when as procurator of the kirk he was voted 1,000 merks a year. Not much, but better than nothing. Soon after, he was again a Scots negotiator, at the Treaty of Ripon, ending the Second Bishops' War in triumph. When Charles came to Scotland in 1641 to ratify a settlement, part of the deal was handouts to the covenanter leaders. Wariston got his share, though the king must have had to grit his teeth unusually hard in this case: appointment as a Lord of Session; a knighthood; a royal pension of £200 sterling. The vanity that was part of the make-up of the man must have been well satisfied with now being Sir Archibald Johnston of Wariston, Lord Wariston.

He was not, however, inclined to settle down into the work of a law lord and build up a good income that way. He remained closely involved in church and state affairs. Then, with the coming of the Solemn League and Covenant, he was one of those dispatched to London, to sit on the committee of both kingdoms co-ordinating the Anglo-Scottish alliance against the king. Simultaneously, he represented his church as a commissioner (with Robert Baillie) attending the Westminster Assembly. Thus he was at the centre of not just Scottish but British affairs in the latter stages of the English civil war. As in 1641, the weakness of the king and his attempts to buy support benefited him. In 1646 Charles was a prisoner of the Scots in Newcastle. Wariston's share of the goodies handed out was the office of king's advocate, conveniently vacant through the death of Sir Thomas Hope of Craighall. The Scots parliament granted him 3,000 merks (£2,000 Scots) in 1646, so it seems likely that Helen and her family had a temporary respite from financial worries.

Wariston was now an eminent statesman, one of the leading figures in the government of Scotland. His energy and skills were widely admired. His religious zeal and the hours he spent in worship won him great respect. But the dark side to his reputation was growing as well. He was hated more than any other covenanter leader. The problem was not just that he was a plain speaker. He was an extremist, and in particular he was always extreme in his demands for harsh action against the enemies of the cause. They were, he would have argued, enemies of God – and therefore, in most cases, deserving of death.

An example of Wariston in this vein was his conduct in the 1645–6 session of parliament. The Marquis of Montrose's royalist rising had only recently been defeated and the covenanting regime was re-establishing itself. On the first day of the session Wariston gave 'a long harangue', in which he urged that the first priority was 'to do justice on delinquents and malignants'. It had been failure to do this in the past that had provoked God into punishing Scotland with bloody rebellion and bubonic plague. In particular those bloodthirsty rebels, those butchers, merited vengeance. As a start in cleansing Wariston demanded an investigation of members of parliament themselves, to see if any had complied with the rebels or had 'dealings' with them. Attention was given to classifying delinquents and defining penalties for the different categories. Some 'first class' delinquents were to be tried and executed. Some were not to be so lucky. Parliament ruled that all Irish prisoners, held in various places across the country, were to be killed without trial. They were especially hated as it had been an Irish force that had supplied Montrose with an army to start his campaigns. Anyway, they were Catholics. Four particularly prominent royalists were tried by parliament itself – and beheaded. In Wariston's eyes, to grant mercy to the bad was to do injustice to the good.

It was a time of particular bitterness in the aftermath of bloody civil war, and the sentences against delinquents were passed by large majorities or unanimously. Wariston was not alone, but was seen to take the lead in pressing for harsh action. Royalists seem to have held him personally responsible for the execution of the four prisoners. He would probably have been flattered at the way he was becoming so hated. The hatred of the enemies of God surely showed he was doing the work of the Lord effectively.

There were ten years of great success, in spite of all difficulties. God was winning, and Wariston, if not by His side, was at least one of His important instruments in fighting the forces of evil. Then came disaster, in the form of the Engagement. The agreement for the Scots to rescue Charles I from his English parliamentary captors split the covenanting movement deeply. But not down the middle. Among the leadership of the state assembled in parliament the majority supported the treaty. The church, represented by the general assembly, voted against it, as contrary to the interests of true religion. Wariston naturally supported the Kirk Party rather than the Engagers, and the notorious advocate of harsh measures against others now found himself in real danger of persecution. Further, his financial problems reached a new intensity. Since 1638 God had employed him on public business, diverting him from money making. He had 'spent all my estate' and was in such 'a desperate condition' that he resolved to leave the country – no doubt to escape his creditors as well as the Engagers.

The crises soon had satisfactory resolutions, however. The defeat of the Engagers in England allowed the Kirk Party to seize power in Scotland. Action against Engagers was limited by terms granted to them in return for their submission, but nonetheless a new act of classes (thought to be largely Wariston's work) was devised. Significantly, one of its classes concerned moral rather than political offences by office holders. Now that moderates had been purged from power (as Engagers), religious radicals, determined to create a truly godly state and society, had far more political influence than in the past. As part of the political settlement Wariston was promoted from the office of king's advocate to clerk register. Perhaps it was the opportunities of the new office that he meant when he referred to the Lord having 'restored my estate and made it better than before and paid all my debt'.

Wariston may have rejoiced at promotion and godly persecution, but the slide into chaos and conquest, destroying all he hoped for, had in fact begun with the execution of Charles I; the proclaiming of Charles II in Scotland (which Wariston supported); the bringing of the new king to Scotland. It is just before this point that Wariston's surviving diaries recommence. To the relief, no doubt, of most readers, the editor of the published version chose to omit not only summaries of sermons but 'all pious reflections saving any that might be of special interest'. However, while this is understandable as saving a huge amount of space, the 'pious reflections' of Wariston's intense spiritual life were major indications of his moods and attitudes, and their loss impoverishes the printed text.

Yet plenty remains. For example, almost the first entry (March 1650) simultaneously shows Wariston at his worst and at a rarely recorded best. Coming out of church, where he had as usual given to the collection for the poor, he angrily hit a beggar who approached him: he had already done his giving, and unauthorised begging was forbidden. But riding home he regretted this, and returned and sought out the beggar, and 'recompensed him largely for my wrong to him'. He was not a man who apologised often.

In military preparations to resist the expected English invasion Wariston played two roles. One was positive: working to get a pretty chaotic army better organised and to hasten recruitment of soldiers. But his other role was negative: the removing from the army of many, especially officers. Wariston played a leading part in this work, which significantly reduced the size and efficiency of the army in the face of the enemy. This was a logical extension of the exclusive, purging policy of the kirk. God wished only the truly godly to fight for His cause. Past disasters could be attributed to God's wrath at being represented by the ungodly. Therefore all 'malignants' were to be purged out of the army – former Engagers, royalists, anyone with the least taint of political or religious misdoing in the past. Those tainted with immorality were to go as well. It would be a thoroughly godly army that confronted the English.

Unfortunately another gap in the diaries means that Wariston's reaction to the massive defeat at Dunbar is not recorded. In significant part the disaster was a result of his purging policy. But whereas after the battle most accepted that 'malignants' should now be allowed to fight for their country, Wariston was one of the Remonstrant minority who rejected worldly common sense and insisted that a small, purged army would ultimately triumph through God's favour. In effect he withdrew from the regime. 'Seeing the State so corrupt I wished to be away, and let them alone.' Most of those who had been his colleagues for years were now defined as too corrupt to associate with.

Wariston, with a good deal of justice, became the scapegoat for Dunbar, hated particularly in the army. In addition it was reported that he was over-friendly with English enemies when they occupied Edinburgh, and had persuaded some Scots to support the English. So bitter were attitudes to him that he feared he would be killed by soldiers. He was in 'extreme danger'. The hatred which he had such a talent for attracting had reached such a pitch that he decided he would be safer among enemy soldiers than those of his own country.

He therefore remained in Edinburgh, but had to face family problems. He was content, but 'oh that my wife were so too, whose discontented humour makes me the more apprehensive of some sharper trial to her, and it may be in my person'. God might punish Helen for being discontented, and He might do this by having something nasty happen to her husband, which would distress her. Her conduct was thus not only dangerous to her, but Wariston as well.

Married to the most hated man in the kingdom, a spiritual egotist whose

God seemed to lack logic when choosing which individual to punish, no wonder Helen was discontent. In addition, she was left to negotiate the return of property that had fallen into the hands of the English, and for some reason she found herself negotiating with Oliver Cromwell in person about the future of the public records of Scotland. Wariston as clerk register was responsible for getting them back from Cromwell. But, it seems, he was too busy worrying about the next stage to deal with the English himself. What was he to do with the records when he got them back? If he returned with them to Scots-held areas in the north, he would be in danger: reports kept coming in of how much he was hated. But if he stayed in Edinburgh he would be regarded as a deserter, as his only excuse for being there was that he he was trying to get hold of the records.

Domestic complications continued:

> There fell some passionate words out between me and my wife, which made me tell her that she had been more uncou [strange] for talk to me, these 6 month since Dunbar than these 16 years.

Indignantly he explained to a doubtless bemused Helen his bizarre theory of how God might well make him ill for the safety of her soul, getting rid of her 'discontented grudging temper' by giving her a fright. Couldn't she see how selfish she was in being discontented and thus endangering him? That Helen being (in her husband's eyes) stroppy dated from Dunbar is likely to be significant. It had been then that they had lost the estate of Wariston and their house in Edinburgh. Perhaps too she had begun to lose whatever belief she had managed to retain until now in the disastrous policies that he supported. His own behaviour may well have been increasingly strange, as his world collapsed around him. He never had been the most stable of men, and his obsession about God getting at his wife through him, and his terror of assassination, suggest near-paranoia. Everything was going wrong, but it was all other people's fault.

Whatever her mood, Helen still came in useful, and when in June a shipload of the records finally sailed, she went with it. Wariston himself didn't dare move. When Helen wrote saying some people were urging him to come north, he sought God's advice with 'tearful prayers', then 'cast the lot' to discover God's decision. To his relief the dice or whatever he used indicated that he should stay in Edinburgh. Helen quickly agreed. She found that it would in fact be highly dangerous for her husband to come north. As his wife, she was repeatedly threatened and abused. Blithely Wariston detected the hand of God, persuading her at last that he was in real danger. That he had sent his wife into danger while he skulked in safety was something he seemed incapable of seeing.

Yet he was not lacking in courage in other ways. He continued to support the policies that had brought such opprobrium on him, and to speak out against many of the policies of an increasingly royalist-inclined regime. He still had confidence that he was striving 'to keep Christ in the land, the greatest and best duty'.

In July 1651 an English army crossed the Forth and defeated the Scots sent against them at the battle of Inverkeithing. Helen had been preparing to cross to Edinburgh, and having decided that the family would have to stay in Edinburgh, she had brought her children back with her. She had a lucky escape. Being at the wrong place at the wrong time, she and the children found themselves in the midst of fleeing Scots soldiers after the battle, with pursuing English cutting them down. They escaped unharmed: God had saved them because they were 'mine', Wariston concluded with insufferable complacency. Soon the family was reunited, but financial problems continued to plague it. Helen revealed that she had had to sell her silverware in order to feed her family. She had also borrowed money, but, humiliatingly, had had to pass herself off under an assumed name, for no one would lend to the Waristons. He leapt energetically into action to deal with the situation – by making a request to the Lord for help.

After Inverkeithing, the Scots regime embarked on the doomed invasion of England which ended in yet another huge defeat, at Worcester. The Scots army had been a malignant one, Wariston had concluded, but perhaps God in his usual mysterious way would use it to defeat English sectaries. Certainly he mourned its defeat, and it was evidently while he was praying about this that he was disconcerted by his wife telling him that his voice was too loud. For how many years had she been repressing the urge to say that? Now with her newly acquired boldness, she said it, and he was deeply shocked. It is as if she had undergone a seventeenth-century course in assertiveness training.

Her problems continued to grow – literally. 1652 saw another addition to the family, a daughter. It was a difficult labour, and at one point Helen nearly died. Wariston organised a campaign of prayer (which included four ministers). It worked, and God brought forth a large child. It was time, Wariston decided, to go through one of his family rituals. He had his own covenant, which had been repeatedly renewed as his family grew. Now it was solemnly renewed for the eighth time by Wariston, Helen, and all their nine surviving children. Wee Janet, only one day old, was taken to church for the ceremony (and for baptism). A month later his second youngest child, Anna, died. With what seems the astounding lack of a sense of proportion in much of Wariston's religious life, he soon worked out why God had taken his child. Her death had brought a Mr James Wallace to Wariston's house. Doubtless he came to pray and condole, but Wariston came to think very highly of him, and realised that God had been arranging an introduction. Presumably at least it occurred to him to hope that the Lord didn't employ this tactic too often in providing him with godly friends. Surely there must be better ways of arranging personal introductions?

By this time Wariston had settled down in occupied Scotland, with a circle of ministers whose principles were similar to his own who could meet to mourn the times and satisfyingly denounce practically everyone else. Other difficulties remained, however. Examples of the hatred felt for him came in an irregular stream. The country's English rulers were deeply suspicious of him, and resentful of his papers denouncing them. He was no longer clerk register: he would not serve under the English, and they would not have him. One of the main sources of income of the office had been selling lesser clerkships. But some of those who had bought offices from Wariston had almost immediately been ejected by English conquerors. Now they wanted their money back — which was over £200 sterling in some cases. Through English invasion, he had lost £11,450 sterling. No one would lend him money.

Problems of money and family went together. 'What would I do about my children?' asked his wife in 1654, worried about their future. 'Leave them upon the Lord' (the Welfare State of the day?) came the smug reply. And if the Lord didn't provide for them any other way, 'let every one of them go to service' — as he himself was prepared to do rather than 'comply with the corruptions of the time'. Helen's bitterness at being told her children could become servants can be imagined. He was no more sympathetic when she became seriously ill. She repeatedly told him that he would only believe that she was gravely ill when she died. When he did at last accept that she really was in danger, his reaction was contemptibly selfish. It is true that he pleaded with his Lord God to preserve her, but the reason he did this was that there was no one else to look after him and his affairs, and the children.

Still, the illness also provoked a rare tribute from him to Helen. God was threatening to remove 'all my outward comforts, helps, reliefs and ease', for she had been that for twenty years. Even that was a pretty self-centred tribute to her, and he spoilt it immediately by worrying that if she died, his enemies would say it was God's judgement on him. Her death would be a social embarrassment.

Wariston had always been an intensely inward-looking, egotistical man, more than usually prone to think the world revolved around him. But now, in the despair of defeat and financial ruin, the frustration of pretending to be busy and useful through attending endless discussions and drafting papers that he knew would achieve nothing, intensified his depressive tendencies and the self-obsession that often accompanies them.

Infuriatingly the final published volume of Wariston's diary, covering 1655–1660, is again printed with 'much abridgement', what does appear covering mainly the author's political activities. Much of what is missing doubtless concerns religion and family. But even in the printed version there is a good deal on a dramatic development in the family which must have added to Wariston's sadness. It became clear that his eldest surviving son Archibald was seriously deranged.

In his confusion, Wariston topped off his career with disastrous political blunders. Many of those, mainly Remonstrants, who refused all cooperation with the English had looked to Wariston as an example of unflinching defiance, whatever suffering was involved. But by the mid-1650s in between firm statements about non-compliance he was beginning to speculate about getting the post of clerk register back. After all, it was really his post anyway, and he had wanted it so badly for so long (since 1640, it turns out, though he had not been appointed until 1649). And he needed the money, as Helen 'wept bitterly' through fears as to how the family was to subsist. Events conspired to push him down the path of collaboration. The English wanted him to take office, and Cromwell ordered payment of an annual pension to him. Then, in a change of policy, the English decided to hold talks with the Scottish religious factions, in the hope of reaching agreement with one at least. The Remonstrants and their opponents the Resolutioners were therefore invited to send representatives to London, and Wariston was one of the former's delegates.

The odds were in favour of the Remonstrants. They might be a minority and extreme in their attitudes, but they had something in common with English puritans – and didn't insist on praying for the exiled Charles II like many Resolutioners. Moreover, there was some rapport between Wariston and Cromwell, who had respect for the former's ability and spirituality. For the English, Wariston would be a major catch, the sea-green incorruptible who had inspired many Scots to refuse to work with the regime now endorsing it by accepting employment. He himself told Cromwell of his 'right' to be clerk register, and of his poverty. Seizing the opportunity, Cromwell chided him for having long been cruel to his wife and children – by not accepting offices. Wariston was flattered by news that he was to be nominated as one of the few Scottish lords in the new house of lords being created.

Issues of conscience over becoming clerk register continued to dominate his thoughts, however. What was God's will? Eventually he resolved to determine this by casting lots. But he convinced himself that it was first necessary to cast lots to decide whether to cast lots! The preliminary round ruled there should be no further lots. Whereupon he concluded that it was divinely lawful for him to accept office. The logic of this is not just hard but totally impossible to understand. He got what he wanted, and that was what mattered.

Clerk register he became, and thus added even further to his enemies – and added to the hatred of existing ones. He had sold out to the enemy. Many Remonstrants felt bitterly betrayed. They too had suffered in varying degrees for their beliefs, and had looked to Wariston as an example to sustain them. He stood for integrity. Now he stood for giving in for worldly gain. 'I am the infamy of the people', and he very quickly repented taking office. Gloomily returning home, he found a family crisis awaiting him. His son Archibald was 'assuredly insane and at times maniacal', dabbling in magic and prepared to invoke Satan. Daughter Helen was showing signs of a similar illness. It seems likely that there was a hereditary element in the mental instability in the family – but perhaps having Wariston as father is on its own enough to account for his children's problems. Daughter Elizabeth was sick and growing weaker. No wonder his wife had pleaded with him to come back from London earlier.

On the public front the sudden death of Oliver Cromwell must have horrified Wariston. The regime he had just sold his soul to join (as he now suspected) began to crumble. He had volunteered for service on the *Titanic*. At first he was closely involved in events, and even if things seldom went well there was plenty that was satisfying to the side of him which craved work and fame. He was summoned to attend the new house of lords in parliament. He became a member of the council of state of the Commonwealth England, Scotland and Ireland, and he was was frequently elected its president or chairman. Perhaps he fooled himself for a time that things were going well. He was a central figure on the British stage, not just the Scottish one, and this had the added advantage of meaning that he was based in London, away from the hostility of his countrymen. That he was also away from his family may have seemed a further bonus.

This late – and brief – flowering of Wariston's career seems surprising at first sight. However, in spite of its resounding name the council had little real power – and he only got appointed to it by default: no other Scots canditate could be agreed on. Even then opposition was expressed, including a fear of having to listen to his long speeches. His appointment to the presidency was hardly a compliment, by one account at least. The president was not permitted to take part in debates, and was not allowed to introduce motions for debate. Wariston was promoted to shut him up. Moreover, in the tense and fragile political situation, competition for the post of president was not intense. The present 'ins' might very soon be the 'outs', and it was the president rather than ordinary members of the council who would be likely to be chosen for punishment. Wariston had been set up.

Still, president of the council of state was a pretty impressive-sounding position, and Wariston revelled in it. 'The Lord thus prefers me in the sight of men.' But soon he realised that for all his posturing about what he would do for Scotland, he was essentially powerless. In J.D. Ogilvie's words, 'His mercurial nature forced him to alternations of self-assurance and despair', and soon he was on the way down again. The presidency he had triumphed about was 'airy, windy, shadowy', achieving nothing but fulfilling fantasies of his importance. Fool's gold.

Wariston tried to play the statesman: no one took much notice. With one of his flashes of insight into his own faults (rather than just indiscriminate grovelling before the Lord about his sins), he sadly admitted that he tended to recognise and act on divine providence only when it suited his worldly ambitions. He had hoped to be a 'muckle laddie' – a big man. But every time he tried to advance himself, God nearly ruined him. And now in 1659 this was happening again as the regime he had given support to collapsed. He saw his danger, and lamented ever sitting in the president's chair, 'That doleful, sinful, wrathful Chair'. In late 1659 orders for his arrest were issued, and he hastily retired to an obscure house, while his wife (who had joined him in London) busied herself collecting information and gossip for him. Exasperated by his skill in making bad worse, she with 'bitter words' chided him for getting involved in politics in London. He replied that he 'found her often a miserable comforter to me in the day of my calamity'. She evidently managed to restrain herself from the obvious retort – that when it came to being a comforter, he himself left something to be desired. In 1660 the couple retreated to Edinburgh, where as usual family problems awaited. His eldest son's condition had so deteriorated that Wariston decided that he needed to be kept in a locked room with 'two strong men' to look after him.

Then, from Wariston's point of view, the worst happened. Charles II was restored to the thrones. He was not against monarchy, or even against Charles. But from Charles's point of view, when he had been in Scotland it had been Wariston who had brought catastrophe to the campaign against the English by purging, who had been mainly responsible for religious divisions which had split the country, who had lectured the king on how godly he must be before he could have power – and on his morals. His supporters wanted vengeance on Wariston, and the king was determined that he would be one of a handful of Scots who paid the ultimate penalty.

Wariston went into hiding, and a manhunt began. He managed to survive for several months on the run. Eventually, disguised as a merchant, he fled to the Continent. Even there he had to remain in hiding, for many were determined to track him to the ends of the earth if necessary. The news that two of his closest associates in the past, the Marquis of Argyll and the Remonstrant minister James Guthrie, had been executed confirmed what fate awaited him if captured. The passing of a death sentence against him in his absence hardly told him anything new.

Holland and Germany were his refuges for two years, as he kept on the move to avoid detection. Helen was with him, or joined him, and she was to have an unwitting part in his detection. Wariston moved to France, and news of this became known. A royalist agent was sent, and first managed to trace Helen. She was then followed until she led to her husband. The French agreed to his extradition, and before long he was in prison in Edinburgh. He is reported to have been in a sorry state, hardly able to speak coherently, with his memory seriously impaired, distressed and melancholic. He didn't recognise his own children. Attempts to question him revealed a pathetic figure. With roaring tears he begged for pity for a poor creature who had forgotten the contents of the Bible. Hardly relevant, but revealing. Brought before parliament, he 'discovered nothing but much weakness'. On his knees he shuffled about, begging for mercy. Propagandists may have exaggerated his abject condition, but he was clearly a pitiful figure.

By the day of execution he had at least recovered his composure. On the scaffold he made a speech reaffirming his faith, confessing sins, admitting to some but denying others, and hoping his enemies would repent. He took leave of his poor afflicted family, and 'dear Scotland'. Mounting the ladder, with some help as he was physically weak, he was duly hanged. His head was then cut off and displayed on one of the town gates, beside that of his friend James Guthrie.

Back to Carlyle: is it possible to love Wariston? Surely even the most dour presbyterian supporters would find it hard to see this man as an example to be held up to others of true religion? There is just so much about him that is simply repulsive. However much allowance is made for a different age, different ideals, it is difficult to like him. And there is no need to try. The interest of the past lies in trying to understand, and through his diaries Wariston becomes comprehensible. He was suffering from severe mental disorder, and tragically his religious context encouraged this and justified the aberrations of conduct that it brought about (though another interpretation would be that his religion was in fact therapeutic, giving meaning to his suffering).

Wariston's God will seem to many God and Devil combined, often arbitrary and cruel. Yet, until quite recently, the typical Christian God has been as much, or more, a figure of wrath and vengeance as of love. With cultural changes, churches have with embarrassment tried to dissociate themselves from the wrath and vengeance aspects. Wariston's God was one he cowered in terror before, but was sure would save him in the end. Nearly every one else had similar basic views, but few treated them with such destructive intensity. He did not expect to understand divine mysteries. That could not be done. But nonetheless, it was his duty to devote his life to trying, and act according to his glimpses of divine will. He was not helped by the fact that he had a game-playing God, often sending his messages in obscurely coded ways. Only when you had worked out the relationship between seemingly quite unrelated events did things begin to make sense.

He was certain of the love of God, but here as well decoding was necessary. Terrible retribution and love could be the same thing. The death of wee Jean Stewart, his child bride, was both punishment of Wariston for loving her too much, and a sign of God's love for Wariston in that it warned him that he was sinning.

Wariston's Calvinism, his search for assurance of that election which would bring him salvation, was extreme even for his own time. But what really distinguished him is that he wrote so much of it down in diaries that have survived. His basic religion was the orthodox Calvinism of much of the Scotland of his day. Thus too much emphasis should not be put on his mental problems as explaining what seems unacceptable in his religion. It has to be realised that in some respects he was typical. The God of Wariston, toned down a bit, was the God of Scotland under the covenanters. If he was 'mad', the surprise is that most of those living in the same mental cage were not mad as well.

FURTHER READING

P.H. Donald, 'Archibald Johnston of Wariston and the Politics of Religion', *Records of the Scottish Church History Society*, xxiv (1990–2), 123–40.

A. Johnston, *Diary of Sir Archibald Johnston of Wariston, 1632–1639*, ed. G.M. Paul (Scottish History Society, 1911).

A. Johnston, 'Fragment of the Diary of Sir Archibald Johnston, Lord Wariston, 1639,' Ed. G.M. Paul, in *Diary of Sir Archibald Johnston, Lord Wariston, 1639; The Preservation of the Honours of Scotland, 1751–52; Lord Mar's Legacies, 1722–27;* . . . (Scottish History Society, 1896), 1–98.

A. Johnston, *Diary of Sir Archibald Johnston of Wariston, 1650–1654*, ed. D.H. Fleming (Scottish History Society, 1919).

A. Johnston, *Diary of Sir Archibald Johnston of Wariston. 1655–1660*, ed. J.D. Ogilvie (Scottish History Society, 1940).

W. Morison, *Johnston of Warriston* (Edinburgh, 1901).

G.W.T. Omond, *The Lord Advocates of Scotland* (2 vols., Edinburgh, 1883), i, 148–67.

A.A.W. Ramsay, 'Johnstone of Wariston', *Challenge to the Highlander* (London, 1933), 132–83.

R. Wodrow, *The History of the Sufferings of the Church of Scotland*, ed. R. Burns (4 vols., Glasgow, 1828–30), i, 355–62.

George Gordon, 2nd Marquis of Huntly. This was PATRICK GORDON'S 'Lost
Leader', a man who potentially had great power to help the royalist cause but
achieved nothing. After being brought up at the royal court in England, Huntly
seemed to have difficulty settling into the aristocratic society of north-east
Scotland, though by status he was its leader. *Scottish National Portrait Gallery.*

TWELVE

HEROIC EPIC AND HARSH REALITY:

Patrick Gordon

PATRICK GORDON WROTE nothing about himself, and evidently shunned involvement in public affairs. He was a north-easterner, a royalist, and wrote an account of the trouble in that region. This begins to sound familiar, with Gordon emerging as a clone of John Spalding. There are also, however, many differences between them. Gordon was proud of his noble lineage, even obsessed by it. Consciousness of it shaped both his life and writings. Spalding, as has been seen, had reason to feel shame for his blood. Spalding chronicled, recorded facts, sometimes with indignation but seldom with analysis or explanation. Patrick Gordon is mainly concerned with interpretation, understanding, frequently wandering away from his accounts of events to pursue their meaning. Spalding is fairly stark: Gordon has style.

As well as history, Gordon wrote epic poetry, but the two types of literary work are separated by a silence of thirty years. When he was born and when he died are both unknown. Indeed that the poet and the historian were one person, and not two of the same name, cannot be proved directly. As with Spalding, the evidence is circumstantial, but so strong as to be convincing. Is it possible to produce a biographical sketch with so unsatisfactory a subject? Not, certainly, in the form of a detailed chronological account of his doings and his personal life and fortunes. A good deal of the internal man can however be resurrected from his writings. The poetry tells of his fantasy world, the history of his personal reactions to an all-too-real world around him. The poems and the history are obviously greatly different in literary form and subject matter, but they have strong elements in common which give confidence that they are products of the same mind. Both sing the glories of the past at the expense of a less satisfactory present. In the epics, whether set in medieval Scotland or a bizarre version of classical Greece, a young man celebrates heroes long ago. In the history a disillusioned old man seeks to understand what has gone wrong with the country and brought the horrors of the troubles on the land. Poet and historian are both obsessed with heroes.

Patrick Gordon was probably born during the 1580s – a guess based on the fact that he was already married in 1606, on the supposition that he was at least in his early twenties when he published his first poem in 1615, and that he lived on until at least 1650. His parentage at least is clear: he was the second son of Sir Thomas Gordon of Cluny, near Monymusk in Aberdeenshire. The family was one of the leading branches of the chiefs of the Gordons, the Earls of Huntly, who dominated the region. From this background Patrick drew an intense loyalty to the earls, and in return could hope for their patronage. By 1606 he was a married man, his wife being one Jean Gordon. Presumably she came of suitable gentry stock, though a bond to which they were parties indicates that she could not write. By this time his elder brother Alexander was laird of Cluny, indicating that their father was dead. Later Patrick is known to have been married to the daughter of a laird of the family of Murray, and he had at least one child living at the time of his death. In 1609 he was made a burgess of Aberdeen at the request of the Marquis of Huntly's son. Apart from being mentioned in passing in a few formal documents, that is all that is known of the man, except what can be deduced from his writings. He is usually know as Gordon of Ruthven, but the title is only given to him in one source (a 1644 Gordon genealogy) during his lifetime.

It seems likely that Patrick lived in Ruthven, six miles from Huntly (now Strathbogie) Castle, the seat of the marquises, but may have lacked the hereditary tenure which would have entitled him to be called 'of Ruthven'.

The exasperatingly elusive Patrick Gordon is, however, dragged into some sort of focus by a sudden, and brief, burst of publications. In 1614 he published a poem on the death of the heir to the throne, Prince Henry, and of congratulation to the new heir, Prince Charles. As if emboldened by this venture, he produced two romances the following year, 'strikingly good prentice attempts at epic', published at Dort in the Netherlands. The first, licensed for publication by the Archbishop of St Andrews in December 1613, drew on the glories of Scotland's past: *The Famous Historie of the Renouned and Valiant Prince Robert Surnamed the Bruce*. This 'Italianate martial epic with romantic trimmings' ran to about 8,000 lines. 'Chivalric nostalgia' prevails, dreams of a glorious past of chivalrous knights of noble blood. In the title the author assures the reader that the work forms 'A History both pleasant and profitable', but the preface includes worried disclaimers, in case he is misinterpreted. He is not, readers are assured, anti-English or anti-Union, and he is anxious to please. He is only venturing to write because 'more excellent Spirits' have failed to do so. Nonetheless he has written out of duty to his country, Scotland, and to stir up in every man's mind desire 'to the following of glorious Actions'. How actions emulating the heroic Bruce were to be performed in his own time remains unexplained.

Thus even before his poem has begun, a fair amount can be deduced about the author: determined but a little apologetic; obsessed with past glories and convinced that the present has not lived up to them. The poem opens with the stirring lines:

> Of martial Deeds, of dreadful Wars I sing,
> Of Potentates, fierce Knights, and Champions bold.

The verse adds to knowledge of the author's interests. There is a good deal of citing of learned scholars (mainly sixteenth-century), and astrology and obsession with royal and noble blood are combined in a prophecy supposedly narrated to Bruce. In this, as in the witches' showing of the line of kings to be descended from Banquo in *Macbeth*, Bruce's royal descendants down to Prince Charles are revealed, each of them linked to a heavenly constellation. But if most of the verse has relevance to its theme, asides do occur as the author wanders off into byways, at once engaging and infuriating: one of them is pedantically labelled 'A Digression, describing the River Po'.

Bruce's career gave Patrick plenty of scope for heroic action – but not enough, it seems. For his second epic abandons even a highly imaginative connection with historical fact. It might loosely, if unkindly, be described as Bruce with knobs on – and plenty of them. The Greek setting for *The First Booke of the famous History of Penardo and Laissa* suggests classical times, but its characters and actions belong to no age and every age. Mike Spiller has described the poem as 'a marvellous Spenserian romp in the world of dungeons and dragons . . . the wizard Mansay, the evil Prince Sigismund, the treacherous Olinda, the unhappy Hungarian princess Vodiva, all crowd in with the Muses, giants and dwarves, to complicate the passionate love of Penardo for the [blonde, inevitably!] warrior-maid Laissa'. Who would have expected such extravagant fantasy to swirl from a remote little Scottish castle? It cries out for adaptation into a computer adventure game.

This was, however, the end of 'Patrick Gordon, Gentleman' (as he signed himself to make clear he was no mere professional scribbler) as a poet – or at least as a published one. He may well in fact have been entitled to prefix his name with 'Mr', or have the initials 'MA' after his name, having attended university. His works show scholarship, and as a younger son, obtaining a qualification that would enable him to earn a living (even if, in the event, he never did) would have been sensible. If he had a degree, however, it was not something to boast about. Claiming to be a gentleman was far more important.

No second book of *Penado* ever appeared to complete the epic – though it can be predicted that Penardo got the girl in the end. Were Gordon's poetic efforts badly received – or even worse, ignored? Was the appearance of the epics an example of vanity publishing, with the author paying the publisher in order to see his name in print? Whatever the reason, the only attempt that Patrick made in his life to be noticed publicly was over.

Presumably during the following decades Gordon busied himself with his estate, his family, and doubtless his scholarly reading and musing. Then, in the 1640s, he felt forced back to the pen by events, by real events rather than dreams of fantastic romances of youth. Disaster struck the society he had lived within securely for so long, and his own decline into old age was paralleled by the decay of the world around him. To sort out his thoughts, he embarked on *A Short Abridgement of Britane's Distemper*. He sought to deal with a number of issues. The wars which had overcome Scotland had to be explained in general terms, and in particular he was bothered by the question of why the regions of the North-East dominated by the Gordons had failed to resist the covenanters' rebellion more effectively, though royalist at heart. How had relations within the landowning aristocracy of the area become fatally weakened? Specifically, he sought to explain the role played by his chief, the Marquis of Huntly, in events. This, indeed, seems to have been the concern that led him to write – though, as in the preface to the Bruce, with protestations that he only did so because those better qualified had not acted.

In 1647 George Wishart, the chaplain to the Marquis of Montrose, published anonymously an account of the role played by his employer during the troubles. Published in Latin in the Netherlands, *De Rebus Auspiciis . . . sub Imperio Illustrissimi Jacobi Montrisrosarum Marchionis . . .* gave international currency to Montrose's great royalist campaign in 1644–6, from his astounding series of victories to his defeat and flight into exile. As a staunch royalist, Patrick Gordon had no quarrel with Montrose. But in Wishart's account Huntly was awarded much of the blame for the failure of the royalist cause in Scotland, and in particular for Montrose's defeat. Patrick Gordon felt compelled to leap to his chief's defence. In his history, as its editors pointed out long ago, Gordon is generally fairly charitable about individuals, even when they stood for all he opposed – with one exception:

he is repeatedly bitter about the anonymous author of the denunciation of Huntly – perhaps all the more frustrated by not knowing Wishart's identity.

Huntly was to be vindicated. But there is a deep tension in the *Short Abridgement*. On the one hand Huntly had to be justified. On the other, Gordon was in fact very much aware of Huntly's many faults, and part of his aim was to show how many of these derived from wider social trends. Montrose, indeed, was the sort of man that, in Patrick's eyes, Huntly ought to have been.

However, general issues rather than local problems came first. The troubles were a disease caused by the ills of modern society. The body politic was diseased through an excess of plenty, peace and pleasure. Luxury and easy times were thus seen as causes of corruption. In religion the body had begun to putrify and rot through ingratitude to God and immorality. But the troubles themselves were, he believed, not symptoms of society's diseases, but on the contrary, part of the cure. God, the Heavenly Physician, had resolved to cure the world. Like a human doctor He was relying on purging. First came the sword: battle, to purge the liver, which comprised the nobility and gentry. This is typical of Patrick's aristocratic assumptions. In reality the casualties of war were of course mainly common people, but for him the true warriors were drawn from the traditional military aristocracy. Second came purging by plague, the bubonic plague which struck Scotland in the later 1640s. This purged society's belly, the merchants, craftsmen and labourers, aptly consigned to the belly as being merely concerned with making money (unlike the honourable aristocracy).

These two purges were already in operation when Gordon was writing. But if this failed to cure society, stronger medicine would have to follow. The terrible purge would be famine – of the spirit as well as the body – purging the stomach (evidently different from the belly). In medical terms, war was phlebotomy, or bloodletting; plague was vomiting; famine was a laxative. Unless Scotland returned to her obedience to the king and true religion, The Good Physician would add famine to war and plague on his prescription. A bizarre National Health Service, specialising in mass destruction but ultimately curing society's ills.

This medical framework allowed Scotland's disasters to be explained as in accordance not only with the will of God, but the will of a *merciful* God. Many saw the troubles as the punishment for human sin, but the mild Patrick Gordon preferred to see them as cures – for sin – rather than vengeance. Strong medicine indeed, but to cure a patient a doctor had to hurt him: medicines had bad tastes and harmful side effects. It was the health of society, not the individual, that mattered, and many such individual components would die as part of the cure. As for why he should write about these things, Patrick explained modestly:

> I, whom God, for my sins, have reserved for these unhappy times, have found an unwonted motion in my soul to leave a memorial to posterity of such observations as I have noticed of this dreadful and never to be matched distemper, although I cannot but confess my own weakness ... This only shall be my best encouragement, that I carry spleen nor hatred to no man, so shall my relation go always accompanied by the truth.

The writer indeed expressed the hope that what he was writing would accompany him to the oblivion of the grave, for the truth would be offensive to those still alive who had taken part in events.

Changing tack, Patrick shows how the heavens themselves had warned of disasters to come, God's way of showing that He 'intends a revolution, a ruin of kingdoms, a fall of high dignities, or change of monarchies for punishment of sin' (sin had crept back in as God's motive). There had been threatening conjunctions of the planets. It seemed the whole fabric of the universe had been shaken. Then there had been 'that fearful and prodigious comet' that had appeared in 1618. The same year the Thirty Years' War had broken out, and like James Turner, Gordon assumed that the comet had been a warning of war to come. Events in Britain were part of that war: prophecies had foretold that a war beginning in Germany would spread through Europe and end up in Britain. A direct link, in Patrick's mind at least, could be established between European wars and the troubles of King Charles I. The French, inspired by Cardinal Richelieu, had stirred up the original troubles in Scotland. Another conspiracy theory.

Patrick Gordon clearly did not see developments in Scotland as parochial. They were part of God's cure and punishment of Europe, related to the shaking of the whole universe, an episode in a great European war and an international conspiracy.

At last events within Britain are reached. Much of the Scottish nobility had joined with 'puritans' to destroy royal power. Patrick was appalled – and bewildered that his own class could do such a thing. Surely they would in time return to their rightful allegiance? Certainly the country's miseries could not end until they did so – a declaration of faith that they were the real backbone of society.

The National Covenant of 1638 had marked the real start of revolution – and resulted from another sinister conspiracy, this time in England. The author's earlier addiction to romance perhaps shows through in his weakness for secret plots. The first man to oppose the rebels in arms in all Britain had been the Marquis of Huntly. For this he deserved a glorious memory – but hadn't got it. Honest Patrick Gordon did not deny that his chief had had faults, for all men had, but bitter and malicious enemies had ruined his name. Now at last the truth was to be told.

Huntly, it is asserted, had stood up staunchly for the king. If he had not fought the covenanters in the Bishops' Wars of 1639–40, no one in Scotland would have. But his strength alone was pitted against the rest of the kingdom, so his failure was not surprising. True, but no hint here that though undoubtedly Huntly was loyal, he was dithering, half-hearted about raising men in arms. Moreover, in one central incident Gordon fails to make the best case for Huntly. For the first time the problem of upholding Huntly without casting any aspersions on Montrose emerges. Montrose, confusingly, was at this time a leader of the covenanters. In 1639 he lured Huntly to a meeting under promise of safe conduct, then arrested him and sent him to imprisonment in Edinburgh. Thus Huntly was neutralised by treachery. But the *Short Abridgement* gives no hint that dishonourable kidnapping was involved, for that would have reflected seriously on Montrose. It also goes a long way to explain why later, when Montrose was a royalist champion, Huntly was so reluctant to cooperate with him. But Patrick can tell none of this. His regard for Montrose meant that he fought for Huntly's reputation with one hand tied behind his back.

In Huntly's absence the forces of his family and allies had brief initial success, but were soon overwhelmed. By 1641 the king had been forced to concede virtually all the covenanters' demands. They had, shockingly, opposed in arms their sovereign king, who stood in an unbroken line of 108 kings. And yet Patrick Gordon seems to have had a sneaking admiration for their success – attributable to the social make-up of their army. In 1639 it had advanced boldly to the border to confront the king 'for it consisted of the gentry, commanded by noble men'. All officers and no men: Gordon's vision of Scotland had no place for the common people.

In 1644, with the covenanters giving military help to the king's enemies in England, came a new opportunity to help the king. Again Huntly was loyal but ineffectual. His family and allies were deeply divided – partly through lack of leadership from Huntly. Even when some Gordon lairds attempted a rising against the rebel regime on their own, clearly showing their opinion of their dithering leader, Huntly refused to act. And when covenanter forces advanced northwards, Huntly's reaction was to retreat, on the grounds that the time was not right for battle. He would bide his time until other royalist plots for armed action were ready. Patrick Gordon, though generally counsel for the defence, was exasperated: 'Here we may see how courage, without resolution, foresight, or mature deliberation, may well intend, but never perform great actions'. Huntly had 'presumed too much on his own judgement'.

This is a hint at a theme that Patrick was to develop later in his work. The potentially great power of the Gordons was nullified by having a chief who failed to consult with those who had a right to be consulted, the Gordon lairds. As a king should consult with his nobles, a nobleman should consult with his leading followers, his officer corps. Huntly didn't, and the result was division and resentment. And these grew when Huntly's 'own judgement' led him to flee to Strathnaver in the far north for safety, abandoning his men. At this point Patrick smugly assures the reader that he has vindicated Huntly from the inveterate malice of hostile interpretations of his conduct. What mattered was that he was unshakeably loyal to his king: there is almost a tacit admission that he was unshakeably feeble as well, with a plea that that was a very minor matter compared with loyalty. Anyway, military reality made it impossible for one family to resist successfully the rest of the nation – especially as Huntly's son and heir, Lord Gordon, temporarily joined the covenanters in exasperation at his father's incompetence.

However, real help for the royalist cause was at hand, in the form of Montrose's rising against the covenanters. As we would expect, Patrick relates supernatural warnings of what was to come. Armies were seen to fight in the air, with the noise of cannon and the clash of arms. Folk were so alarmed they carried their valuables off to hide in bogs. The sun shone with a strange faint light, and sometimes was blood-red. Cannons, muskets, drums and trumpets were heard over wide areas. The sun shone at night. Choirs sang in an empty church – accompanied by a *viola da gamba*! And the final heavenly sign of heavenly wrath to come: at the moment when the Irish forces which were to join Montrose landed in the West Highlands, a tremendous cannon shot was heard throughout the kingdom. It all sounds rather like the advertising build-up to some great media event.

Alas, by the time of the Irish landing Huntly had fled to the remote north. If only the Irish had been able to join Huntly, the king's party would undoubtedly have prevailed, asserts Gordon, with more family piety than credibility. Soon Montrose was winning support, and among the reasons for this were his personality and manners. He scorned ostentation, and the keeping of state, and therefore conquered the hearts of those who came into contact with him.

Patrick now, at last, explains his theory of social decay in the upper classes. Traditionally, those of high rank among the nobility and gentry had treated those of lower rank fairly informally, with courtesy and respect. A noble or chief would indicate by his behaviour that he recognised that the gentry within his following were of noble blood, even if blood junior to his own. He would accept them as natural leaders of his people, would consult them and take their views seriously. And he in turn would expect respect from them, behaviour which recognised his seniority, but this could be conveyed in informal, friendly ways, without any deferential fuss and bootlicking ceremonial. Perhaps this was in part one of Patrick Gordon's idealistic fantasies about the superiority of the past, but he was emphatic that things had changed drastically by the mid-seventeenth century.

'That English devil, keeping of state' gained popularity among the Scots nobility. Influenced, through the Union of the Crowns, by a much more formal and deferential code of manners, they widened the gap between themselves and the gentry:

> They began to keep a distance, as if there was some divinity in them, and gentlemen therefore must put off their shoes, the ground is so holy whereon they tread: but [just] as he is an evil bred gentleman that understands not what distance he should keep with a noble man, so that noble man that claims his due with a high look, as if it did best fit his nobleness to slight his inferiors,

might get deference but he would not win the heart of a freeborn gentleman. In an aside, he adds that keeping of state was tolerable to the English, because that nation had been so often conquered that it had become slavish, and men accepted being the slaves of their superiors:

> But our nation, I mean the gentry not the commons, having never been conquered, but always a free born people, are only won with courtesies, and the humble, mild, cheerful, and affable behaviour of their superiors.

'Our Scots nation' turns out to be composed of the nobles and gentry: the commons don't count. Occasionally it is admitted that the commons have some useful qualities, and those from northern Scotland more courage and martial spirit than those of the south. Nonetheless, they were 'born slaves and boundmen', and 'in our gentry only consisteth the strength and valour of our nation'. It is ironic that Patrick Gordon resents the growing gap between nobles and gentry, but is anxious to emphasise and widen the gap between gentry and commons.

Montrose had a demeanour which meant he could win the hearts of gentlemen. So did the great covenanter leader, the Marquis of Argyll. But there is no mention of Huntly as one of those resisting the tide of destructive, if fashionable, manners: his name seems to hover unsaid. Only gradually, as if reluctantly, does Patrick admit, after much more narrative, that Huntly was an example of the ill brought by the new manners. Patrick Gordon's passionate denunciation of keeping of state seems to have something personal in it, and it is a safe guess that he himself had felt insulted by Huntly's haughty, distant manner. It didn't accord with his high ideals of chivalrous conduct, with manners between ranks regulated by tacit understanding, gentleman's agreements, rather than by rigid rules and deference on the one side, snobbish remoteness on the other.

Aided by his courteous manners, Montrose went from victory to victory. Huntly remained sulking in the north, refusing to put his name behind the cause of his hated rival in spite of their common royalism. Bizarrely, only when Montrose was finally defeated did Huntly emerge from his ignoble retreat, return to his Gordon homeland and lead a rising. By then there was virtually no hope of success – especially as he refused to join his forces with Montrose's efforts to rebuild a royalist army. Soon Montrose was in exile, and Huntly captured. Through all this ignominious time Patrick Gordon strives manfully to extract his chief's name from the mud: his only fault, it is urged, was to over-value his own opinion.

At last, Huntly paid the ultimate price of his loyalty, being executed in Edinburgh in 1649, just weeks after the king he had served with unswerving loyalty and consistent incompetence had been beheaded in London. Death was the point at which a character sketch was traditionally expected of the historian, and Patrick Gordon rises to the occasion. Like everyone else, Huntly had been a mixture of good and bad. But his good had been superlatively good, and his bad had injured himself alone. The greatest faults were self-will and obstinate opinion, refusing to accept advice: he had a nimble mind which could find reasons for whatever he had decided on. Obstinacy often led him to ingratitude when things went badly. Services done to him were forgotten, and old servants, for whom there was no use, must be brushed or rubbed off, as spots from clothes. But, Patrick argued with awesome special pleading, this fault – if indeed it was a fault – 'was truly a noble one', for all nobles behaved like that; and anyway, it hurt Huntly more than it hurt those he cast off, for in the end it alienated the hearts of his followers. Nonetheless, it was just part of his mistreatment of others. He desired 'to keep a distance with his inferiors, without distinction of quality; for friends and followers were equalled with domestics'. He could, indeed, be familiar and obsequious when he needed help from others, but this only bought outward, reluctant obedience.

At last Gordon admits it openly: there was antipathy between the genius of the Scottish nation and English keeping of state, and Huntly was tainted with the latter. But there was, of course, an excuse. Huntly had been affable, courteous and sociable before being sent when young to the English court to be brought up. There he had been corrupted, against his natural inclination.

Still, claims Patrick, rallying his own loyalty, Huntly was like the martyred Charles I in most respects – an argument that seems to claim for him the same reverence, even if in both cases it arose as much from death on the scaffold as from their lives. Death at the right time and in the right way does great things for reputations. They were the two wisest and most accurate in judgement of the three kingdoms, among the most just and upright of men, merciful, not ambitious or vainglorious. And yet in the end falsehood prevailed over their justice, deceit over their upright dealings, gross errors and absurd folly over their wisest resolutions, cruelty over their mildness.

Why had God permitted this? Patrick Gordon had no answer. But he was confident that this would be revealed in the next generation. There, rather abruptly, the *Short Abridgement* ends.

'With friends like that, who needs enemies', Huntly might well have reflected if he had ever read Patrick Gordon's work. The Gordon chief comes across as thoroughly disagreeable and inadequate for the tasks that faced him, in spite of his loyalty to the king. Why does Patrick make such a mess of defending his master? Quite simply, he had written with a number of objectives in mind, and some conflicted with others. Gordon might place great emphasis on the loyalty of Huntly, but he was obsessed with glorious action as well, and couldn't disguise the fact that here his chief was a complete failure. He felt compelled to point out how relationships in the upper classes, mutual respect combined with easy familiarity, had been fatally undermined by the loathsome keeping of state, and Huntly was a prime example of that decay. The desire to defend Huntly fights uneasily with these other motivations for writing. There may have been personal and family frustration as well.

Patrick had daydreamed of heroic action, chivalrously fighting for the cause of his country, in his youth. But the occasion had not arisen. Then in the 1640s, when a rightful cause to fight for had appeared, he was too old to take the field – and in military affairs Huntly had failed the Gordons. If Montrose was the man Patrick Gordon wanted Huntly to be, Montrose was also the man he wanted to be himself.

His own branch of the Gordons faced him with crisis locally as well. His elder brother, Sir Alexander, had at first played a respectable part in local public life, as befitted a laird, and became a baronet. But by 1630 he was in prison for debt, and spent much of the following years fighting to keep ahead of his creditors – a pretty inglorious battle. Some time, evidently in the 1630s, he was succeeded by his son – though as the latter was also a Sir Alexander there is a good deal of uncertainty. Financial troubles continued, and became mixed up with moral scandal. Sir Alexander (presumably the younger), 'a lewd man', became involved with Elizabeth Gordon, 'an infamous woman', 'of suspect chastity'. Not only was she the wife of another laird, but her husband accused Sir Alexander of cheating him out of his property. Eventually the husband died and Sir Alexander married Elizabeth, but it was claimed her evil influence was partly responsible for his financial ruin. Admittedly Sir Alexander was active for the king in the 1639–40 Bishops Wars – though as an agent shuttling back and forward rather than on the battlefield. The record of the Gordons of Cluny was hardly the glorious one that Patrick expected of those of noble blood.

No wonder Patrick Gordon was melancholic. His king had been defeated and executed; his chief had been executed and his heir killed in battle; his own brother and nephew had let the side down; the old society of a military aristocracy was falling apart. It may be a cliché that old men see the past through rose-tinted spectacles, lamenting lost glories, despising a debased present. But in Gordon's case he had good reasons for nostalgia. One almost hopes that the sad old man did not long survive the point at which *A Short Abridgement* ends in early 1650. A few months later Montrose too was executed. Then came the ultimate disaster, English invasion and conquest. The great days of Robert the Bruce were indeed long over.

FURTHER READING

P. Gordon of Ruthven, *A Short Abridgement of Britane's Distemper* (Spalding Club, 1844).

M. Spiller, 'Poetry after the Union, 1603–1660', in R.D.S. Jack (ed.), *The History of Scottish Literature: Origins to 1660* (Aberdeen, 1988). The comments on Gordon's poetry quoted in the text are from this work.

D. Stevenson, 'The English Devil of Keeping State: Élite Manners and the Downfall of Charles I', in R. Mason and N. Macdougall (eds.), *People and Power in Scotland. Essays in Honour of T.C. Smout* (Edinburgh, 1992), 126–44.

THE CORONATION OF CHARLES II, 1651. This Dutch print is the only known
depiction of the coronation – unfortunately, as it is almost entirely imaginary. At
least three events are shown in the one engraving. On the left, the young king
is symbolically dressed for battle against the English 'rebels' – the commonwealth
regime. He already holds the sword denoting his authority: Ireland, kneeling
on a harp, helps him put on his armour, while Scotland hands him a pistol
– the military force that will bring him victory. The church (in a remarkably
broad-brimmed hat) stands approvingly alongside. On the right Charles sits on
a dais, being crowned by the Marquis of Argyll, while behind him money is
thrown to the crowd in celebration. In the background, the king rides off with his
parliament and troops.

THIRTEEN

A LADY AND HER LOVERS:

Anne, Lady Halkett

PATRICK GORDON WAS not alone in stressing the enormous gap in status between the gentry and the commons. It was the widest gap in society, and yet for many – including many of those considered in this book – gentility was something that could be lost all too easily. Usually gentry status came with birth, but it was not retained automatically, especially by younger sons and daughters. If your family's resources were limited, you could fall out of the gentry, struggling to maintain a status but finding it no longer recognised by others. Girls had to marry below them in many cases. Boys had to earn livings in ungenteel ways, but on the fringes of the gap there was a good deal of confusion. Having to earn money, unless you had an official post or served at court, was thought servile, common. But having money was not, even if it was servilely earned. Merchants were common, but if a merchant became rich enough and bought land he might be accepted as gentry – or his son might be. Successful lawyers or soldiers could merge into the gentry. Blood and land might come first, but money and success could be useful substitutes. Declining out of the gentry usually followed loss of land. In Major Weir's case, the family's scrap of land may well have been so small that his parents had difficulty in being counted as gentry, and certainly once they had sold it he was not a gentleman. Yet Urquhart of Cromarty could have his lands seized and still pass as a gentleman. Was a parish minister a gentleman by virtue of education and occupation? James Turner seemingly had no doubts on the matter. Andrew Melvill thought it best to keep quiet about his father's job. Probably it depended partly on the individual minister's wealth and family background, partly on the attitude of the local gentry in a parish, whether a minister was seen as a genteel sort of servant or a sort of honorary (but inferior) gentleman. Or both. Like most concepts of social status, gentility was fuzzy round the edges.

For women, gentility was dependent on others. If your father was genteel, you were gentle – at first. The status of your husband determined genteelness after marriage. If you were a younger daughter of a small landed gentleman, with virtually no dowry, you might well find yourself a common wife, though claiming genteel descent. If you didn't marry, you could retain status if your family could – and would – provide for you. There was virtually no way for an unmarried woman to earn a living and retain status. An acceptable marriage allowed a woman to maintain status. A good marriage was one which increased status and wealth. Sometimes there were dilemmas. Would it be better to marry a well-off merchant and live in comfort, or an impoverished gentleman and shiver in a mouldering tower house?

These conditions of life for women were of course nothing new. They had existed for, and would continue to exist for, centuries. Anne Murray, later Lady Halkett, provides in her diary the life of a woman whose prospects on the marriage market fluctuated. She was the daughter of a well-connected minor courtier who did well, but who died when she was an infant. Undoubtedly she was born gentry. The possibility of alliance with a noble family beckoned, then collapsed: the proposed groom had status but lacked the means to maintain it. Anne's family fortunes then declined, so she had no dowry to offer, but there was for years a prospect of marriage with a gentleman – but one whom some claimed was a rogue and no gentleman in the true sense. In the end she married a middle-aged, well-established Scots laird, a widower – only to experience financial problems after his death. She then faced the difficulty of having to work to supplement her income, by finding an occupation as approaching the genteel as possible. Eventually she turned to taking in orphans from gentry families to look after and educate.

In these bald terms Anne's fate sounds like that of cattle at market, value and status assigning her passively to her fate. There was vastly more to her life than that. Suitable marriage as for any woman was naturally a central obsession. She had strong views, however, on who she would and would not marry. She would choose for herself. She wanted love. As a result, she married late, and probably was lucky to marry at all.

Her so-called diary – it is really a memoir – provides an autobiography that contains seeming paradoxes. She was deeply pious, spending many hours in her religious devotions, and she was obsessive in regretting any faults in her conduct. Yet she was outspoken, bold in action, prepared to stick up for herself and her opinions. She was very feminine in how and what she writes, but submissiveness would not have featured largely in her definition of the word. Her religious obsessions were combined with romanticism, a tendency to fall passionately and tenaciously in love – even if most unsuitably in conventional terms on two out of three occasions. And this independent, strong-willed lady was determined on marriage, even though the conventions of the time would inevitably mean that she would have to surrender much of her prized independence.

In fact the seeming contradictions can be reconciled. It was strength of religious conviction which enabled her to act for herself with confidence, for she was backed by her conscience and belief in a providence which would see her through her troubles in the end. The passionate commitment which dominated her love-life and inspired her religious devotions was a central aspect of her character, the tendency to feel very strongly, even stubbornly, in all aspects of life. Strength of emotion as much as reason carried her along. That she was known for bad temper when frustrated fits in well with her determination to get her own way. As to marriage, of course she sought the things it could bring her: love and companionship, security, a settled, defined position in society, children to be hoped for. Still, she was well aware of the element of surrender of freedom it involved. That was why she was so picky, and married late.

Anne Murray was Scots by blood, English by birth and upbringing. Her father was typical of many ambitious Scots in the generation following the 1603 Union of the Crowns who made their way south in the hope of rich rewards as a Scots dynasty established itself in England. Thomas Murray was one of the minority of these hopefuls who thrived at the new court. He became tutor and then secretary to the young Prince Charles, and was rewarded by appointment as provost of Eton College and other favours – in spite of occasionally earning disfavour for his presbyterian sympathies. Alas, it is not known how the playing fields of Eton took to being invaded by a broad Scots accent. Later Anne's mother became temporarily governess to two other royal children.

However, family fortunes changed within months of Anne's birth in 1623, when her father died. The beginnings of Anne's memoirs are unfortunately fragmentary, but what can be deciphered suggests a typical determination to prove that her parents were of good birth, derivation from noble stock being claimed on both sides of the family. The Murrays were clearly in reasonably comfortable circumstances even after the death of Anne's father. Masters were paid to teach Anne and her sister French, to play on the lute and virginals, and to dance; and a gentlewoman taught them needlework. Anne was anxious to stress this tuition to demonstrate that she was 'not brought up in an idle life', for idleness was abhorrent. Good birth was not to be demonstrated by doing nothing.

Thus Anne received an appropriate education for a gentlewoman, and though it was hardly a scholarly one her memoirs show she acquired an attractive and effective writing style – perhaps indeed all the more attractive to the modern eye because she wrote freely and not pedantically, writing as she thought and felt. There was evidently one unusual – and unladylike – element in Anne's education. She studied medicine, informally, while young, evidently wanting some useful skill for helping others – and, it may be suspected, out of determination to do something distinctive for herself.

Anne did not bother recording her 'childish actions', which extended, it seems, until 1644. Until then all her conversation was innocent, she was guilty of no immodesty in thought or action, and never disobeyed her mother. Perhaps we are lucky to be spared an account of this tediously righteous childhood! The only events she mentions are walking in the Spring Gardens in London and going to plays. She loved doing both – but is anxious to assure us that it was all very proper, she always being respectably accompanied. Even here, however, she showed something of her later spirit. Overhearing some gentlemen talking about which ladies they had taken to plays and how much it had cost them, she indignantly determined not to be the subject of such gossip – or of complaints about expense. She got two or three other young girls together, and they went to plays 'without any man', each paying for herself. In fact they had a footman with them – but in their eyes no doubt such a servant was not really 'with' them, and not a 'man'. They gave him the money and he paid it at the theatre, this not being a suitable task for ladies. Nonetheless, it was a declaration of independence, however limited. She would be with or without men at her own choice.

Adulthood came, in Anne's eyes, with romantic love. Thomas Howard, the eldest son of Lord Howard of Escrick, fell in love with her. Anne at first felt no inclination to accept his passionate proposals of marriage, and her mother was furiously opposed to the relationship. This might seem strange: surely the heir of a noble would be a good catch? But blood was not the only consideration in choosing a partner. Money was of equal importance, and the Howards were not considered able to support Anne in suitable style – and Anne, by not being able to bring the Howards the money they needed to maintain a noble lifestyle, would bring disgrace to her own family.

Nonetheless, after a slow start the relationship blossomed for a while. How much did Anne's mother's denunciations strengthen a strong-minded girl's determination to proceed? But in the end Anne accepted the inevitable, and the liaison was broken off after a last secret meeting – which Anne attended blindfold so as not to break her oath to her mother never to see

Howard again! In her frustration she went so far as to swear never to love or marry any other. This made reconciliation with her mother (who had a prospective husband for her in mind) impossible, and reveals that her mother shared something of Anne's determination to get her own way and furious reactions to being thwarted. It also reveals the strength of Anne's commitment to Howard.

Over a year of great family bitterness followed, during which Anne's mother declared that she hated her daughter and could not bear the sight of her. Anne decided on drastic action. She wrote to her mother's cousin, Sir Patrick Drummond (Thomas Cuningham's rival for the post of Scots conservator at Veere) to ask him for information on a Protestant nunnery she had heard about in the Netherlands. There she could retire from her mother's enmity. This would provide a solution to her problem, though not the one she really wanted. Drummond responded by writing to her mother urging her to change her attitude to Anne: and she did so. 'From that time she received me again to her favour, and ever after used me more like a friend than a child'. It was acknowledged that Anne was an adult with some freedom of action – more, indeed, than was usual for an unmarried girl living at home.

The finale of the Thomas Howard episode soon followed. In spite of all his declarations of undying love for Anne, news arrived (1646) that he had married another:

> I was alone in my sister's chamber when I read the letter, and flinging myself down upon her bed, I said 'Is this the man for whom I have suffered so much? Since he hath made himself unworthy my love, he is unworthy [of] my anger or concern'. And rising, I immediately went out into the next room to my supper as unconcernedly as if I had never had an interest in him.

Pride would not let her show her devastation, but she could not keep the news secret, and had to endure her mother's cruel laughter. So much for their new found friendship. Death soon removed the tension between the two women: and it is notable that the page of the memoir which would have recorded her mother's death in 1647 is missing. Anne's feelings must have been ambivalent, and on reflection she may have decided that she had been too frank for filial duty.

She moved to stay with her brother and his wife. Now free of all parental control, she soon had a new admirer: Colonel Joseph Bampfield – though as he was married she at first regarded him merely as a friend. She was attracted by his 'piety, loyalty, and virtue'. None of these words would be used by a biographer of the man. The colonel was an ingenious, plausible, unscrupulous rogue, as Anne was eventually to discover. A born intriguer, Bampfield was deep in royalist plots, and was currently (1648) engaged in contriving the escape of James, Duke of York, from St James's Palace, where he was held prisoner by parliament. The prince was to be disguised as a girl, and Bampfield, with the king's approval, recruited Anne to get suitable clothes made for him. The assumption was presumably that a woman was less likely to arouse suspicion ordering women's clothes than a man, but in the event this was not entirely the case. Measurements of the prince were taken and submitted to the tailor, but he was deeply puzzled by them, confessing he had never before made clothes for a woman of such a shape. However, the escape went well, Anne having personally dressed the prince, recording that she thought he looked 'very pretty'. It would be interesting to know whether she told the prince this.

Anne remained in touch with Bampfield, bringing him news and doing what she could to further his royalist plots: innocent contacts, from a personal standpoint, but ones which began to give rise to rumours of an affair between them. One of the things Anne sacrificed for the royalist cause was her reputation, and reputation was just about her most valuable possession.

One day Bampfield had news: his wife (whom Anne had never met as she lived in the country) had died. Shortly thereafter, he proposed marriage. After some hesitation Anne accepted. Even years after the 'misfortune' he brought on her, she justified her decision. He was loyal (in the royalist sense), handsome, a good scholar, and above all devout in life and conversation, teaching her many lessons in piety and virtue. It was decided to delay the marriage until the political situation clarified itself. Bampfield had been promised (or so he said) the post of a member of the king's bedchamber if Charles was restored to power, a potentially very profitable position. But all their plans soon collapsed. Bampfield reported that he had heard that his wife was not dead after all: and then that he had double-checked and she was indeed dead. Quite what this unsettling episode was about is hard to say. Perhaps Banfield had occasional twinges of conscience about deceiving Anne.

Rumours began to circulate in London that Anne had been involved in the Duke of York's escape. Other problems followed. Charles I was executed (Anne confessed that she spent more time on imprecations on those guilty than prayers for the martyr king). Her brother died. Not only did she lose a secure home, but acting as executor she was defrauded and left deeply in debt. Then her only other brother died suddenly. Fearing arrest for her part in the York affair, she fled from London to stay with friends at Naworth Castle in Cumberland. There she received further bad news. Bampfield had been arrested and was likely to be sentenced to death: and his wife was indeed still alive!

Under the strain of all these disasters Anne fell seriously ill, and her death was expected: 'I lay waiting till my change should come'. But she lived, and wishful thinking led her to the conclusion that Bampfield's wife was indeed dead, malice having led to the rumours that she was still living. Bampfield escaped from prison, but fled to the Netherlands, where the young Charles II was negotiating with Scottish representatives about terms for coming to Scotland. One of the Scots involved was the Earl of Dunfermline, and Bampfield talked to him about Anne's situation. The earl advised that she go to Scotland, giving two reasons: personally, with her Scots connections she would find many friends ready to help her gain possession of some property she had inherited there; and politically, the king would soon be in Scotland. Bampfield urged her to accept the advice, adding that if the king landed in Scotland, Oliver Cromwell would probably march his army to the north of England, thus endangering her.

So Anne at last visited the country of her blood. Her English breeding led her to expect very little of it. The sight of a pretty, well-dressed, well-mannered lady caused her amazement. The Marquis of Argyll, the most powerful man in Scotland, had invited Anne to visit his house:

> I was met in the outward room by my Lady Anne Campbell [Argyll's daughter], a sight I must confess did so much surprise me that I could hardly believe I was in Scotland. For she was very handsome, extremely obliging, and her behaviour and dress was equal to any that I had seen in the court of England. This gave me so good impressions of Scotland that I began to see it had been much injured by those who represented it under another character than what I found it.

A visit to Sir James Douglas at Aberdour in Fife reinforced such impressions: his garden was 'so fragrant and delightful that I thought I was still in England'. Whereas so many visitors to Scotland could only see what confirmed their prejudices, Anne was ready to make her own judgements.

Charles II had now landed, and accepted the Earl of Dunfermline's invitation to stay with him. Hearing of Anne's desire to be presented to the king, the countess invited her to join them. Anne was duly presented, but she was offended when the days passed and Charles failed to talk to her. She was not one to accept such a slight. Finding a sympathetic courtier, she explained the troubles that had followed on her helping in the escape of the Duke of York, having to flee from London, and then to Scotland. Seeing her so little regarded by the king, those who were being civil to her were likely to lose respect for her. 'I could not utter this without tears.' This approach worked. Charles came up to her, handsomely acknowledged her services, and promised he was ready to do anything in his power for her. 'And with that the King laid his hand upon both mine as they lay upon my breast. I humbly bowed down and kissed His Majesty's hand.' Given the reputation that the young Charles had already acquired for an obsession with female anatomy, it may be doubted whether his gesture was solely one of respect.

The effect of the king having promised favour was immediate: two courtiers took her by the hands to lead her out. Anne immediately reminded them of a play in which those ignoring a woman at court immediately began to trouble her with their attentions when the king took notice of her. This implication that they were insincere sycophants not surprisingly 'put them both a little out'. Her sneering comment was really rather hypocritical, since the courtiers' conduct displayed the very increased honour and respect that she was seeking. But she was never one to resist saying what she really thought.

Anne's life was soon disrupted again by public events, however. Cromwell had invaded Scotland, and one day letters arrived from the Scots army at Dunbar announcing triumphantly that the enemy was surrounded and 'there was no possibility for them to escape'. A few days later the news came that the Scots had in fact been totally routed. It was almost immediately realised that not even Fife was now safe from the English, and the Dunfermline family decided to retreat north to their castle at Fyvie in Aberdeenshire. The first stop on the journey was at Kinross. On the way there Anne passed a couple of soldiers who looked desperately ill, and asked them what was wrong. On their replying that they had been wounded at Dunbar she told them to come to her at Kinross and she would treat their wounds. In two days she and her servant dressed the wounds of at least sixty soldiers – a man being employed to deal with wounds 'unfit for me to dress', there being limits to what could be expected from even the most charitable of maiden ladies.

Most of the soldiers had received no treatment whatever up to this point, and word had clearly spread fast among these unfortunates that

PALATIVM REGIVM EDINENSE,
quod & Cænobium S. Crucis.
The royal palace of holy rood-hous. by J.G.

HOLYROOD PALACE, residence of Charles I and Charles II on their visits to
Scotland in 1633, 1641 and 1650, engraved from a drawing by James Gordon. The
print dates from the 1640s, thus providing an illustration of the old palace just
before it was burnt – accidentally – by occupying English troops in 1650, after
the battle of Dunbar.

some help was available. If sixty wounded could gather in Kinross in two
days without notice or advertisement, how many walking wounded must
have been wandering the countryside of southern Scotland as a whole,
many dying by the wayside? Anne's action had some wider influence. It
was reported to the king, discussed in the council, and orders were issued
to pay surgeons in a number of towns to treat wounded soldiers. It seems
astounding that no such simple measures had been taken before. Given the
chaotic state of the country, it may be doubted that the order had much
practical effect. Anne herself, however, did derive some advantage from her
actions. The king sent her his thanks, and shortly after she reached Fyvie he
sent her fifty gold pieces (she having requested financial aid). Since fleeing
from London and virtually abandoning her property there to the English
parliamentarians, she had had money problems. Most of what money she
had started out with had been used to help pay her way with the various
hosts with which she had stayed, for she hated to feel that she was living
on their charity, however freely and tactfully offered. But sometimes she
had had to, and sometimes she had to write round to relatives and friends
seeking loans.

The royal gift eased one problem in her life, but another one re-emerged. The irrepressible Colonel Bampfield arrived in Aberdeen and asked permission to come to see her at Fyvie. She refused, having determined not to see him until the question of whether his wife lived or not had been conclusively settled. For years now she had been pursued with whispers that she was involved with a married man. The colonel persisted, and got Lady Dunfermline's agreement that he should come. At last Anne gave way. It was a conflict between 'love and honour', and so intense was the emotional turmoil that Anne again fell seriously ill. But the Lord decided that He 'had some further use for me in the world' and she recovered and was able to meet with Bampfield. All his protestations failed to influence her stance. She would keep a 'due distance' from him until not only she but everyone else was convinced that his wife was dead. Once this happened, no misfortune under heaven would prevent her making good 'what I had designed'. It would be interesting to know how the colonel took this firm statement that she was taking the initiative and had decided to marry him if appropriate.

Anne spent nearly two years (1650–2) at Fyvie: 'in all my life I never was so long together so truly contented'. The statement is all the more surprising as in 1651 the conquering English reached the castle. First were some 'scattering soldiers' without officers. They were 'very rude', beating up all the men, frightening the women, threatening to shoot anyone who did not give them what they wanted. And, reported Anne, 'I hear they say they are informed there is an English woman in the house, and if they get her, they will be worse to her than any', she being regarded as a traitor.

She was therefore particularly disconcerted when Lady Dunfermline (the earl was not at home), who was pregnant, asked Anne to try to calm the soldiers: she was the best person to do it, as being English (by upbringing) she was their countrywoman! Anne braced herself with prayer, and then, accompanied by her servant woman, went down to where the soldiers were, 'though naturally [by nature] I am the greatest coward living'.

She was greeted with demands to know if she was 'the English whore' that had come to meet the king, 'and all set their pistols just against me'. She acknowledged herself to be English – and to honour the king. But the English were 'generally esteemed the most civil in the world' and she was sorry English soldiers were being so barbarously rude as to terrorise the inhabitants of the castle who consisted mainly of women, children, and a pregnant noblewoman – especially when they were being given all they wanted.

An Exact Ground-Plot of ỹ City of
WORCESTER,
As it ſtood fortifyd 3.Sept.1651.

THE BATTLE OF WORCESTER, 3 September 1651. A meticulous street-plan of the
city by Robert Vaughan – with some fighting crudely sketched in on the right,
as if as an afterthought. This was the culminating defeat of the Scots, after which
resistance to the English collapsed. No fewer than three of the subjects of this
book were captured: Andrew Melvill, James Turner and Urquhart of Cromarty.
None had fought at Dunbar exactly a year before, as they had been excluded from
the army as 'ungodly'.

Typically, even in these circumstances, she had been unable to avoid a
provocative declaration of loyalty to the king. Otherwise, she could hardly
have chosen a better message. Flatter the English; express nanny-like
indignation at the behaviour of the soldiers; show them they are getting what
they want. They backed down, shamefaced. One thing Anne's upbringing
had brought her was knowledge of how to deal with the lower classes. The
men, 'flinging down their pistols', agreed to behave.

Shortly afterwards several English regiments under proper discipline
arrived. When the officers dined at Fyvie, Anne was provoked by Colonel
Overton's talk – of the wonders God had performed in bringing the English
parliament victory – into a spirited denunciation of the murder of a lawful
king and other deeds. As on other occasions her outspokenness seems to
have won her respect rather than the fury that might have been expected.

One can imagine the Scots round the table, nervously trying to butter up the English officers, gritting their teeth and wishing this stupid girl would shut up before they were all locked up.

One of the main reasons for Anne's contentment at Fyvie was undoubtedly that she found a useful role to play. News of her medical exploits at Kinross had spread, and the sick and wounded made their way to the castle for help. Some were English soldiers. The price they had to pay for treatment was having to listen to her exhortations 'to repent their sin of rebellion and become loyal'. Eventually she resolved to leave Fyvie, rather than presume too far on the kindness of the Dunfermlines, and she decided to begin a lawsuit in Edinburgh to regain lost property.

Her time in Edinburgh had mixed effects on her fortunes. Her case in the courts dragged on for years, and ended badly. By her account the problem was that the judges were English republicans, and her antagonist was favoured because he supported their principles, while her own royalism made her a 'malignant'.

The more positive result of her stay started unpromisingly. Lord Dunfermline visited her one day accompanied by a gentleman who immediately earned her dislike because he wore a sword. What was normally the badge of a gentleman was now 'a mark of slavery', for the English conquerors would only allow the wearing of swords by 'such as served their interest and disowned the King, which made me hate to see a Scotch man with a sword'. Luckily she soon found that she was mistaken. The 'sword' she thought she had discerned under his coat was in fact just a stick. The gentleman concerned, Sir James Halkett of Pitfirrane, in Fife, proceeded to visit her frequently on one pretext or another, and 'any that saw him in my company could not but take notice but he had a more than ordinary respect for me'. With her usual forthrightness Anne explained that she was already engaged to Colonel Bampfield (who was now in the north of England and corresponding with her). Sir James continued to see her, however, as he was one of a group of royalists plotting a rebellion against the English occupiers which met in the house she was staying in. Before long Bampfield appeared in Edinburgh and joined the plotters.

However, one day Halkett brought her news that must have delighted him – but which he knew would devastate her. It was certain that Bampfield's wife was after all alive. This time Anne believed the report – indicating an unusual trust in Halkett. As at the time of the death of Anne's mother, a page of her memoirs is missing here. Evidently on reflection she decided what she had written of her reaction to the news was too bitter to leave to posterity.

After a suitable interval Sir James began to try to renew his declarations of affection, now Anne was free of obligations to Bampfield. She repeatedly declared she would never marry because, in spite of the circumstances, she was still bound by her promises to Bampfield! Beyond this, though she was the victim, she felt demeaned by the Bampfield episode: her 'injured virtue', her damaged reputation, made it unfit that she marry. She may also have given consideration to the fact that Sir James was a middle-aged widower with four children (though two or three of them were evidently virtually adults).

By late 1654 Anne's lawsuit was at last coming to an end, and she decided that she would return to London, not least to vindicate herself from her 'supposed guilt'. She was not long in London when, almost predictably, Bampfield turned up, and with remarkable audacity proceeded to protest his innocence, claiming that he had something to propose that 'might be both for his advantage and mine' – unless she was married to Sir James Halkett. If she was married he would 'never trouble me more'.

> I said nothing a little while, for I hated lying and I saw there might be some inconvenience to tell the truth, and (Lord pardon the equivocation) I said, 'I am' (out aloud, and secretly said, 'not').

For once the colonel was as good as his word. He left immediately, and Anne never saw him again.

Seeking to settle her financial affairs in London turned out to be a prolonged process. She had been there for about a year when Sir James arrived to visit her – and renew his pleas to her to marry him. Anne records that this made the settling of her debts – or at least the most pressing ones – all the more urgent. This is the first indication she gives that she was after all contemplating marriage, and was anxious not to bring financial burdens to the marriage. Time was modifying her first, extreme, reactions to Bampfield's betrayal. No doubt she could now see her own past conduct as foolish, perhaps, but not scandalous, and the friends she had feared would despise her had proved true.

Anne had no doubts as to Sir James's worth. She was deeply grateful for his support in difficult times, and she was much impressed by his persistence. She must also have reflected that she was now in her thirties, and not (with her determined character) to many men's taste. But it still took her a great deal of fasting and prayer before she finally agreed to the marriage. 'I intended to give him myself.' The decision to enter into marriage seen in such terms must have been all the harder to take for so independent a woman. In March

1656 the marriage at last took place – a very small-scale affair as it was not wise for royalists to hold large gatherings – and soon afterwards the couple left for Scotland.

Infuriatingly, after their arrival the manuscript of the memoirs ends abruptly in the middle of a sentence. She was writing in the later 1670s, and how far she carried her narrative on from the 1650s is impossible to know. And as with the missing pages earlier in the memoir, it is tempting to speculate that the destruction was deliberate. Did she for some reason become unhappy at her description of her married life?

After marriage came sorrow in one aspect of Anne's life. She gave birth to four children. Three were still-born or died in infancy. But one, Robert, lived, and proved true to his parents' royalist sympathies. He fought for the dethroned James VII in Ireland (having become a soldier, not a lawyer as his mother had wanted), but was captured and imprisoned, dying in 1692 shortly after his release. Childbearing apart, married life was fairly quiet – but secure. Sir James was an amiable country gentleman, comfortably off from the proceeds of coal mining rather than farming, who 'loved to be at home, and diverted himself in useful contrivances for improving his House, Gardens, and Enclosures' at Pitfirrane. He died in 1670, leaving her to a widowhood that was to last twenty-nine years, spent largely living quietly in Dunfermline. Whether or not she still considered herself English, she was well acclimatised in the Scotland she had once considered so barbarous. On her husband's death she consulted the Bible to learn how to be a good widow. St Paul told her to wash people's feet, but she briskly decided this was not meant to be taken literally in the Scottish climate. Better dirty feet than cold ones, it seems.

Married or widowed, Anne devoted much of her time to developing her own existing interests. Religion was the centre of her life, and she was said to have spent five hours a day in her devotions. She developed a passion for writing, producing twenty volumes of mainly religious writings, which seem to have been worthy but little more. Especially poignant – and ironic considering her obstetrical history, was 'The Mother's Will to her Unborn Child'. She wanted to leave a message for her child if she died in childbirth: but it was to be the children who died. Far more interesting than the religious works was her autobiography, evidently written without any intention that anyone else would ever read it. Rather she was attempting to sort out for herself the confused pattern of her life – and confess the errors she had made as well as the misfortunes that had befallen her.

She now had an opportunity to develop her medical interests, closely related to her religious concerns in being a form of charity. Gathering herbs, snails and worms, she busily boiled and distilled to produce potions and ointments. Each Wednesday she held a surgery, and the sick gathered from the locality for treatment. In addition, her reputation evidently spread until 'persons of all ranks' sent from all over the country for her advice and medicaments. All this she did free, and in addition evidently gave to charity. But she was dogged by her debts dating back to the 1640s. The civil wars and the problems of her brother's estate had lost her a great deal. The Restoration of Charles II in 1660 brought her a welcome grant of £500 sterling, but this was a mere fraction of what she owed. In the 1680s she thought of moving to London and making a living for herself by charging for her medical services. News of her skills had evidently spread far enough for her to think this possible. Her income from her jointure (the Halkett family funds from which she had an income for life) could then be devoted entirely to paying off her debts. It might not be a genteel occupation, but she would be tackling her debts honourably, and there would be an element of charity in it.

Friends dissuaded her from this upheaval late in life. Instead, they suggested that she set up a school to board and educate orphans of local gentry. This she agreed to do. Looking after orphans who were supported by their families gave her an income without reflecting too much on her status. Soon she had seven children in her care who had lost their mothers, and one who had no father. Typically, this inspired her to put pen to paper, and two years after her death her brief *Instructions for youth . . . For the Use of those young Noblemen and Gentlemen whose Education was committed to her Care* was published. It is little more than conventional notes closely based on the Bible, starting from the standard premise that all youth is 'infected with the contagion of sin' and needs cleansing. Doubtless she would not have been amused that changes in the usages of words have rendered her order that youths begin every day with a 'short Ejaculation' a bit startling, even if it was to be addressed to God. Life became easier financially with the accession of James VII in 1685, for he awarded her a pension of £100 a year in gratitude for her help in his escape from imprisonment (as Duke of York) nearly forty years before.

If financial problems dogged her later years, solace came from religion. Her views were settled and intense, but her zeal was not the sort that measured piety by bigotry. In spite of the depth of her commitment to the Church of England, she was ready to work or socialise with those of other faiths. At Naworth Castle she had worked with an old Catholic priest in helping the sick. Of two gentlemen she talked with on a coach journey she concluded, 'I could not have met with civiler gentlemen', though 'I regretted to find they were Roman Catholics'. That they were Catholics did not alter her otherwise favourable judgement of them. At the other religious extreme, while in Scotland in the 1650s Anne attended presbyterian services in parish churches regularly, though she was unhappy with the Scots habit of only holding communion services very occasionally, and travelled round in search of such services. More surprising, she developed a great enough respect for some parish ministers to consult them. David Dickson might be one of the leading covenanting divines, a rebel against the king, but she had sought his advice on the Bampfield business – and he had taken to coming to see her once a week when she had lived in Edinburgh.

Anne Murray, dowager Lady Halkett, died in 1699 aged seventy-six. The course of her life had been very different from anything she could have predicted. Playing a part in a plot to free a prince from captivity; losing the financial security she had had every reason to take for granted; becoming involved in a prolonged liaison with a married man which became a widely known scandal; marrying a Scot; and living more than half her life in Scotland. In some ways she could claim to have suffered much misfortune. But in others she was fortunate. She escaped the clutches of the infamous Colonel Bampfield (who turned out to have been spying on royalists for Cromwell in the late 1650s) while still young enough to marry and have at least one child who lived to adulthood. For nearly a decade before her marriage her situation was financially precarious – though in keeping with her status as a gentlewoman she had always had her 'woman', her servant, with her. However, most nobles and gentry she came into contact with offered her hospitality, and often slipped her a few pounds.

In spite of her dependence on others, the main impression left by her memoirs is of independence. Her father had died when she was an infant. In the strength of the authority her mother sought to assert she was almost a father figure, but Anne struggled hard to reject her authority in the Thomas Howard affair. She seems to have made no attempt to turn to her elder brothers as masculine authorities to guide her. In getting involved in the plot to free the Duke of York, an involvement which could have had disastrous consequences for her, she acted for herself. In the entanglement with Bampfield she may have been foolish, but she was acting according to the dictates of her own heart. She much regretted being an object of suggestive gossip: but she would not let it change her stance. She often asked the advice of those she respected, and listened to it attentively; but often she did not take it, having weighed it against her own judgement.

Why did she write her diary? Apart from the Bampfield affair, she seems to feel no need to exonerate and justify herself. As the years passed, she doubtless looked back over the adventures of her early life, and wished to record them. Why does she choose the chunk of her life to narrate that she did? Childhood is left out as boring. Does the period after her marriage get omitted for the same reason – or because she felt it not appropriate to comment on relations with her husband? Perhaps the marriage was dealt with originally, but part of the manuscript has been lost.

It is probably significant, however, that her story starts with her first experience of love, and ends when love is at long last consummated through marriage. Surely she was writing about her struggle for love. She has crafted her work, given it a shape and theme, a beginning and an end, from love sought to love achieved. The bits and pieces have a coherent theme chosen from her life. Oddly, the only other memoir featured in this volume about which the same can be said is Father Blakhal's, and the theme is surprisingly similar. Under the surface of emphasis on ingratitude shown to him, it is a story of frustrated love, going beyond that expected of a priest, for three ladies. He begins when he meets the first, finishes when the last breaks away from him. Lady Anne Halkett and Father Gilbert Blakhal have in common that what they wanted to record of their lives was their relations with those of the opposite sex whom they had loved.

It has been observed by others that Anne's diary is, of all seventeenth-century memoirs, closest to a great deal of later fiction – in subject matter and, in parts, in style. Heroine deprived of her young noble lover; heroine betrayed by plausible scoundrel; heroine at last finds a husband and implication of 'lives happily ever after'. Heroine emotional, but strong and resilient under the surface, winning through in the end. Take the passage quoted earlier where Anne flings herself on her bed in despair on hearing of Thomas Howard's marriage, but pulls herself together, dismisses her betrayer as unworthy, and goes out to face her family. There is a nineteenth-century romantic novel struggling to get out, as a middle-aged lady sits in seventeenth-century Dunfermline and recalls her youth.

The 'novelistic' aspects of her writing are obviously linked to her sex. The aspects of life she tends to emphasise are ones of particular concern to women, and she treats them from a female angle. As she was a woman, that may seem too obvious to be worth commenting on, but it is interesting that this is not a woman trying to write like a man, but confident enough to be herself. She takes a distinctive and refreshing look at living in the troubles from a woman's viewpoint. Public events only appear because they disrupt her life; there is no need to describe debates and military campaigns. The slaughter of battle only appears when she helps the wounded. No one else in this book ever mentions doing such an odd thing (except for Andrew Melvill's brief shudder at a horrific hospital in Flanders, and that may well have been run by nuns). At the other extreme of experience, no one else writes so much about love and so intimately about their emotion – except Johnston of Wariston!

Arguably one aspect of the development of the early romantic novels and their popularity was the insinuation into fashionable culture of areas of interest and feeling that had formerly been regarded as specifically feminine. Earlier fiction had tended to concentrate on the boisterous, rollicking, physically active world of the male – a sort of equivalent of the cheerfully amoral and violent memoirs of a Melvill or a Turner. Adventure stories. If they are factual forerunners of, say, Smollett, can one say Anne Halkett is a distant – very distant but perceptible – forerunner of Jane Austen in some respects? A glint of a female sensibility showing in a culture so male-dominated in the records that it is seldom detected?

FURTHER READING

M. Bottrall, *Every Man a Phoenix. Studies in Seventeenth-Century Autobiography* (London, 1958).

L.M. Cumming, 'Anne, Lady Halkett', *Blackwood's Magazine*, 216 (1924), 654–76.

[S. Couper], *Life of Lady Halkett* (Edinburgh,, 1701).

Paul Delany, *British Autobiography in the Seventeenth Century* (London, 1969).

J. Loftis (ed.), *The Memoirs of Anne, Lady Halkett and Ann, Lady Fanshawe* (Oxford, 1979).

M.B. Rose, 'Gender, Genre, and History. Seventeenth-Century English Women and the Art of Autobiography', in M.B. Rose (ed.), *Women in the Middle Ages and the Renaissance. Literary and Historical Perspectives* (Syracuse, 1986), 245–78.

W. Shumaker, *English Autobiography: Its Emergence, Materials and Form* (Berkeley, 1954).

D.A. Stauffer, *English Biography before 1700* (Cambridge, Mass., 1930).

INDEX